Captivating the Simple-Hearted:

A Struggle for Human Dignity
in the Indian Subcontinent

Captivating the Simple-Hearted:

A Struggle for Human Dignity in the Indian Subcontinent

by Pieter Friedrich and Bhajan Singh

"You must take the stand that Buddha took. You must take the stand which Guru Nanak took. You must not only discard the Shastras, you must deny their authority, as did Buddha and Nanak. You must have courage to tell the Hindus that what is wrong with them is their religion — the religion which has produced in them this notion of the sacredness of caste."
— **Dr. Bhim Rao Ambedkar** —

SOVEREIGN STAR
P U B L I S H I N G
California, USA

Published 2017 by Sovereign Star Publishing, Inc.

Captivating the Simple-Hearted: A Struggle for Human Dignity in the Indian Subcontinent

Front cover features Sikh students in Uttar Pradesh. They belong to a community commonly called "Sikligar Sikhs" who originated from a Mulnivasi group who manufactured weapons for the Sikh Gurus, beginning with Guru Hargobind. The back cover features Harmandir Sahib in a simpler time.

Inquiries should be addressed to:
Sovereign Star Publishing, Inc.
California, USA
wwww.SovStar.com

Softcover: ISBN 978-0-9814992-9-1; 0-9814992-9-5

Hardcover: ISBN 978-0-9814992-1-5; 0-9814992-1-X

— TABLE OF CONTENTS —

Foreword

by Dr. Vislavath Rajunayak

Histories about India have been written and re-written. Many Indian historical narratives are written from a dominant perspective to justify Brahmanical Hindutva ideology. The facts have been completely removed from history.

Authoritarian forces antagonize the history of marginalized communities as well as the struggle of "other" *Mulnivasi* martyrs. *Captivating the Simple-Hearted* challenges historians who appropriate merely ideological interpretations to write histories of the marginalized people of the Indian subcontinent. The authors demonstrate that one can see history through *Mulnivasi* eyes.

In order to fully understand the community, a detailed study of the Sikh history needs to be read. It has been provided in this book. *Captivating* narrates both individual and community historical accounts with accurate dates and contemporary references. Moreover, it opens up a new area of scholarly inquiry that has been pushed underground to conform to the hegemony of the prevailing narratives.

Captivating is an eye-opener for any reader to understand the dynamic and humanitarian approach and vision of the Sikh Gurus towards the *Mulnivasi* in India. The authors reveal the historical and systematic processes which tried to thwart that vision. They bring to light the dominant and exploitative role played by an alliance of Mughal nobles and Brahman elites to suppress the desires of *Mulnivasi* people to claim their humanity. The authors underline the need to reexamine history to authentically understand the struggles of marginalized communities.

The authors bring to life proper histories in a technical sense; nevertheless, the histories are not simply imaginative negotiations with the past but are also relevant to contemporary conditions of life and identity.

Even today, histories of these marginalized communities are not accessible to their members. Due to this ambiguous relationship with historical narratives, we can say that this book enlightens the *Mulnivasi* on their past by giving accurate, contemporary references and disproving dominant historical narratives. I am sure this book will help readers to reclaim their own identity.

A quick examination of this literature creates an immense pride in the Sikh Gurus. If you read *Captivating the Simple-Hearted*, you will be amazed to know about the Gurus' wonderful proclivity towards the *Mulnivasi*. Anyone who wants freedom in this world should partake of this history to learn about facing today's challenges.

Dr. Vislavath Rajunayak is an Assistant Professor in the Department of Indian and World Literatures at the The English And Foreign Languages University, Hyderabad and a Visiting Scholar at the Institute for South Asian Studies at University of California, Berkeley

Prologue

"India needs such a history that germinates revolutionary consciousness for social change because history plays a very significant role in this respect," writes Indian advocate Dr. Santokh Lal Virdi. "Society assumes a character and shape as molded by its history."[1]

From before the point of recorded history, the issue of caste — that is, the hereditary and hierarchical division of humanity — has been at the epicenter of sociopolitical conflict in South Asia. Therefore, South Asian struggles for equality and liberty (or, in short, human dignity) can be best understood in context of resistance to the caste system. Within that paradigm, the Sikh Revolution is central to the struggle for emancipation of those enslaved by caste.

Within that context, Dr. Rajkumar Hans (an Indian intellectual who was considered a Dalit or "Untouchable" by virtue of his ancestry) summarizes the significance of the rise of the Sikhs.

> Growing out of the powerful, anticaste *sant* tradition of the fourteenth and fifteenth centuries in northern India, the Sikh variant of Guru Nanak and his successors evolved into an organized religious movement in the sixteenth and seventeenth centuries. It became a rallying cry for the Untouchables and members of the "lower castes" that they be allowed a respectable social existence....
>
> Guru Nanak felt that the real cause of the misery of the people was the disunity born of caste prejudices. To do away with caste differences and discords, he laid the foundation of *sangat* (congregation) and *pangat* (collective dining). Thus, all ten of the gurus took necessary steps to eliminate the differences of varna and caste.[2]

This book shows how the Sikh Revolution developed with the specific intent of eliminating the social divisions of caste, instilling the masses with a sense of the universal nobility of the common person, and empowering the people to defy and prevail against sociopolitical tyranny.

Offering a survey of many critical points of the history of the Indian subcontinent from the 5th century to the 21st century, we present the struggle for liberation as the principal theme. *Captivating the Simple-Hearted* details the eradication of Buddhism in the 500s to 900s, the emergence of Bhagats (saints) in the 1200s to 1500s, the establishment of the Delhi Sultanate in the 1200s and of the Mughal Empire in the 1500s, and the development of the Sikh philosophy from the 1500s to 1700s. Our narrative reveals the unbroken thread connecting all of these historical developments.

Along the way, we examine the origins and impact of Brahmanism (the underlying philosophy of the Hindu religion), the alliance between Brahmans and Mughals, the lives and teachings of several of the Sikh Gurus, the schemes perpetrated against the lives of the Gurus by a Mughal-Brahman alliance, the martyrdom of three Gurus, the wars waged against the Mughal Empire and the Hindu Rajas by the Sikhs, the spread of the Sikh philosophy across the Indian subcontinent, the independence of Punjab, the rise and fall of the Sikh Empire, the occupation of the subcontinent by the British Empire, the emergence of social reformers in the 1800s, the interactions between Dr. Bhim Rao Ambedkar and Mohandas Gandhi as the Indian subcontinent pursued independence from British rule, and the impact of these historical realities on the present conditions of the Republic of India.

"There is no work on Sikh history and tradition that has been produced from the Dalit history perspective," wrote Dr. Hans.[3] Thus, we hope that *Captivating the Simple-Hearted* will clearly demonstrate (especially as we rely on objective Persian and European primary sources for evidence) that Sikhism, at its core, seeks alliance with those considered "low born." This history brings to light how the Sikh *Panth* (path) sought — and secured — liberation of the subjugated masses.

Bhai Jaita (c. 1649-1704), a poet and a warrior in service of Guru Gobind Singh, the tenth Sikh Guru, exemplified the fulfillment of that goal. Jaita was born as a Dalit. Yet, according to Dr. Hans, "Jaita emerged as a fearless Sikh warrior who so endeared himself to the tenth guru that he was proclaimed by the guru as the *panjwan sahibjada* (fifth son) in addition to the guru's own four sons." Renamed by the Guru as "Baba Jiwan Singh," he was "killed in a fierce battle with Mughal armies in 1704."[4] His legacy lives on, however, in his poetry. In one of his verses, a *rahit* (code) for the Sikhs,

Baba Jiwan Singh declares,

> Now listen to the *rahit* of the Singhs.
> The Singh should pray to God, keeping war in mind.
> When a victim and a needy person beseeches help,
> Forgetting his own, a Singh should remove others' suffering.
> Not keeping in mind differences of high and low caste,
> The Singh should consider all humans as children of God.
> Abandoning the Brahmanical rituals and customs,
> The Singh should seek liberation by following the Guru's ideas.[5]

Ideas have consequences. The ideology of Brahmanism has deadly consequences, but the contrasting idea of Sikhism restores life to a desolate land. Beliefs influence behavior. The beliefs of Brahmanism produced a society of inequality and tyranny, but the contrasting beliefs of Sikhism inspired a devotion to the universal equality and right to liberty of all humanity.

Today, Sikhism has not only taken root in South Asia but spread across the globe. However, its rival of Brahmanism has yet to be fully uprooted. Indeed, it remains a predominant, coercive, and treacherous force in modern India and threatens to spread. From its origins as an ancient prejudice, Brahmanism has evolved into a politicized form of violent nationalism which is menacing to every citizen of the Republic of India who wants a free and peaceful society.

We hope that examining one of the Indian subcontinent's central struggles for human dignity will expose the impact of historical realities on current events. To transform our future, we must first comprehend our past.

Citations

1 Rawat, S. Ramnarayan and K. Satyanarayana (eds.). *Dalit Studies*. Durham: Duke University Press. 2016. 136.
2 Ibid., 131 & 134.
3 Ibid., 136.
4 Ibid., 137.
5 Ibid., 135-136.

— 1 —
Mulnivasi Flock to the Warm Shop

The martyrdom of Guru Arjun (1563-1606), carried out in Lahore under the orders of Delhi Emperor Jahangir (1569-1627), was a turning point in the struggle of the people of the Indian subcontinent to secure their human dignity. This struggle was compounded by foreign invasions which imposed a dehumanizing sociopolitical structure.

Guru Arjun's persecution was instigated by the elite who benefited from the centuries of oppression produced by the caste system, a power structure which enslaved South Asia's indigenous people. The diverse indigenous communities, ranging from Punjab to Nagaland and Kashmir to the Tamil country, included Adivasis (tribal peoples), Shudras (the lowest of the four castes), and Ati-Shudras (outcastes). United by their exclusion from society, which is dictated by the caste system, these communities represent the majority of the population. In company with others who fundamentally reject caste and its hierarchical system of repression, they are collectively known as the *Mulnivasi Bahujan* (original people in the majority).

From 20th century civil rights champions like Dr. Bhim Rao Ambedkar, the *Mulnivasi* (original people) can trace their fight for equality and liberty back to South Asian Gurus (spiritual teachers) like Arjun, Nanak, Ravidas, Kabir, Namdev, Farid, and other torchbearers in the struggle to secure the human dignity of the common person.

Occurring at the height of Guru Arjun's endeavor to institutionalize that struggle as the Sikh *Panth*, his arrest, torture, and execution was a landmark attempt by Brahmans (the high-caste elite), in collaboration with Mughal invaders, to suppress a flourishing movement to secure the liberation of the downtrodden *Mulnivasi*.

The Warm Shop — In his memoirs, Jahangir (whose great-grandfather, Babur, established the Mughal Empire's foreign rule of India) clearly details his reasons for persecuting the Guru.

There lived a Hindu named Arjun in the garb of *Pir* [saint] and *Sheikh* [king], so much so that, having captivated many simple-hearted Hindus — nay, even foolish and stupid Muslims — by his ways and manners, he had noised himself about as a religious and worldly leader. They called him *Guru*, and from all directions fools and fool-worshippers were attracted towards him and expressed full faith in him. For three or four generations, they had kept this shop warm. For years, the thought had been presenting itself to me that either I should put an end to this false traffic or he should be brought into the fold of Islam....

When this came to the ears of our majesty, and I fully knew his heresies, I ordered that he should be brought into my presence, and having handed over his houses, dwelling places, and children... and having confiscated his property, I ordered that he should be put to death with tortures.[1]

This historical account produces an ocean of questions. Who was Arjun? Who were the simple-hearted? What heresies was Arjun accused of teaching? If Jahangir saw simple-hearted, did he also see complex-hearted? If the simple-hearted were swayed by Arjun's "ways and manners," why were the complex-hearted not swayed? How did Jahangir believe Arjun captivated the hearts of the simple? Who lost if the hearts of the simple remained captivated? Who won if the simple-hearted lost their attraction to the Guru's message? Indeed, who were the simple-hearted — and who were the foolish and stupid?

Answers are found in the origins of the "warm shop" of "three or four generations" which disturbed Jahangir — so deeply did it disturb him, in fact, that he even describes members of his own Islamic religion who were attracted to Arjun as "foolish and stupid."

In 1604, under the auspices of Guru Arjun, this warm shop took physical form in completion in Amritsar, Punjab of the simple structure of Harmandir Sahib (later known as the Golden Temple), an institution whose four doors brought fresh air to the lungs of the suffocated *Mulnivasi*.

The *Gurdwara* (God's doorway) was open to all and designed to empower the common people to embrace their intrinsic self-worth. From this focal point in Amritsar, the Sikh (a lifelong "disciple" or "student") community carried out its work of liberating the masses by preaching equality, educating the ignorant, and practicing *langar* — a free kitchen that defied caste taboos by providing people with a place to sit together, touch each other, and break barriers by eating and drinking with one another regardless of social status.

At this warm shop, the Shudras and Ati-Shudras, previously indoctrinated by the prevailing Brahmanical culture to be terrified of their own shadows, were shown how to love themselves and their neighbors. They discovered new life in the uranium of everlasting energy flowing from the *Adi Granth*, the collected teachings of South Asian saints who proclaimed the human dignity of all people. The spines of these enslaved masses, broken from being forced to bow and scrape before Brahmans and Emperors, found relief in voluntary surrender to the ideas of liberty contained within the *Granth*.

Once victims of a power structure that enslaved them, those mocked by their oppressors as "simple-hearted," "foolish," and "stupid" were inescapably captivated by a message that offered liberation. As these sons and daughters of the soil lived out the teachings of the *Granth*, Harmandir Sahib produced a monsoon to water the hopes of the hopeless while simultaneously flooding the strongholds of their oppressors. The ruling elite were understandably terrified by this flourishing institution — or "shop" — which was so heavily patronized by free people.

This shop, which Jahangir said was kept warm "for three to four generations," was opened by the first Sikh Guru, Nanak (1469-1539), who declared, "There is neither Hindu nor Muslim, so whose path shall I follow? I shall follow God's path."[2] As he began following that path, traffic trickled after him. It was a path less travelled and entirely unfamiliar to the complex-hearted because, as Guru Nanak explains, God's path requires intentional association with the downtrodden,

ਨੀਚਾ ਅੰਦਰਿ ਨੀਚ ਜਾਤਿ ਨੀਚੀ ਹੁ ਅਤਿ ਨੀਚੁ ॥
ਨਾਨਕੁ ਤਿਨ ਕੈ ਸੰਗਿ ਸਾਥਿ ਵਡਿਆ ਸਿਉ ਕਿਆ ਰੀਸ ॥
ਜਿਥੈ ਨੀਚ ਸਮਾਲੀਅਨਿ ਤਿਥੈ ਨਦਰਿ ਤੇਰੀ ਬਖਸੀਸ ॥

The lowliest of the lowly, the lowest of the low born,
Nanak seeks their company. The friendship of great is in vain.
For, where the weak are cared for, there Thy Mercy rains.[3]

Guru Nanak's friendship with the "low born" signified a declaration of war against the Indian subcontinent's reigning power structure. According to the elites, only those born at the top of the culture's caste system had access to God; those at the bottom were not even considered human. Yet the Guru preached the equality of everyone, saying, "Recognize the Lord's Light within all, and do not consider social class or status; there are no classes or castes in the world hereafter."[4]

Those who stopped considering caste, the Guru suggested, gained emancipation. As he says, "That slave, whom God has released from the restrictions of social status, who can now hold him in bondage?"[5] Caste, he explained, is irrelevant to a person's natural right to liberty because all are equal before the Creator. Everyone, no matter his or her origins, obtains liberty through the same method. As he stated, "The Brahmans, the Kshatriyas, the Vaishyas, the Shudras, and even the low wretches are all emancipated by contemplating their Lord."[6]

Laying the foundation for a recurring doctrine of the *Panth*, Guru Nanak emphasized the irrelevance of royal birth. "Even kings and emperors with mountains of property and oceans of wealth cannot compare with an ant filled with the love of God," he declared.[7] The concept that the lowest creatures can be superior to those born as royalty was embraced and expanded by his successors, especially Guru Arjun (who taught that paupers can become princes). Furthermore, Guru Nanak explains,

ਖਸਮੈ ਖੁੰਦਕਾਰੁ ਸਾਹ ਆਲਮੁ ਕਰਿ ਖਰੀਦਿ ਜਿਨਿ ਖਰਚੁ ਦੀਆ ॥
ਬੰਧਨਿ ਜਾ ਕੈ ਸਭੁ ਜਗੁ ਬਾਧਿਆ ਅਵਰੀ ਕਾ ਨਹੀ ਹੁਕਮੁ ਪਇਆ ॥

The Creator is the King of the world;
He enslaves by giving nourishment.
By His Binding, all the world is bound;
No other Command prevails.[8]

The battle lines were thus clearly drawn between society's Touchables and Untouchables — between those who sought to command others and those who understood they do not have to answer to the command of anyone except the Creator.

Guru Nanak developed this message by weaving together the threads of liberty spun by preceding saints. Traveling throughout the world, he became the Steward of the *Mulnivasi* by knitting together into a single fabric the records of resistance and celebrations of human dignity of others who similarly pursued emancipation of the oppressed. As the originator of the

Panth, it was left to him to institutionalize the message of social, economic, and spiritual freedom proclaimed by the saintly Bhagats who preceded him.[9]

One of the earliest of these Bhagats was Baba Farid (1179-1266), a poet whose compositions formed the foundation for the Punjabi language.

Brahmanism Cripples India — Farid lived in a transformative era for the *Mulnivasi* as historical events found them torn between two vicious forces. On one side were Islamic invaders who, during Farid's lifetime, achieved a conquest of Delhi that lasted until the 19th-century. On the other side were Brahmans who imposed and brutally enforced the intense segregation of the Hindu caste system. Detailing the significance of the caste system, German sociologist Max Weber writes,

> Caste, that is, the ritual rights and duties it gives and imposes, and the position of the Brahmans, is the fundamental institution of Hinduism. Before everything else, without caste, there is no Hindu.... "Caste" is, and remains essentially, social rank, and the central position of the Brahmans in Hinduism rests primarily upon the fact that social rank is determined with reference to Brahmans.[10]

Because caste hierarchy ranks a person's social status in "reference to Brahmans," the practice is also known as "Brahmanism." One of the most penetrating analyses of Brahmanism was written in the 20th century by a Hindu named Swami Dharma Theertha. An attorney from Kerala who gave up his practice to become a monk, he devoted his life to teaching against caste. In 1941, after decades of studying the Hindu religion, he published a book entitled *History of Hindu Imperialism*. Subsequently, he renounced Hinduism entirely.

Referring to Brahmans, Theertha writes, "So far as the Hindus are concerned, all power has remained for many centuries in the hands of a small group of hereditary exploiters whose life and interests are even today antagonistic to the welfare of the masses of India."[11] In *History of Hindu Imperialism*, he defines Brahmanism.

> Brahmanism is the name used by historians to denote the exploiters and their civilization. It may be defined as a system of socioreligious domination and exploitation of the Hindus based on caste, priestcraft, and false philosophy — caste representing the scheme

of domination, priestcraft the means of exploitation, and false phi-losophy a justification of both caste and priestcraft. Started by the Brahman priests and developed by them through many centuries of varying fortunes and compromises with numerous ramifica-tions, it has, under foreign rule, become the general culture of the Hindus and is, at the present day, almost identical with organised Hinduism....

Its strength depends on an ingenious organization of society in which the hereditary priest is supreme, priestcraft is the high-est religion, and philosophy is the handmaid of priestcraft. Origi-nally, the scheme contemplated only four caste divisions, but the process of classification by birth and social exclusiveness, once brought into fashion, gave rise to many thousands of castes and sub-castes.[12]

In the 12th century, at the time of Farid, Buddhism was South Asia's only indigenous religion which suggested temporal equality. Approximate-ly 1700 years before Farid, Gautama Buddha traveled and taught through-out eastern parts of the subcontinent; his philosophy took deep root and flourished for a time.

Describing Buddhism's impact on a caste-ridden society, Theertha writes, "Wherever the Buddha's teachings spread, they created a revolution in the mentality of the people. Liberated from the artificial restrictions of caste, they delighted to mingle their thoughts, activities, and destinies in the free flow of human friendships, attachments, and love, and many Brahmans even broke through their orthodoxy to share in this new freedom."[13]

Ultimately, however, the free expression of liberated human beings was intolerable to those who benefited from censoring it. As Sikh historian Dr. Sangat Singh reveals, "Gautama Buddha, like the Sikh Gurus, earned the deep-rooted hostility of Brahmanism because of his revolt against the Brah-manical caste system, priestcraft, and rituals." Consequently, the Buddhists were mercilessly, brutally, and almost completely driven out of South Asia. From the 5th century onwards, Dr. Singh describes an "ongoing... attack on the Buddhists and their places of worship." Frequently, the Brahmans were "cooperating with foreign invaders like Huns and early Kushans to strike at the roots of Buddhist power." Ancient Buddhist cities were eradicated; "Kapilvastu [in Nepal] had become a jungle and Gaya [in Bihar] had been laid waste and desolate." In Bengal, King Shashanka "carried out acts of vandalism against the Buddhists, destroyed the footprints of Lord Buddha at Pataliputra [in Bihar], burnt the Bodhi tree under which he had meditated, and devastated numerous monasteries, and scattered their monks."[14]

Facing constant persecution, thousands of Buddhist monks fled the Indian subcontinent. "All of them and others who followed later to China, Tibet, or to Korea and Japan, were fugitives from oppressive Brahmanism, which threatened their very existence." Subsequently, in the 9th century, philosopher Adi Shankaracharya oversaw "an all-out Brahmanical assault on Buddhism." Dr. Singh explains,

> Shankaracharya himself killed hundreds of Buddhists of Nagarju-nakonda [in Andhra Pradesh] and… "wantonly smashed" the Buddhist temples there…. Shankaracharya, thereafter, led the group of marauders to Mahabodhi temple in Gaya, and they indulged in large-scale destruction of Buddhist monasteries and stupas. The Brahmans took over the temple under their control.
>
> His appetite whetted, Shankaracharya personally led a motivated group through the Himalayas. The object now was the Buddhist centre at Badrinath [in Uttarakhand]. His reputation of wholesale destruction of Buddhists preceded him. The Buddhists chose to abandon Badrinath. They threw the statue of the presiding deity in Alakananda river at the foot of the temple and escaped to Tibet. The centre was taken over by the Brahmans.[15]

Thereafter, Muslim occupation — which took root in the heart of the subcontinent with the establishment of the Delhi Sultanate in 1206 — created ideal conditions for Brahmans to expand the slavery of the caste system. "It was only when the country ultimately fell a victim into the hands of foreigners that Buddhism was crushed to death and Brahmanism spread its fangs over the prostrate people," explains Theertha. "Brahmans favored the religion of gods and goddesses and rituals, and not the religion of righteousness."[16]

While foreign occupation enabled Brahmanism to finally eradicate Buddhism, it was Brahmanism itself that enabled foreign occupation to take root. Muslim warlords invaded the Indian subcontinent from the northwest by passing through Afghanistan, Pakistan, and Punjab. In 711, Muhammad bin Qasim (born in Arabia) secured the earliest successful Islamic foothold in the subcontinent when he conquered Sindh and part of Punjab (areas now in eastern Pakistan). "Many causes contributed to the subjugation of Sindh," writes Indian historian Ashirbadi Lal Srivastava. Chief among those causes, he explains, were caste divisions.

> The province was internally disunited and unable to resist a mighty invader like the Arabs. Its population was sparse and heterogeneous.... The lower orders of the society were badly treated. The Jats, the Meds, and certain other castes were looked down upon and subjected to humiliation by the ruler, the court, and the official class no less than by the higher caste people. They were not allowed to ride on saddled horses, to carry arms, or to put on fine clothes. Owing to these circumstances, social solidarity, the best guarantee of political independence, was conspicuously lacking.[17]

Qasim's conquest enabled further inroads by other Islamic warlords, which continued for several centuries until, finally, Turkic warlord Qutb al-Din Aibak (1150-1210) established the Delhi Sultanate in 1206. In 1526, Ibrahim Lodi became the last ruler of the Delhi Sultanate when he was killed in battle by Uzbek warlord Zahir-ud-Din Muhammad (1483-1530) — commonly known as "Babur," meaning "tiger" — who established the Mughal Empire.

From 1206 to 1947, the majority of the Indian subcontinent largely remained under uninterrupted foreign rule.

Jean-Baptiste Tavernier, a 17th-century French merchant who wrote about his travels in the Mughal Empire, corroborated Srivastava's 20th-century conclusion that the caste system enabled India's subjugation by foreign invaders. "The idolaters of India are so numerous that for one Muhammadan there are five or six Gentiles," writes Tavernier. Nevertheless, their numerical superiority did not empower them to resist invasion. He continues,

> It is astonishing to see how this enormous multitude of men has allowed itself to be subjected by so small a number of persons, and has bent readily under the yoke of the Muhammadan princes. But the astonishment ceases when one considers that these idolaters have no union among themselves, and that superstition has introduced so strange a diversity of opinions and customs that they never agree with one another. An idolater will not eat bread nor drink water in a house belonging to any one of a different caste

from his own.[18]

Foreign occupation was irresistible by a society divided into castes. Even then, however, the occupation might have inspired the common people to jettison caste and unite in resistance to the invaders. Yet this was prevented by the high-caste — the Brahmans — who ingratiated themselves with the conquerors, secured privileged positions in the courts of the foreign Emperors, and used the occupation as an opportunity to entrench Brahmanism. According to Theertha, the caste system took deeper root as Brahmans collaborated with the occupiers.

The disappearance of Buddhism and the passing of political power into the hands of Muhammadans, though they meant the extermination of national life, was a still triumph for Brahmanism…. One prominent result of the invasion of India by the Muhammadans was that, so far as Hindu society was concerned, Brahmans became its undisputed leaders and law-givers…. When the Muhammadans had overcome all opposition and settled down as rulers, unless some of them were fanatically inclined to make forcible conversions, they left the Hindus in the hands of their religious leaders and, whenever they wanted to pacify them by quiet methods, they made use of the Brahmans as their accredited representatives.

Another great advantage was that, for the first time in history, all the peoples of India, of all sects and denominations, were brought under the supremacy of the Brahmans. Till then, they had claimed to be priests of only the three higher castes and did not presume to speak for the Shudras and other Indian peoples except to keep them at a safe distance. The Muhammadans called all the non-Muslim inhabitants, without any discrimination, by the common name "Hindu," which practically meant non-Muslim and nothing more. This simple fact… condemned the dumb millions of the country to perpetual subjection to their priestly exploiters. Indians became "Hindus," their religion became Hinduism, and Brahmans became their masters…. Brahmanism became Hinduism, that is, the religion of all who were not followers of the Prophet of Mecca. Fortified thus in an unassailable position of sole religious authority, Brahmans commenced to establish their theocratic overlordship of all India.[19]

The Bhagats Seek Begampura — In the 12th century, at the outset of the Delhi Sultanate, lived Farid. A Sufi Muslim born in Punjab and one of the earliest Bhagats who preceded Guru Nanak, Farid faced the dark condition of the Indian subcontinent with calmness as he taught a path of love rooted in human worth. Amidst great sociopolitical upheaval, Farid declares, "The Lord Eternal in all abides: Break no heart – know, each being is a priceless jewel."[20]

Championing the equally divine origins of *all* humanity, he proclaims, "The Creation is in the Creator, and the Creator is in the Creation."[21] For Farid, because of the inherent sacredness of all creatures, no one is an infidel or an Untouchable. While the majority of the population languished under a system that called them outcastes, he suggested the way to cast out the hatred practiced by the elites was to respond with love. As Farid says, "Do not turn around and strike those who strike you with their fists."[22] Instead, he admonishes, "Return thou good for evil, bear no revenge in thy heart."[23]

Over ensuing centuries, other Bhagats charted paths to guide the most wretched members of society towards freedom.

Bhagat Namdev (c. 1270-1350), a tailor and poet from Maharashtra, asks, "What do I have to do with social status? What do I have to do with ancestry?"[24] He believed God cares for all humans, no matter their flaws. He writes, "You saved the prostitute and the ugly hunch-back."[25]

This simple-hearted saint, who knew that all people are created equal, was himself regularly treated as inferior. Describing his experience being thrown out of a temple, he writes, "Calling me low-caste and Untouchable, they beat me and drove me out; what should I do now, O Beloved Father Lord? If You liberate me after I am dead, no one will know that I am liberated."[26] In another verse about being ejected from a temple because of his caste, he expresses the pain and injustice felt by all the *Mulnivasi* as he cried out to his Creator.

ਹਸਤ ਖੇਲਤ ਤੇਰੇ ਦੇਹੁਰੇ ਆਇਆ ॥
ਭਗਤਿ ਕਰਤ ਨਾਮਾ ਪਕਰਿ ਉਠਾਇਆ ॥
ਹੀਨੜੀ ਜਾਤਿ ਮੇਰੀ ਜਾਦਿਮ ਰਾਇਆ ॥
ਛੀਪੇ ਕੇ ਜਨਮਿ ਕਾਹੇ ਕਉ ਆਇਆ ॥
ਲੈ ਕਮਲੀ ਚਲਿਓ ਪਲਟਾਇ ॥
ਦੇਹੁਰੈ ਪਾਛੈ ਬੈਠਾ ਜਾਇ ॥

Laughing and playing, I came to Your Temple, O Lord.
While Namdev was worshipping,
he was grabbed and driven out.
I am of a low social class, O Lord;
why was I born into a family of fabric dyers?
I picked up my blanket and went back,
to sit behind the temple.[27]

In the 15th century, a weaver from Uttar Pradesh named Bhagat Kabir (c. 1398-1448) voiced the equality of all which is found in the mortality of all. He writes, "The king and his subjects are equally killed; such is the power of Death."[28] Whether a person is considered high born or low born, all enter and leave the world in the same way, as he states, "Naked we come, and naked we go. No one, not even the kings and queens, shall remain."[29] Consequently, he denounces the concept of hereditary caste in a verse opposing the superiority of Brahmans.

ਗਰਭ ਵਾਸ ਮਹਿ ਕੁਲੁ ਨਹੀ ਜਾਤੀ ॥
ਬ੍ਰਹਮ ਬਿੰਦੁ ਤੇ ਸਭ ਉਤਪਾਤੀ ॥੧॥
ਕਹੁ ਰੇ ਪੰਡਿਤ ਬਾਮਨ ਕਬ ਕੇ ਹੋਏ ॥
ਬਾਮਨ ਕਹਿ ਕਹਿ ਜਨਮੁ ਮਤ ਖੋਏ ॥
ਜੌ ਤੂੰ ਬ੍ਰਾਹਮਣੁ ਬ੍ਰਹਮਣੀ ਜਾਇਆ ॥
ਤਉ ਆਨ ਬਾਟ ਕਾਹੇ ਨਹੀ ਆਇਆ ॥
ਤੁਮ ਕਤ ਬ੍ਰਾਹਮਣ ਹਮ ਕਤ ਸੂਦ ॥
ਹਮ ਕਤ ਲੋਹੂ ਤੁਮ ਕਤ ਦੂਧ ॥

In the dwelling of the womb, there is no ancestry or social status.
All have originated from the Seed of God.
Tell me, O Pandit, O religious scholar:
since when have you been a Brahman?
Don't waste your life by continually claiming to be a Brahman.
If you are indeed a Brahman, born of a Brahman mother,
Then why didn't you come by some other way?
How is it that you are a Brahman, and I am of a low social status?
How is it that I am formed of blood, and you are made of milk?[30]

Guru Ravidas (1450-1520), a contemporary of Guru Nanak, was a cobbler who, like Bhagat Kabir, was also from Uttar Pradesh. He continued spreading ideals against social division by declaring one Creator God who loves His creatures equally regardless of the caste his followers were born into. He proclaims, "Whether he is a Brahman, a Vaishya, a Shudra, or a Kshatriya; whether he is a poet, an outcaste, or a filthy-minded person, he becomes pure by meditating on the Creator."[31]

Instead of a segregated society, in which the masses live in fear of their shadows because they are divided into castes of increasingly degraded value, Bhagat Ravidas presents a vision of an heavenly city where all are equal and free.

ਬੇਗਮ ਪੁਰਾ ਸਹਰ ਕੋ ਨਾਉ ॥
ਦੂਖੁ ਅੰਦੋਹੁ ਨਹੀ ਤਿਹਿ ਠਾਉ ॥
ਨਾਂ ਤਸਵੀਸ ਖਿਰਾਜੁ ਨ ਮਾਲੁ ॥
ਖਉਫੁ ਨ ਖਤਾ ਨ ਤਰਸੁ ਜਵਾਲੁ ॥
ਅਬ ਮੋਹਿ ਖੂਬ ਵਤਨ ਗਹ ਪਾਈ ॥
ਊਹਾਂ ਖੈਰਿ ਸਦਾ ਮੇਰੇ ਭਾਈ ॥
ਕਾਇਮੁ ਦਾਇਮੁ ਸਦਾ ਪਾਤਿਸਾਹੀ ॥
ਦੋਮ ਨ ਸੇਮ ਏਕ ਸੋ ਆਹੀ ॥
ਆਬਾਦਾਨੁ ਸਦਾ ਮਸਹੂਰ ॥
ਊਹਾਂ ਗਨੀ ਬਸਹਿ ਮਾਮੂਰ ॥
ਤਿਉ ਤਿਉ ਸੈਲ ਕਰਹਿ ਜਿਉ ਭਾਵੈ ॥

Begampura, "the city without sorrow," is the name of the town.
There is no suffering or anxiety there.
There are no troubles or taxes on commodities there.
There is no fear, blemish, or downfall there.
Now I have found this most excellent city.
There is lasting peace and safety there, O Siblings of Destiny.
God's Kingdom is steady, stable and eternal.
There is no second or third status; all are equal there.
That city is populous and eternally famous.
Those who live there are wealthy and contented.
They stroll about freely, just as they please.[32]

Guru Nanak's *Panth* — Under the guidance of Guru Nanak, these liberating messages were united as the foundational doctrines of the Sikh Revolution. As a Sikh, Guru Nanak exhausted all points of travel in his mission to discover truths that might topple tyranny. Traveling to the East as far as Assam and Burma, to the South as far as Sri Lanka, to the West as far as Mecca, and to the North into Tibet and China, he listened, learned, and dialogued. In the process, he constructed an institution called the *Panth* with the intention of overturning the conventions of falsehood which enslaved the common people of the Indian subcontinent. His vision was to give them (and those beyond the subcontinent) a guiding light for the future.

In his lifetime, new burdens were placed upon the downtrodden as armed foreign invaders again swept into India. Since the 12th century, the Bhagats had challenged Brahmanism by composing poetry, dialoguing, and educating the masses. In the 16th century, however, circumstances deteriorated further as Babur — the "tiger" who founded the Mughal Empire — conquered Afghanistan and then swept through northern India to seize Delhi.

Historically, the Brahmanical strategy for survival was alliance with invaders. With the arrival of the Mughals, the voice of the *Mulnivasi* risked total strangulation as Brahmans united with the State to suppress any strain of resistance. The "lowest of the low" faced a two-headed hawk — one head being the Mughals, who devoured the people's possessions; the other head being the Brahmans, who devoured the people's souls. Thus, as Guru Nanak recognized these fresh challenges placed on the backs of the *Mulnivasi*, he developed the *Panth* as a new and relevant institution — a unique path entirely distinct from any other existing tradition.

A hallmark of the *Panth* was its condemnation of both social *and* political tyrannies. Setting the precedent of resistance to tyranny, Guru Nanak observed the bloodshed perpetrated by the Mughal invaders and mournfully provided his eyewitness account.

Babur terrified Hindustan. The Creator Himself does not take the blame, but has sent the Mughal as the messenger of death. There was so much slaughter that the people screamed. Didn't You feel compassion, Lord? O Creator Lord, You are the Master of all. If some powerful man strikes out against another man, then no one feels any grief in their mind. But if a powerful tiger attacks a flock of sheep and kills them, then its master must answer for it. This priceless country has been laid waste and defiled by dogs, and no one pays any attention to the dead.[33]

As he denounced the invasion, Guru Nanak developed a policy of the

Panth which would be carried forward by his successors for generations. As he lamented the brutal subjugation of Hindus and Muslims alike, he emerged as an equal opportunity activist for all oppressed peoples. He not only exposed the exploitations of Brahmanism, but also raised his voice in protest against the atrocities committed by the State. As the powerful waged war for territorial control, he warned those caught in the confluence of events.

He writes, "You are engrossed in worldly entanglements, O Siblings of Destiny, and you are practicing falsehood." Ultimately, Babur's massacres led the Guru to conclude that the fact of human mortality reveals the value of things of an eternal rather than a temporary nature. The atrocities, as he describes, inspired him to call out to the Creator for hope.

> Those heads adorned with braided hair, with their parts painted with vermillion. Those heads were shaved with scissors, and their throats were choked with dust. They lived in palatial mansions, but now they cannot even sit near the palaces.... They came in palanquins, decorated with ivory. Water was sprinkled over their heads, and glittering fans were waved above them. They were given hundreds of thousands of coins when they sat, and hundreds of thousands of coins when they stood. They ate coconuts and dates and rested comfortably upon their beds. But ropes were put around their necks, and their strings of pearls were broken. Their wealth and youthful beauty, which gave them so much pleasure, have now become their enemies. The order was given to the soldiers, who dishonored them, and carried them away....
>
> Since Babur's rule has been proclaimed, even the princes have no food to eat. The Muslims have lost their five times of daily prayer, and the Hindus have lost their worship as well. Millions of religious leaders failed to halt the invader,when they heard of the Emperor's invasion. He burned the rest-houses and the ancient temples; he cut the princes limb from limb, and cast them into the dust. None of the Mughals went blind, and no one performed any miracle. The battle raged between the Mughals and the Pathans, and the swords clashed on the battlefield. They took aim and fired their guns, and they attacked with their elephants.... The Hindu women, the Muslim women, the Bhattis and the Rajputs, some had their robes torn away, from head to foot, while others came

to dwell in the cremation ground. Their husbands did not return home....

The body shall fall, and the soul shall depart; if only they knew this. Why do you cry out and mourn for the dead? The Lord is, and shall always be. You mourn for that person, but who will mourn for you? You are engrossed in worldly entanglements, O Siblings of Destiny, and you are practicing falsehood. The dead person does not hear anything at all; your cries are heard only by other people. Only the Lord, who causes the mortal to sleep, O Nanak, can awaken him again. One who understands his true home does not sleep. If the departing mortal can take his wealth with him, then go ahead and gather wealth yourself.... I have searched in the four directions, but no one is mine. If it pleases You, O Lord Master, then You are mine, and I am Yours. There is no other door for me; where shall I go to worship? You are my only Lord; Your True Name is in my mouth.[34]

Thus, Guru Nanak lived in a land caught between the rival and equally vicious forces of Islamic invaders and the Brahmans. Amidst this chaos, he constructed the *Panth*. In the process, he denounced virtually every orthodoxy of Brahmanism — caste, fundamentalism, the practice of *sati*, prohibition of remarriage by widows, degradation of women, the dowry system, the hypocrisy of empty rituals, and a culture of brutal subjugation of the masses by a handful of elite.

The masses flocked to this new "shop" as they joined the Guru's reverence for reason and celebrated the equality and liberty produced by this freedom from delusion. This new shop, which grew warm with "traffic" over time, was giving away freedom. When the shop opened, however, its chief competition was the shops of the Brahmans which peddled superstition.

Praising the establishment of Sikhism as "a highly important event," British historian Edward Thornton simultaneously describes Brahmanism as "a vast system of superstition, probably the most influential, as well as the most tyrannical and mischievous, that has ever enthralled and depraved human nature."[35] A principal way in which Brahmanism enthralled human nature was through its myriad of idols. Then as now, idol-worship was promoted by Brahmans — the priests and curators of the temples which housed the idols — as the cornerstone of devotion.

The premier example of how Brahmanism harnessed the superstitions of the masses to control and exploit them was the floating Shiva-linga idol at Somnath Temple in Gujarat. Among the many smoke and mirrors experiments fraudulently thrusted on the public throughout the long annals of human history, the idol at Somnath stands out as one of the most successful attempts to fleece people of their wealth and dignity.

Although suspended by a scientifically-advanced magnetic levitation mechanism, the idol was mischievously portrayed as supernaturally self-levitating. Worshippers came from far and wide to pay to see this marvel. The idol's secret was discovered in 1024, however, when the temple was captured by the invading army of Sultan Mahmud of Ghazni. Persian scientist Zakariya al-Qazwini simultaneously describes the idol and its fate, writing,

The idol was in the middle of the temple without anything to support it from below, or suspend it from above. It was regarded with great veneration by the Hindus, and whoever beheld it floating in the air was struck with amazement, whether he was a Mussulman or an infidel....

Everything that was most precious was brought there as offerings, and the temple was endowed with the taxes gathered from more than ten thousand villages. There is a river, the Ganges, which is held sacred.... They used to bring the water of this river to Somnath every day and wash the temple with it. A thousand Brahmans were employed in worshipping the idol and attending on the visitors and five hundred damsels sang and danced at the door — all these were maintained upon the endowments of the temple. The edifice was built upon fifty-six pillars of teak, covered with lead....

When... [Mahmud of Ghazni] asked his companions what they had to say about the marvel of the idol, and of it staying in the air without prop or support, several maintained that it was upheld by some hidden support. The king directed a person to go and feel all around above and below it with a spear, which he did, but met with no obstacle. One of the attendants then stated his opinion that the canopy was made of loadstone [magnetite], and the idol of iron, and that the ingenious builder had skillfully contrived that the magnet should not exercise a greater force on any one side — hence the idol was suspended in the middle.... Permission was obtained from the Sultan to remove some stones from the top of the canopy to settle the point. When two stones were removed from the summit, the idol swerved on one side; when more were taken away, it inclined still further, until at last it rested on the ground.[36]

How could human intelligence so easily fall prey to such a scam? The masses were an easy target for such frauds because, for generation after generation, the caste status imposed on them denied them access to even basic education. According to caste laws, they were forbidden to obtain education. All learning was preserved in the Sanskrit language. As explained by 17th-century French physician François Bernier, who lived in the Mughal Empire, Sanskrit signified "pure language." The Brahmans "call it the holy and divine language," and it was "a language known only to the Pandits, and totally different from that which is ordinarily spoken in Hindustan."[37] With all knowledge kept under lock and key, the common people remained in a state of abject ignorance.

The elites isolated their community, banned others from learning their language, and propagated religious teachings forbidding non-Brahmans from accessing education. An educated public was to their disadvantage. "The Brahmans encourage and promote these gross errors and superstitions to which they are indebted for their wealth and consequence," wrote Bernier. "As persons attached and consecrated to important mysteries, they are held in general veneration, and enriched by the alms of the people."[38]

In the midst of this cultural context arose Farid, Namdev, Kabir, Ravidas, and Nanak, who denounced the exploitive system of Brahmanism, taught that all are made equal and free in the sight of our Creator, and presented a hopeful vision of a city without sorrow called Begampura. They championed the premier importance of embracing universal human dignity and reaching out to those who are considered low born. Furthermore, they taught that idol-worship is foolish because it involves humans worshipping their own lifeless creations. Idols cannot respond to those who cry out for help. As Guru Nanak advises,

ਹਿੰਦੂ ਮੂਲੇ ਭੂਲੇ ਅਖੁਟੀ ਜਾਂਹੀ ॥
ਨਾਰਦਿ ਕਹਿਆ ਸਿ ਪੂਜ ਕਰਾਂਹੀ ॥
ਅੰਧੇ ਗੁੰਗੇ ਅੰਧ ਅੰਧਾਰੁ ॥
ਪਾਥਰੁ ਲੇ ਪੂਜਹਿ ਮੁਗਧ ਗਵਾਰ ॥
ਓਹਿ ਜਾ ਆਪਿ ਡੁਬੇ ਤੁਮ ਕਹਾ ਤਰਣਹਾਰੁ ॥੨॥

The Hindus have forgotten the Primal Lord;
they are going the wrong way.... They are worshipping idols.
They are blind and mute, the blindest of the blind.
The ignorant fools pick up stones and worship them.
But when those stones themselves sink,
who will carry you across?[39]

Instead of seeking God in statues set in temples, the Bhagats agreed that people must recognize the presence of "the Lord's Light in all." With the arrival of the Mughals, however, a unique institution was necessary to continue propagating this teaching. Thus, Guru Nanak conceived the *Panth*.

The response to the teachings of the *Panth* was revolutionary. Rationality replaced superstition. Enlightenment replaced delusion. Exposition replaced exploitation. Liberty replaced tyranny. In contrast to the "system of superstition" propagated by Brahmanism, humanitarian Puran Singh (1881-1931) writes,

> Guru Nanak condemns false creeds and crooked politics and the unjust social order. He condemns the hollow scriptures and isms of the times; he condemns barren pieties, asceticisms, trances, sound-hearing yogas, bead-telling, *namazes'* fasts, and all the formal vagaries of religious and political hypocrisies. He condemns them without sparing any, for it was all darkness in the world....
>
> Guru Nanak takes up, like a giant, the long-rooted conventions of Hindu and Muslim on the palm of his hand and pitches them into the sea. Off with cant. Away with nonsense. Down with lies....
>
> Here, in the Punjab, was the wholesale destruction of all such systems in a glance, in a smile, in a presence. Down with the dead form and the evil minded social order. Down with false Islam and false Hinduism; take to the true creeds.[40]

Most notably, Guru Nanak reached out to the "lowest of the low." Indian historian Dr. Rajkumar Hans explains, "The Sikh Guru embraced Untouchables by distinctly aligning himself with them to challenge the Hindu caste system. He destroyed the Hindu hierarchical systems — social as well as political."[41]

The Guru chose to live as a son of the soil, exemplifying his teachings by taking up a profession of honest labor. "Truth is higher than everything; but higher still is truthful living," he taught.[42] "Guru Nanak cast off the costume of a hermit and spent the last 18 years of his life as a householder at Kartarpur," reports Sangat Singh. There, in a town he founded in 1522, he worked as a farmer.

> Here, he set up a human laboratory to practice the new faith, the Sikh *Panth*, to give practical shape to his over two decades of teachings…. Here was Guru Nanak, tilling the land, living with his wife and sons, preaching the name of God and his philosophy, a positive reaffirmation of all human beings and their right to a dignified life, free from religious coercion, social bondage, and political oppression.[43]

As Guru Nanak denounced unjust social orders, challenged invaders, and showed the path to emancipation through the "true creeds" of equality and liberty, he set the stage for his successors. For 169 years after his death, nine Sikh Gurus continued his sacred mission to institutionalize the *Mulnivasi*'s centuries of struggle for liberation. In place of "false creeds and crooked politics" which taught elitism and entrenched oppression, these Gurus introduced and cultivated teachings of human dignity. They brought mental, spiritual, and physical liberty to an oppressed community. As a result, in the words of Guru Arjun, "The egg of superstition has burst; the mind is illumined: the Guru has shattered the fetters of the feet and freed the captive."[44]

With the advent of the tenth Guru, Gobind Singh, and his establishment of the *Khalsa* in 1699, the original intent of Guru Nanak was finally fulfilled. The downtrodden embraced a *Panth* in which they will never be victims, always be victorious, and constantly fight for the oppressed. First, however, it was destined for Arjun, the fifth Guru, to sacrifice his life.

Citations

1 Madra, Amandeep Singh and Parmjit Singh (eds.). *"Sicques, Tigers, or Thieves": Eyewitness Accounts of the Sikhs*. New York: Palgrave MacMillan. 2004. 4.
2 Cole, W. Owen and Piara Singh Sambhi. *A Popular Dictionary of Sikhism*. 1990. London: Routledge. 1997. 3.
3 *Guru Granth Sahib*. 15.
4 Ibid., 349.
5 Ibid., 376.

6 Ibid., 300.

7 Ibid., 5.

8 Ibid., 432.

9 Usage of terms "*Bhagats* and Gurus" should in no way be construed as placing the status of one above the other. Both terms are equal in accordance with the teachings of *Guru Granth Sahib*.

10 Weber, Max. *The Religion of India: The Sociology Of Hinduism And Buddhism*. Glencoe: The Free Press. Tr. by Gerth, Hans H. and Don Martindale. 1958. 29-30.

11 Theertha, Dharma Swami. *History of Hindu Imperialism*. 1941. Kottayam, Kerala: Babasaheb Ambedkar Foundation. 1992. 6.

12 Ibid., 6-7.

13 Ibid., 76-77.

14 Singh, Sangat. *The Sikhs in History*. 1995. Amritsar: Singh Brothers. 2005. 4.

15 Ibid., 5.

16 Theertha. *History*. 100-101.

17 Srivastava, Ashirbadi Lal. *The Sultanate of Delhi*. 1950. Agra: Shiva Lal Agarwala & Company. 1966. 17.

18 Tavernier, Jean Baptiste. *Travels in India* (vol. 2). V. Ball (tr.). London: Macmillan and Co. 1889. 181.

19 Theertha. *History*. 114.

20 *Granth*. 1384.

21 Ibid., 1350.

22 Ibid., 1378.

23 Ibid., 1381.

24 Ibid., 485.

25 Ibid., 345.

26 Ibid., 1292.

27 Ibid., 1164.

28 Ibid., 855.

29 Ibid., 1157.

30 Ibid., 324.

31 Ibid., 858.

32 Ibid., 345.

33 Ibid., 360.

34 Ibid., 417-418.

35 Thornton, Edward. *A Gazetteer of the Territories Under the Government of the East-India Company and of the Native States on the Continent of India*. London: Wm. H. Allen & Co. 1858. 911.

36 Jackson, A.V. Williams (ed). *A History of India* (Vol. 9). London: The Grolier Society. 1906. 201-203.

37 Bernier, François. *Travels in the Mogul Empire: A.D. 1656-1668*. Archibald Constable (Tr.). London: Oxford University Press. 1916. 335.

38 Ibid., 305.

39 *Granth*. 556.

40 Singh, Puran. *Spirit of the Sikh* (Vol 2, Part 2). Patiala: Punjabi University. 1981. 3-4.

41 Rawat. *Studies*. 134.

42 *Granth*. 62.
43 Singh. *Sikh*. 20.
44 *Granth*. 1002.

— 2 —
Guru Arjun Carries the Caravan Forward

A succession of Gurus after Nanak expanded on the vision of Begampu-ra — the city without sorrow. Like his predecessors, Guru Arjun, the fifth Guru, boldly denounced the Brahmanical caste system taught by the *Shas-tras* (Hindu scriptures). Like the sons and daughters of the soil in whose footsteps he followed, he was tasked with the mission of "moving the cara-van forward" — that is, progressing the emancipation of the downtrodden.

Under the patronage of his father, Guru Ram Das (1534-1581), Arjun was prepared to sacrifice himself for the sake of the despised and deprived. His mother, Bibi Bani, was also central to preparing her son and inspiring the generations which followed in his footsteps. Summing up the importance of family and a mother's role in nurturing her children, Guru Arjun writes, "O son, this is a mother's blessing, that you may never even for a mere moment forget the Creator, forever worshipping the Lord of the Universe."[1] In turn, Guru Arjun prepared his son, Hargobind, to sacrifice himself.

As he was called to sacrifice, the Guru was not naive to the difficulty of his assignment or the dangers it entailed. Yet he knew he must fulfill his duty at any cost — even at the cost of his life.

Guru Arjun's legacy included two of the most significant achievements of the *Panth*. First, the completion in Amritsar, Punjab of Harmandir Sahib. Second, he compiled the *Adi Granth* (the Sikh noble book which eventually became the *Guru Granth*) and installed it in the completed Gurdwara.

"*Guru Granth Sahib*, the sacred text of the Sikhs, consists of the com-positions of six of the ten Sikh gurus and contributions of fifteen Sikh bards and fifteen non-Sikh *sant* poets of various social, ethnic, and religious back-grounds, including the eminent Muslim Sufi, Sheikh Farid," explains Dr. Rajkumar Hans. "This makes the sacred text an inclusive expression of spir-ituality in the history of world religions."[2]

Guru Arjun became the Steward of Begampura as he compiled the *Adi Granth* by collecting the writings of Farid, Namdev, Kabir, Ravidas, Nanak, and many other Bhagats. Guided by the *Shabads* (hymns) recorded in the *Adi Granth,* the Guru put the wisdom of the saints into practice. At this time, he was the leading light who took upon himself the duty to guide the *Mulnivasi* in a victorious march towards freedom.

In a dark age, Guru Arjun shouldered the tremendous burden of preserving the flickering flame of Begampura to shine hope for the wretched. Standing against the flow of history, the Guru yelled "stop" in the faces of the Brahmans and Mughals who collaboratively trampled the commoners under their feet. As Guru Nanak counseled, this was a dangerous position to hold.

ਜਉ ਤਉ ਪ੍ਰੇਮ ਖੇਲਣ ਕਾ ਚਾਉ ॥
ਸਿਰੁ ਧਰਿ ਤਲੀ ਗਲੀ ਮੇਰੀ ਆਉ ॥
ਇਤੁ ਮਾਰਗਿ ਪੈਰੁ ਧਰੀਜੈ ॥
ਸਿਰੁ ਦੀਜੈ ਕਾਣਿ ਨ ਕੀਜੈ ॥

If you desire to play this game of love with Me,
Then step onto My Path with your head in hand.
When you place your feet on this Path,
Give Me your head, and do not pay any attention to public opinion.[3]

Nonetheless, Guru Arjun was willing to sacrifice his head. Playing the game of love, he stepped onto the path with his head in his hand, sought the company of "the lowest of the low," and ignored all the critics. Despite knowing the most brutal tortures awaited him, he embraced the opportunity to help the simple-hearted break the shackles placed upon them by the Brahmans and Mughals. The ruling elites, as detailed in the words of Jahangir, perceived his "ways and manners" as a direct threat to their powerhouse.

For centuries, Brahmans secured their upper-echelon position by brutal maintenance of a totalitarian caste system which denied education, resources, and fundamental human dignity to the masses — all under the guise of honoring religious tradition. These common people were the "simple-hearted" described by Jahangir as flocking to Guru Arjun. Meanwhile, as the *Adi Granth*'s message progressively chipped away at the power structure of the Brahmans, the Mughals expanded their rule over northern India. The downtrodden in both Hindu and Muslim communities found no hope in either religion and little difference between either creed. "Islam then established in India as a religion had become a tyranny," explains Puran Singh.[4] "It was just lip profession."

Despite these continued oppressions, the *Panth* flourished as it showed the people how to obtain spiritual, social, economic, and political liberty. As it flourished, Amritsar began to represent the people's power. Essentially, it arose as the capital of a parallel government — the government of a nation of people who were subjects by choice, not birth. Autonomy, however, was intolerable to the ruling elites. British journalist Fergus Nicoll explains,

> Jahangir was not willing to take any risk with such an influential Punjabi community leader; he also found it irritating that Arjun Dev and his predecessors had represented an alternative source of authority to his own dynasty ever since the early years of the Mughal invasion. It has been argued that Jahangir would ideally have liked to end Amritsar's autonomy and force all Sikhs into the embrace of Islam, a recourse that would have been wholly objectionable to his father Akbar.[5]

Nicoll's explanation that Guru Arjun "represented an alternative source of authority" was collaborated by Jahangir's testimony about his reasons for ordering the Guru's execution. The Guru, wrote Jahangir, was "in the garb of *Pir* [saint] and *Sheikh* [king]." Thus, Guru Arjun was manifesting both temporal and spiritual authority.

Nicoll's description of Guru Arjun as an "influential Punjabi community leader" was collaborated by Father Jerome Xavier, a Jesuit priest living in the Mughal court. Describing Guru Arjun in a September 1606 letter, Fr. Xavier writes, "[He was] a Gentile called Guru, who amongst the Gentiles is like the Pope amongst us. He was held as a saint and was as such venerated." The Guru's reputation, notes Xavier, was of "high dignity."

Mughal-Brahman Co-Rule — Efforts to eliminate this man of "high dignity" owed their origins to a joint alliance between the Mughals and the Brahmans.

The caste system enabled India's subjugation by foreign invaders. According to Lieutenant Colonel John Malcolm of the British East India Company, "The Muhammadan conquerors of India... saw the religious prejudices of the Hindus, which they had calculated upon as one of the pillars of their safety."[6] Meanwhile, alliance with the Mughals benefited the Brahmans as it enabled them to protect themselves, maintain sociopolitical power, and continue to impose the caste system with the sanction of the Mughals.

Consequently, Brahmans were welcomed as key members of the Mughal government and they were more than willing to fill those positions. American historian Dr. Audrey Truschke explains, "The Mughal elite poured immense energy into drawing Sanskrit thinkers to their courts, adopting and adapting Sanskrit-based practices, translating dozens of Sanskrit texts into Persian and composing Persian accounts of Indian philosophy."[7] Seizing the chance to maintain their stranglehold on social power, Brahmans (already the wealthiest and most-educated by virtue of their position in the caste system) "became influential members of the Mughal court, composed Sanskrit works for Mughal readers, and wrote about their imperial experiences."[8]

Some of the most prominent of these "Sanskrit thinkers" were Birbal (1528–1586), Bhagwant Das (1537-1589), Todar Mal (died 1589), Pandit Jagannath (1590-1641), Raghunath Ray Kayastha (died 1663), Chandar Bhan Brahman (died c. 1670), and Bhimsen Saxena (lived c. 1700). Birbal and Bhagwant Das were generals under Akbar. Todar Mal was the Chief Finance Minister under Akbar. Jagannath was a poet under Jahangir and Shah Jahan. Raghunath was a Finance Minister (eventually Chief Finance Minister) under Shah Jahan and Aurangzeb. Chandar Bhan was a *munshi* (secretary) under Akbar, Jahangir, Shah Jahan, and Aurangzeb. Bhimsen was a general under Shah Jahan and Aurangzeb.

While these men stood out as prominent examples of the partnership between Brahmans and Mughals, they represent a mere handful of the many others who joined in the Mughal-Brahman co-rule of India. The backbone of the civil service was composed of upper-caste Hindus. "From the middle of the 17th century onwards, most of the *munshis* were Hindus, and their proportion rapidly increased," writes Indian historian Jadunath Sarkar. "The Hindus had made a monopoly of the lower ranks of the revenue department (*diwani*) from long before the time of Todar Mal."[9]

The privileged castes not only swelled the civil service ranks of the Mughals, but they also provided much of the muscle for the imperial military. In particular, the high-caste Rajputs stepped forward to exercise force on behalf of the Empire. Indian historian Satish Chandra reports,

The policy of seeking a special relationship with the Rajputs emerged under Akbar, and was one of the most abiding features of Mughal rule in India....

Apart from being loyal allies, the Rajputs begin to emerge as the sword-arm of the empire.... The Rajputs emerge as partners in the kingdom....

The Rajputs not only emerged as dependable allies who could be used anywhere for fighting, even against princes of blood, they also began to be employed in tasks of governance....

The Mughal-Rajput alliance was mutually beneficial.... The steadfast loyalty of the Rajputs was an important factor in the consolidation and further expansion of the Mughal empire. On the other hand, service in the Mughal empire enabled the Rajput rajas to serve in distant places far away from their homes, and to hold important administrative posts. This further raised their prestige and social status. Service with the Mughals was also financially rewarding. beginning with Akbar.[10]

On one hand, this dual alliance between two oppressive systems created fertile ground for the growth of the doctrines of the Gurus. "Sikhism arose where fallen and corrupt Brahmanical doctrines were most strongly acted on by the vital and spreading Muhammadan belief," wrote Scottish historian Joseph Davey Cunningham in 1849.[11] On the other hand, when Sikhism emerged as the subcontinent's leading defender of the doctrine of human dignity, it provoked the wrath of both the Mughals and the Brahmans.

Just as in times past when Brahmans collaborated with foreign invaders during the eradication of Buddhism, they again joined forces with the occupying Mughals. The Mughal Empire was established in 1526. By the mid-1500s, Brahmans began employing their intimate relationship with the Mughals to attempt to instigate the State against the Sikhs.

According to British historian Max Arthur Macauliffe, who wrote a six-volume history of the Sikhs, a group of Brahmans approached Emperor Akbar (1542-1605) to lodge a complaint against the third Sikh Guru, Amar Das (1479-1574). The basis of their grievance was the Guru's opposition to caste. As Macauliffe reported, the Brahmans told Akbar:

Thy Majesty is the protector of our customs and the redresser of our wrongs.... Guru Amar Das of Goindwal hath abandoned the religious and social customs of the Hindus, and abolished the distinction of the four castes. Such heterodoxy hath never before been heard of.... There is now no twilight prayer, no *gayatri* [Sanskrit hymns], no offering of water to ancestors, no pilgrimages, no obsequies, and no worship of idols.... The Guru hath abandoned all these, and established the repetition of *Waheguru* instead of Ram; and no one now acteth according to the Vedas or the *Smritis*. The Guru reverenceth not Jogis [yogis], Jatis [castes], or Brahmans. He worshippeth no gods or goddesses, and he ordered his Sikh to refrain from doing so forevermore. He seateth all his followers in a line, and causeth them to eat together from his kitchen, irrespective of caste — whether they are Jats, strolling minstrels, Muhammadans, Brahmans, Khatris, shopkeepers sweepers, barbers, washermen, fishermen, or carpenters. We pray thee restrain him now, else it will be difficult hereafter. And may thy religion and Empire increase and extend over the world.[12]

Thus, the Mughal-Brahman alliance began with the Brahmans turning the attention of the Mughals to the distinct "ways and manners" of the warm shop of the Sikhs. Akbar did not act on their complaint, but the Brahmans continued attempting to use State power to undermine the rise of the *Panth*. In the late 1500s, their attempts expanded with Birbal.

Birbal — During the reign of Akbar, one of the "Sanskrit thinkers" drawn to the Mughal courts was Raja Birbal, a Brahman from Uttar Pradesh. Birbal was "Akbar's constant companion for many years," explained Indian historian Abraham Eraly. "A celebrated litterateur," he was nicknamed "Kavi Rai, King of Poets" by Akbar.[13] The Mughal and the Brahman were so close that the Emperor opened his mind to Brahmanism. According to Eraly, "When Raja Birbal became a major influence on Akbar, he... persuaded the Emperor to worship the sun and the fire, and venerate 'water, stones, and trees, and all natural objects, even down to cows and their dung; that he should adopt the sectarian mark, and the Brahmanical thread.'"[14]

Birbal planted the seeds of conflict between the ruling elite and the Sikhs. "Birbal, a learned and accomplished man, was on religious grounds hostile to the Guru and jealous of his daily increasing influence and popularity," writes Macauliffe.[15] Corroborating Macauliffe's perspective on Birbal, British historian Vincent Arthur Smith continues, "He was hostile to the Sikhs, whom he considered to be heretics."[16]

In 1586, Akbar sent Birbal on a military campaign to subdue a rebellion in Afghanistan. First, the Brahman "made up his mind to harass the Guru and the people at Amritsar," reports Sikh historian Prithi Pal Singh. He stopped in Punjab and, on the excuse of raising funds for his expedition, he "ordered his collectors to collect a fixed levy from the people of Punjab with a special reference to Amritsar." Guru Arjun replied that the Sikhs sought an exemption and, following his lead, the simple-hearted people of Amritsar refused to pay.[17]

Unable to delay his military campaign any longer, Birbal was forced to depart. "He ordered his staff to remind him of the Guru on his return, and said that if he did not then get a rupee from each house in Amritsar, he would raze the city to its foundations," explains Macauliffe.[18] However, he never got the chance to do so. According to American historian John F. Richards, during the Raja's war in Afghanistan, "about 8,000 imperial soldiers, including Raja Birbal, were killed in the greatest disaster to Mughal arms in Akbar's reign."[19] The Sikhs, writes Smith, "consequently regard his miserable death as the just penalty for his threats of violence to Arjun."[20]

According to Eraly, Akbar "avenged Birbal's death by sending Todar Mal to hunt down the Afghans."[21] Bhagwant Das, meanwhile, was sent in 1586 to conquer Kashmir. Francisco Pelsaert, a 17th-century merchant with the Dutch East India Company, notes, "Raja Bhagwant Das overcame the country by craft and subtlety, the lofty mountains and difficult roads rendering forcible conquest impossible."[22] Thus, while Guru Arjun was peacefully developing the *Panth* and the *Granth* in Punjab, Brahmans led armies in aggressive wars of conquest to expand the borders of the Mughal Empire.

Chandu Shah — Birbal planted seeds of conflict between Sikhs and the Empire. Twenty years after his death, the seeds were watered and eventually harvested by another "Sanskrit thinker" named Chandu Shah, who worked as "the finance administrator of Lahore province."[23]

Chandu is referenced in contemporary accounts of Guru Arjun's persecution — one in 1606 from Fr. Xavier and one in the mid-1600s from the Persian history *Dabistan-i Mazahib*. The accounts refer, respectively, to a "rich gentile" (a Hindu) and "collectors" who orchestrated the Guru's torments.

Later accounts by agents of the British East India Company also reference Chandu. In 1783, for instance, George Forster writes, "Arjun, who having incurred the displeasure of a Hindu (named Chandu) favored by Jahangir, was committed by that prince to the persecution of his enemy; and his death... was caused, it is said, by the rigor of confinement."[24] Writing in 1812, Lt. Col. Malcolm mentions Chandu as well, referring to him as "Danichand."

The *Adi Granth...* was partly composed by Nanak and his immediate successors, but received its present form and arrangement from Arjunmal, who has blended his own additions with what he deemed most valuable in the compositions of his predecessors. It is Arjun, then, who ought, from this act, to be deemed the first who gave consistent form and order to the religion of the Sikhs: an act which, though it has produced the effect he wished of uniting that nation more closely and of increasing their numbers, proved fatal to himself. The jealousy of the Muhammadan government was excited, and he was made its sacrifice. The mode of his death... is related very differently by different authorities: but several of the most respectable agree in stating that his martyrdom, for such they term it, was caused by the active hatred of a rival Hindu zealot, Danichand Kshatriya, whose writings he refused to admit into the *Adi Granth* on the ground that the tenets in them were irreconcilable to the pure doctrine of the unity and omnipotence of God taught in that sacred volume. This rival had sufficient influence with the Muhammadan governor of the province to procure the imprisonment of Arjun; who is affirmed, by some writers, to have died from the severity of his confinement; and, by others, to have been put to death in the most cruel manner. In whatever way his life was terminated, there can be no doubt, from its consequences, that it was considered by his followers as an atrocious murder.... The Sikhs, who had been till then an inoffensive, peaceable sect, took arms under Hargobind, the son of Arjunmal.[25]

Chandu, who Malcolm describes as a "rival," initially attempted to buy Guru Arjun's allegiance by proposing the marriage of his daughter to the Guru's son. However, Guru Arjun's only desire was to liberate humanity. He saw through the scheme and understood the marriage proposal as a devious attempt to trap him, neutralize the Sikhs, and consolidate their power with that of the tyrants who ruled from the throne of Delhi. Writing a little over 100 years after the incident, 18th-century Indian author Seva Das reports that Chandu "was reeling from the rejection of the marriage of his daughter to the Guru's son." According to his account, "Chandu is identified as feeding false reports against Guru Arjun, thereby contributing to his arrest and torture."[26]

In his memoirs, Jahangir confesses to maintaining hawk-eyed surveillance of the *Panth* and desiring to put an end to their "false traffic." The Emperor, who was already agitated by the Guru, was emboldened to act when the upper-caste State agent, Chandu, campaigned against the Guru. Once again, Brahman bureaucrats collaborated with Imperial forces to assail this irritating group of liberators. "The Guru was summoned to the Emperor's presence, and fined and imprisoned at the instigation chiefly, it is said, of Chandu Shah, whose alliance he had rejected, and who represented him as a man of dangerous ambition," reports Joseph Davey Cunningham.[27]

Guru Arjun's "Objectionable Passages" — Subsequently, the campaign against Guru Arjun was joined by a broader coalition of Brahman and Mughal courtiers who felt equally endangered by the independence of the Sikh people as manifested in the Guru sitting in Amritsar at Harmandir Sahib. The elite were angered by this sovereign source of power and the elevation it gave the oppressed. The power of the elite depended on suppressing the *Mulnivasi Bahujan* by maintaining both the Brahman's caste system and the Mughal's foreign occupation.

"The *pandits* and the *qazis*," notes Macauliffe, "also thought it a favorable opportunity to institute new proceedings against the Guru on the old charge of having compiled a book which blasphemed the worship and rules of the Hindus and the prayers and fastings of the Muhammadans."[28] Jahangir imposed a fine of 200,000 rupees on Guru Arjun as a condition for his freedom. The Guru's followers offered to pay it, but he defied the Emperor's demand and refused monetary assistance. Macauliffe reports, "As the Guru would not allow the fine to be paid, he was placed under the surveillance of Chandu. The *qazis* and Brahmans offered the Guru the alternative of being put to death or of expunging the alleged objectionable passages in the *Granth Sahib* and inserting the praises of Muhammad and of the Hindu deities."[29]

What were these "objectionable passages"? The teachings of the Bhagats, who spoke against caste, defended the equality of all humanity, and shared their vision of Begampura were naturally offensive to these powerful people. Also objectionable was Guru Arjun's teaching that royalty is attainable by even the commonest of people. For instance, the Guru writes,

ਸਗਲ ਪੁਰਖ ਮਹਿ ਪੁਰਖੁ ਪ੍ਰਧਾਨੁ ॥
ਸਾਧਸੰਗਿ ਜਾ ਕਾ ਮਿਟੈ ਅਭਿਮਾਨੁ ॥
ਆਪਸ ਕਉ ਜੋ ਜਾਣੈ ਨੀਚਾ ॥
ਸੋਊ ਗਨੀਐ ਸਭ ਤੇ ਊਚਾ ॥
ਜਾ ਕਾ ਮਨੁ ਹੋਇ ਸਗਲ ਕੀ ਰੀਨਾ ॥

ਹਰਿ ਹਰਿ ਨਾਮੁ ਤਿਨਿ ਘਟਿ ਘਟਿ ਚੀਨਾ ॥

He is a prince among men
Who has effaced his pride in the company of the good,
He who deems himself as of the lowly,
Shall be esteemed as the highest of the high.
He who lowers his mind to the dust of all men's feet,
Sees the Name of God enshrined in every heart.[30]

Guru Arjun asserts that a person is not noble because of any social status obtained through an accident of birth. Lineage and bloodlines are not the source of royalty. Instead, humility, self-sacrifice, and recognition of the divine image present in all people are the attributes by which a person can become a prince. He went even further, insisting a pauper can be a king — even the "king of the whole world." All that is necessary is love. He writes,

ਬਸਤਾ ਤੂਟੀ ਝੁੰਪੜੀ ਚੀਰ ਸਭਿ ਛਿੰਨਾ ॥
ਜਾਤਿ ਨ ਪਤਿ ਨ ਆਦਰੋ ਉਦਿਆਨ ਭ੍ਰਮਿੰਨਾ ॥
ਮਿਤ੍ਰ ਨ ਇਠ ਧਨ ਰੂਪ ਹੀਣ ਕਿਛੁ ਸਾਕੁ ਨ ਸਿੰਨਾ ॥
ਰਾਜਾ ਸਗਲੀ ਸ੍ਰਿਸਟਿ ਕਾ ਹਰਿ ਨਾਮਿ ਮਨੁ ਭਿੰਨਾ ॥

He who lives in a ruined hut, with all his clothes torn:
Who has neither caste, nor lineage, nor respect,
Who wanders in the wilderness,
Who has no friend or lover, who is without wealth or beauty,
And who has no relation or kinsmen,
Is yet the king of the whole world,
If his heart is imbued with the love of God.[31]

The Brahmans, who propagated their hereditary superiority based on an accident of birth, and Emperors, who premised their nobility on the same argument, were equally infuriated by Guru Arjun's assault on their claims to supremacy. The Guru was no respecter of titles, or wealth, or power. Instead, he accorded royalty to those who demonstrate humility by making themselves the servants of the downtrodden. In his eyes, a man becomes a king by serving rather than being served. Leadership means being a servant instead of a dictator.

Guru Arjun developed this concept but he did not originate it. Sikh propagation of the idea that a true king earns his title rather than being born to it — that is, the idea that a king only rules by consent of the governed — traced back to Guru Nanak. Sikh historian Dr. Gurmit Singh notes, "He denied to the kings their divine right to rule with absolute authority. According to him, authority in every sphere ultimately derives from God." Consequently, while he was certainly regarded as a superior spiritual authority, Singh reports, "The followers of Guru Nanak had started looking upon him and his successors as a superior temporal authority."[32]

Guru Arjun also repeated and expanded another idea originally articulated by the Bhagats and specifically detailed in Guru Nanak's declaration, "There is neither Hindu nor Muslim." He affirmed the separate identity of the Sikhs by distinguishing the Sikh *Panth* from the religions of the ruling elite.

ਵਰਤ ਨ ਰਹਉ ਨ ਮਹ ਰਮਦਾਨਾ ॥
ਤਿਸੁ ਸੇਵੀ ਜੋ ਰਖੈ ਨਿਦਾਨਾ ॥
ਏਕੁ ਗੁਸਾਈ ਅਲਹੁ ਮੇਰਾ ॥
ਹਿੰਦੂ ਤੁਰਕ ਦੁਹਾਂ ਨੇਬੇਰਾ ॥
ਹਜ ਕਾਬੈ ਜਾਉ ਨ ਤੀਰਥ ਪੂਜਾ ॥
ਏਕੋ ਸੇਵੀ ਅਵਰੁ ਨ ਦੂਜਾ ॥
ਪੂਜਾ ਕਰਉ ਨ ਨਿਵਾਜ ਗੁਜਾਰਉ ॥
ਏੱਕ ਨਿਰੰਕਾਰ ਲੇ ਰਿਦੈ ਨਮਸਕਾਰਉ ॥
ਨਾ ਹਮ ਹਿੰਦੂ ਨ ਮੁਸਲਮਾਨ ॥

I do not keep the Hindu fast nor the Muslim Ramadan.
I serve Him alone who is my refuge.
I serve the one Master, who is also Allah.
I will not worship with the Hindu, nor like the Muslim go to Mecca;
I shall serve Him and no other.
I will not pray to idols nor heed the Muslim's adhan [call to worship];
I shall put my heart at the feet of the one Formless Lord,
For we are neither Hindus nor Muslims.[33]

His words succinctly express centuries of struggle by the *Mulnivasi*. They only found freedom in rejecting all oppressors and establishing a distinct, separate identity apart from any label imposed on them by the ruling elite. This separation, as well as the declaration of the nobility of the common person, naturally deepened the hostility of the Mughal-Brahman alliance against the Sikhs.

These passages in the Adi Granth to which the *qazis* and *pandits* objected must have also shocked the Emperor. Not only was Guru Arjun teaching that a pauper can become a prince, but he appeared, as Jahangir describes, "in the garb of *Pir* [saint] and *Sheikh* [king]." Scottish missionary John Nicol Farquhar corroborates this idea, writing, "While Akbar honored Arjun, his son Jahangir was suspicious of the *Granth* and subjected him to tortures to which he succumbed."[34]

So dire was the need for liberation of the downtrodden, however, that Guru Arjun refused to give even the smallest ground despite facing tortures. He would not remove the teachings of the Bhagats. He would not remove his own teachings. Nor would he insert praises of religions from which he and his predecessors had entirely separated. "My main object is the spread of truth and the destruction of falsehood; and if, in pursuance of this object, this perishable body must depart, I shall account it great good fortune," the Guru tells his persecutors.[35]

Guru Arjun's Martyrdom — According to the *Dabistan*, "Jahangir mulcted [extracted money from] Guru Arjun Mal…. A large amount was demanded from him [and] he found himself powerless to pay it."[36] According to Fr. Xavier, Guru Arjun was then abused by Chandu, who he describes as "a rich gentile who remained his guarantor." To cover the 200,000 rupee fine, this guarantor "seized… everything he could find, not sparing his clothes nor the clothes of his wife and sons; and seeing that all this was not enough… each and every day he gave new torments and new affronts to the poor saint."[37]

Under Chandu's direction, Guru Arjun was tortured to death. "He ordered him to be beaten many times with shoes on his face and forbade him to eat… and thus, amongst many trials, pains, and torments… the poor Guru died," reports Xavier. According to Macauliffe, "They poured burning sand on him, seated him in red-hot caldrons, and bathed him in boiling water."[38] The *Dabistan* concludes, "He was tied up and kept [in the open] in the desert around Lahore. He gave up his life there owing to the strong sun, summer heat, and injuries inflicted by the collectors."[39]

On May 30, 1606, Guru Arjun became the first Sikh Guru to be martyred. Relentlessly refusing to succumb to the tyrannies of the Emperor and his courtiers, Guru Arjun defended the *Adi Granth* with every fiber of his being. To his last breath, he willingly risked his life, his property, and even the lives of his own family down to his children.

Only the *Mulnivasi* can comprehend the Guru's pain as he was punished for challenging the system. He knew what price he had to pay. Yet he took up the challenge and sacrificed his life for the sake of liberating the oppressed. Every shoe on his face, every broken bone, every inch of skin dragged across hot sands, every hour of starvation, every second of thirst, every moment he was spit upon, jeered at, and tormented represent his willingness to endure the sufferings, sorrows, and persecutions of others so that the children of the *Mulnivasi* might escape dehumanization and achieve emancipation. Afflicted, wounded, and martyred, Guru Arjun accepted his death so that others might be set free. He was imprisoned, impoverished, mocked, beaten, tortured, and murdered, but he bore the abuse with a spirit of love. In the midst of his torments, he declares, "No one is my enemy, none a stranger, and everyone is my friend."[40]

Despite the massive sufferings they have endured, all the *Mulnivasi* saints have faced their torments with this same attitude of unconditional love — dying just as they lived.

Citations

1 *Granth*. 496.

2 Rawat. *Studies*. 133

3 *Granth*. 1412.

4 Singh. *Spirit*. 3-4.

5 Nicoll, Fergus. *Shah Jahan: The Rise and Fall of the Mughal Emperor*. London: Haus Publishing Ltd. 2009. 59.

6 Malcolm, John. *Sketch of the Sikhs*. Prithipal Singh Kapur (ed.). Amritsar: Satvic Media Pvt. Limited. 2007. 46.

7 Truschke, Audrey. *Culture of Encounters: Sanskrit at the Mughal Court*. New York: Columbia University Press. 2016. Preface.

8 Rigoglioso, Marguerite. "Stanford scholar casts new light on Hindu-Muslim relations." stanford.edu. September 9, 2015.

9 Kinra, Rajeev. *Writing Self, Writing Empire: Chandar Bhan Brahman and the Cultural World of the Indo-Persian State Secretary*. Oakland: University of California Press. 2015. 291-292.

10 Chandra, Satish. *Medieval India: From Sultanat to the Mughals* (vol. 2). 1999. Har-Anand Publications Pvt. Ltd. 2006. 110, 115-117.

11 Cunningham, Joseph Davey. *A History of the Sikhs From the Origin of the Nation to the Battles of the Sutlej*. London: John Murray. 1849. 96.

12 Macauliffe, Max Arthur. *The Sikh Religion: Its Gurus, Sacred Writings, and Authors* (Vol. 2). Oxford: Clarendon Press. 1909. 104-105.

13 Eraly, Abraham. *The Mughal Throne: The Saga of India's Great Emperors*. 1997. London: Phoenix. 2004. 155.

14 Ibid., 193-194

15 Macauliffe, Max Arthur. *The Sikh Religion: Its Gurus, Sacred Writings, and Authors* (Vol. 3). Oxford: Clarendon Press. 1909. 15.

16 Smith, Vincent A. *Akbar the Great Mogul, 1542-1605*. Oxford: Clarendon Press. 1917. 237.

17 Singh, Prithi Pal. *The History of Sikh Gurus*. New Delhi: Lotus Press. 2006. 65-66.

18 Macauliffe. *Religion* (Vol. 3). 16.

19 Richards, John F. *The Mughal Empire*. Cambridge: Cambridge University Press. 1995. 50-51.

20 Smith. *Akbar the Great Mogul, 1542-1605*. 237.

21 Eraly. *Mughal*. 156.

22 Pelsaert, Francisco. *Jahangir's India*. Cambridge: W. Heffer & Sons Ltd. 1925. 35.

23 Cunningham. *History*. 50.

24 Madra and Singh. *Sicques*. 137.

25 Malcolm. *Sketch*. 38.

26 Madra and Singh. *Sicques*. 5.

27 Cunningham. *History*. 58.

28 Macauliffe. *Sikh Religion* (Vol. 3). 90.

29 Ibid. 92.

30 *Granth*. 266.

31 Ibid., 707.

32 Singh, Gurmit. *History of Sikh Struggles* (Vol. 1). New Delhi: Atlantic Publishers & Distributors. 1989. 21.

33 Ibid., 1136.

34 Farquhar, J.N. *The Religious Quest of India: An Outline of the Religious Literature of India*. Oxford: Oxford University Press. 1920. 338.

35 Macauliffe. *Religion* (Vol. 3). 92.

36 Grewal, J.S. (ed). *Sikh History from Persian Sources*. Irfan Habib (tr.). 2001. New Delhi: Tulika Books, 2011. 67.

37 Madra and Singh. *Sicques*. 7.

38 Macauliffe. *Religion* (Vol. 3). 93.

39 Madra and Singh. *Sicques*. 5.

40 *Granth*. 1299.

The Simple-Hearted:
Progressing From "Worms" to Free People

Guru Arjun's death by extreme torture was designed to send a chilling message to those contemplating the path of equality and liberty which he proposed, terrify those spreading the message of human dignity, and demonstrate the superiority of the powerful over the weak.

The Guru stewarded over 400 years of teachings by others who offered a ray of hope. From Farid to Namdev, Kabir to Ravidas, and Guru Nanak onwards, their teachings of emancipation, as encapsulated within the *Adi Granth,* represent the suffering, sorrows, and hopes of the Indian subcontinent's downtrodden people in a divine context. As they carried out a mission to overthrow successive, oppressive systems of dehumanization, they united a diverse, scattered, and subjugated population under their aegis.

The complex-hearted desired to squelch the rising tide of free people who were breaking the shackles of slavery bound upon them by the caste system. The alliance between Jahangir and Chandu intended to achieve this goal by killing Guru Arjun. Yet the Guru willingly played the "game of love" spoken of by Guru Nanak. He stepped onto God's path with his head in the palm of his hand. Bhagat Kabir, over 150 years earlier, describes such people as spiritual heroes.

ਗਗਨ ਦਮਾਮਾ ਬਾਜਿਓ ਪਰਿਓ ਨੀਸਾਨੈ ਘਾਉ ॥
ਖੇਤੁ ਜੁ ਮਾਂਡਿਓ ਸੂਰਮਾ ਅਬ ਜੁਝਨ ਕੋ ਦਾਉ ॥
ਸੂਰਾ ਸੋ ਪਹਿਚਾਨੀਐ ਜੁ ਲਰੈ ਦੀਨ ਕੇ ਹੇਤ ॥
ਪੁਰਜਾ ਪੁਰਜਾ ਕਟਿ ਮਰੈ ਕਬਹੂ ਨ ਛਾਡੈ ਖੇਤੁ ॥

The battle-drum beats in the sky of the mind;
aim is taken, and the wound is inflicted.
The spiritual warriors enter the field of battle;

now is the time to fight!
He alone is known as a spiritual hero,
who fights in defense of righteousness.
He may be cut apart, piece by piece,
but he never leaves the field of battle.[1]

Guru Arjun heard the battle-drum beating in the sky of his mind. Like his predecessors, who heard the same beat, he took aim against dehumanizing systems. His "ways and manners," which so offended Jahangir, morally wounded the oppressors. Interpreting those "ways and manners" as "heresies," they responded by cutting him apart. Yet he never left the field of battle. His successors heard the beat of the same battle-drum, entered the field, and refused to leave even at the cost of their lives. The caste system — indeed, any system of inequality — was the chief target of these spiritual heroes.

The Lowest of the Low — According to the Hindu scriptures, the system of *Varnashrama Dharma* — meaning the duties (*dharma*) of each class (*varna*) in each life stage (*ashrama*) — was divinely ordained at the creation of humankind.

According to the *Shastras*,[2] explains American religious studies professor Brian K. Smith, "The social classes and the *dharma* assigned to each were created in the beginning from the body parts of the creator god."[3] *Rigveda*, the oldest of the *Shastras*, teaches that the caste system originated at the creation of humanity. According to *Rigveda*, humans were created when "the gods" killed a Cosmic Being and split his body into parts. "His mouth became the Brahman.... From his two feet the Shudra was born."[4] *Manusmriti*, known as the Hindu law book, repeats the same creation myth but claims the god, Brahma, was the Cosmic Being from whose body humankind was created.

"Indian castes are grounded in a social theory positing four principal, hierarchically ordered classes (*varnas*)," writes Smith. Originally, the system of *Varnashrama Dharma* classified humans into four separate *varnas*. As it was imposed and practiced, however, it evolved into a more intricate system. "*Varna*... provides the historical roots and theoretical backbone for the later caste system, a social institution that many regard as distinctively, perhaps uniquely, South Asian. Furthermore, caste is sometimes identified as one of the only, if not *the* only, definitional features of the many-sided religion we call 'Hinduism.'"[5]

Manusmriti extensively details the value, purpose, and required conduct of these four separate classes. The edicts it contains were, supposedly, issued by Manu, the "first man." Writing in 1841, Scottish historian Mountstuart Elphinstone describes the importance of the "Laws of Manu" to shaping Hindu society.

> The first complete picture of the state of society is afforded by the code of laws which bears the name of Manu.... With that code, therefore, every history of the Hindus must begin....
>
> The first feature that strikes us in the society described by Manu is the division into four classes or castes.... In these we are struck with the prodigious elevation and sanctity of the Brahmans and the studied degradation of the lowest class.... The fourth class and the outcastes are no further considered than as they contribute to the advantage of the superior castes.[6]

Brahmans, at the top of the caste system, were the prime beneficiaries of the system. At the bottom were the Shudras. Below the Shudras were the Ati-Shudras — also called outcastes, Untouchables, or *Chandalas* — who belonged to no caste. Regarding the value of Brahmans, *Manusmriti* states,

> A Brahman, coming into existence, is born as the highest on earth, the lord of all created beings.... Whatever exists in the world is the property of the Brahman; on account of the excellence of his origin, the Brahman is, indeed, entitled to all.... Other mortals subsist through the benevolence of the Brahman.[7]

In practice, Smith writes, this meant that "the Brahman social class are 'gods on earth.'"[8] According to the *Shastras*, Brahmans were superhuman — or, at least, all others were subhuman. "In the classification of society, the Brahmans are also and always given the highest position.... The Brahman is the most complete manifestation of the human being and encompasses within his lordship all the domains of the other social classes," explains Smith.[9] This claim of supremacy was premised on the teachings in *Rigveda* and *Manusmriti* about the origins of humanity. "The priority the Brahmans claim in creation stories establishes the precedence of that class in social affairs."[10]

In contrast to the elite Brahmans, who were identified as superhuman "lords of all," the Shudras at the bottom were identified as subhuman slaves of all. According to *Manusmriti*, "One occupation only the lord prescribed to the Shudra, to serve meekly even these (other) three castes."[11] Ati-Shudras, on the other hand, had no place in society. "He who associates with an outcast, himself becomes an outcast after a year... by using the same... seat, or by eating with him."[12]

Shudras and Ati-Shudras, however, have historically constituted the majority of the population of the Indian subcontinent. As described by French Catholic missionary Jean-Antoine Dubois in his 1816 book, *Hindu Manners, Customs, and Ceremonies*, "The Shudras are the most numerous of the four main castes. They form, in fact, the mass of the population, and added to the Pariahs, or Outcastes, they represent at least nine-tenths of the inhabitants."[13] Thus, the caste system appears as an artificial construct which, by its design, subjugates the majority of the indigenous people — the *Mulnivasi Bahujan*.

Many scholars believe the Vedic society which invented Brahmanism and enslaved these *Mulnivasi Bahujan* originated from an invasion of the Indian subcontinent by an ancient Aryan people who are known as Indo-Aryans or Indo-Europeans. "The *varna* system does appear to have ancient roots," notes Smith. "It is fundamentally a version of a classification strategy brought to India by the Indo-European invaders during the second millennium BC."[14] He argues that identification of a people group as Shudras (and Ati-Shudras) was caused by an "historical expansion of Vedic society to include within it the non-Aryan indigenous inhabitants of South Asia." Smith further suggests,

> These natives the Indo-European invaders originally called *dasas* or *dasyus*, "slaves." Over time, as the invaders themselves became natives and as some of the original inhabitants were assimilated to some degree within Aryan society, the latter came to be known as "Shudras" and took over the bottom rung in the social order.[15]

This social order benefitted the Brahman class at the expense of the masses. The *Shastras* taught that humans classed as "Brahmans" originated from the head of Brahma. The *Shastras* taught that only Brahmans could be priests. The *Shastras* were written in Sanskrit. The *Shastras* forbade non-Brahmans from learning Sanskrit. The *Shastras* taught the superiority of Brahmans. The *Shastras* taught the other classes that their sole purpose was to fulfill their *dharma* in this life with the hope they might become a Brahman in the "next life." The *Shastras* taught that the *dharma* of all the other classes was to serve and obey the Brahmans. Thus, as Smith concludes, "The Brahmans derived economic as well as social advantages from their exclusive claim to the priesthood."[16]

"Such privileges… were… authorized by the teachings of the very Veda the Brahmans have preserved," explains Smith. "This is not surprising given the fact that it was members of the Brahman class who were not only the historical perpetuators but also the authors of these authoritative texts."[17] In other words, the *Shastras*, which were written by Brahmans, taught the supremacy of Brahmans. The irony did not escape European observers like Niccolao Manucci, an Italian who traveled to India and spent his life working as a writer in the Mughal court. Writing in 1707, Manucci reports on the contemporary teachings about caste.

> [From] Brahma's countenance… they assert, the Brahmans were produced. This class of men is, among them, the most considered and the noblest. Being themselves the authors of all these fables, they accept without any hesitation the origin I have just stated.[18]

Manucci personally witnessed how these teachings were implemented and the social ramifications of the concept of Brahman superiority. His observations confirm how 18th-century Hinduism embraced the creation myth taught by *Rigveda* and *Manusmriti*, how society was broken into four castes, how the castes were further broken into sub-castes, how the system produced outcastes, and how the isolation of the outcastes was enforced by social ostracism of those who reached out to the low. Manucci writes,

> The Hindus divided all mankind into four kinds or classes. Some men they make out to be born from Brahma's face, and these people are called Brahmans, who are divided into several branches. The second kind of men they make out to have been born from the shoulders of the said Brahma, and these they call Rajas, also divided into several branches. The third kind are said to be born from the thighs of the said Brahma, and these are the merchants or shopkeepers, of whom also there are many varieties. Finally, there is the fourth or last kind, born, as they say, from the feet of Brahma; these are the Shudra, who, just like the others, have many

subdivisions, and it is difficult even to count them.

To these four kinds or classes they add one more, which is not counted along with the above, but is held by them to be separated from the general body of men. These people are called, in their language, *Chandala*, or blacks.

All these people that they call blacks are, and pass among the natives of the country as, so low and infamous that it is an irremediable contamination and disgrace, not only to eat with them, but even to behold them drink or eat. Thus, other castes never do one or the other, happen what may. Nor can any one of the other castes live in the house of any of these blacks, or take from their hand anything to eat or drink. They would much rather be left to die unheeded than touch, or allow themselves to be touched by, one of those blacks, or take from their hands anything to eat or drink. For if that happens… if the fact comes to the knowledge of the magistrate, all the family and descendants are marked with infamy, and become on a level with the blacks themselves, and have no hope of ever being able to re-enter their caste.[19]

Shudras were low, but Ati-Shudras were truly the "lowest of the low" whose company Guru Nanak sought. In 1626, Dutch merchant Francisco Pelsaert described the masses as "poor wretches who, in their submissive bondage, may be compared to poor, contemptible earthworms, or to little fishes, which, however closely they may conceal themselves, are swallowed up by the great monsters of a wild sea."[20] American historian Katherine Mayo echoes Pelsaert. Describing the condition of Ati-Shudras in the early 20th century, she writes, "You live not like men but like worms."[21]

Like his predecessors, Guru Arjun sought to transform these people, who were treated like "worms," into humans by teaching them to recognize, respect, and protect their rights and dignity. He wanted them to reject the concept of a hereditary hierarchy of value. He wanted them to accept their humanity. He wanted them to realize that caste is a fraud. He wanted to destroy their imposed self-image of "worms" by teaching them how to have the confidence of free people. Ultimately, once they progressed from "worms" to free people, he wanted them to understand how even the commonest person can be royal if they are filled with the love of God.

When Guru Nanak established the battle lines between society's Touchables and Untouchables by aligning himself with the outcastes, he knew it would provoke the hostility of the ruling elite. "Caste prejudice and the practice of untouchability being central to Hinduism, any individual, organization, or ideology questioning it was always seen as an enemy, and no effort was spared to eliminate the challenge," notes Dr. Rajkumar Hans.[22] Thus, as Guru Arjun carried on the mission of Guru Nanak, the complex-hearted responded by killing him so they could continue grinding the "worms" beneath their feet.

The complex-hearted failed. The fledgling Sikh Revolution was so resilient and the parched souls of the oppressed were so thirsty that, rather than dissipate away after Guru Arjun's martyrdom, the revolution sprang back with greater force as it came under leadership of Guru Hargobind. Nevertheless, this seemed to be the darkest period for the abolitionists who had worked for centuries to secure emancipation of the *Mulnivasi*.

Guru Hargobind (1595-1644) — After Guru Arjun's death, his property was destroyed, his family was bankrupted, and his following appeared fractured. The most venerated guru of the common people had been cruelly eliminated in the most torturous manner imaginable. Only time would tell whether or not the Sikhs could survive this devastating blow.

Mughal Emperor Jahangir hoped Guru Arjun would be "brought into the fold of Islam." The Brahmans hoped to thwart his assault on the caste system. However, the nefarious designs of the Mughal-Brahman nexus were frustrated by the Guru's resolute spirit. The teachings of the *Adi Granth* had already made Harmandir Sahib a source of power from which the aspirations of the suffering people of India were being realized. In the end, martyring Guru Arjun only strengthened his message; his blood was the seed from which sprung a stronger tree with deeper roots and brighter blossoms.

As a result of the persecution of Guru Arjun and the murderous collaboration of the Brahmans with the Mughals, five things happened.

First — Hargobind, son of Guru Arjun, was installed as the sixth steward of the mission to liberate the downtrodden and preserve the institution of Harmandir Sahib and the *Granth*.

Although the *Panth* (those who followed the path of the *Adi Granth*) knew full well that their new Guru faced the same dangers as his father if he took up the torch, the young Hargobind stepped forward to stoke the fire of freedom sparked centuries earlier. He sought to fan it into an inferno whose blaze might shed light on all the weakest, poorest, and most vulnerable in society. He did this by advancing and developing the same philosophies as his predecessors.

The *Dabistan*, an unparalleled examination of South Asian religious traditions, was composed by an unknown Persian author who records personally meeting Guru Hargobind around 1643. Confirming how the Guru perpetuated the vast contrast between the Sikhs and the prevailing culture, the *Dabistan* explains,

> The Guru believes in one God. His followers put not their faith in idol worship. They never pray or practice austerities like the Hindus. They believe not in their incarnations, or places of pilgrimage, nor the Sanskrit language which the Hindus deem to be the language of their gods.[23]

Second — In the greatest of victories, Guru Hargobind constructed the Akal Takht (Eternal Throne) and established a doctrine of synthesis between the temporal and the spiritual.

In June 1606, the month following his father's execution, Guru Hargobind laid the foundations for the Akal Takht directly across from Harmandir Sahib. Construction began with a 12-foot tall platform "resembling the platform for the Emperors, while construction of even an ordinary pedestal of a height of more than 2 feet was prohibited by the then government."[24]

The Akal Takht, explains Dr. Gurmit Singh, was intended to be a "royal throne, a sovereign chair of the State, a seat from where the State-law is promulgated and enforced."[25] It represented the Capitol of a nation of people who owed allegiance to no one, were subjected by no one, and were ruled directly by the principles of God rather than an earthly State. According to Sikh statesman and philosopher Kapur Singh, "The peculiar Sikh doctrine of Double Sovereignty took birth, the essence of which is that a man of religion must always owe his primary allegiance to Truth and morality, and he must never submit to the exclusive claim of the secular State to govern the bodies and minds of men."[26]

When Guru Hargobind first revealed the platform of the Takht, he strapped on two swords — one representing *miri* (or kingly) authority and the other *piri* (or spiritual) authority. He then called for the Sikhs to arm themselves and began forming an army. The message was clear. "Construction of [the] Takht was an open declaration by the Sikh community of its character as political sovereigns," writes Kapur Singh.[27] This declaration of independence affirmed the Sikhs as a decentralized people governed by the principle of universal royalty — that is, the individual sovereignty — of every person which was proclaimed by the Bhagats and Gurus and enshrined within the *Adi Granth*.

Finally, in 1608, the Sikhs first hoisted their national flag — *Nishan Sahib* — at the Akal Takht. This banner and the throne over which it flew represented a direct challenge to rule by Mughals, Brahmans, and every other tyrant.

Third — The traffic to the warm shop increased and the growth of the Sikh *Panth* became so significant that it prevented the Mughals from taking direct action against it.

In 1609, Jahangir arrested the Guru and temporarily imprisoned him, reported the *Dabistan*, "on account of the demand for the balance of the fine he had imposed on Arjun Mal." However, while the Guru was in prison, "Sikhs went and knelt down in *sijda* [i.e., with foreheads touching the ground] before the wall of the fort."[28] The Emperor could no longer ignore the power of the people. Thus, Jahangir released Guru Hargobind.

The Sikhs were reaping the reward of centuries of effort. For 400 years, from Bhagat Farid to Guru Arjun, the *Mulnivasi* organized themselves with a comprehensive, ideological approach to life which developed into an institution with a geographical center in Amritsar. From Guru Nanak's advent to Guru Arjun's martyrdom, this center was heavily trafficked by the *Panth*. Empowered by 100 years of practiced discipline, the *Panth* was also united across a wide geographical region that included most of the northern regions of the Indian subcontinent — from Maharashtra to Uttar Pradesh to Delhi and across Punjab. According to *Dabistan*, "The Sikhs increased in numbers, till in the reign of Guru Arjun Mal, they became very numerous. Not many cities remained in the inhabited region where the Sikhs had not settled in some number."[29]

Fourth — Guru Hargobind put into practice the doctrine of the nobility of the common person by establishing an army in direct contradiction to the laws of the Mughal Empire and of the Brahmanical caste system.

Speaking of Guru Arjun's execution, Mountstuart Elphinstone explains, "This act of tyranny changed the Sikhs from inoffensive quietists into fanatical warriors. They took up arms under Hargobind, the son of their martyred pontiff."[30] The Mughals respected his military strength. As the *Dabistan* reports, "He had seven hundred horses in his stable. Three hundred battle-tested horsemen and sixty musketeers were always in his service."[31] Acknowledging the joint spiritual and temporal authority they had recognized in Guru Nanak, the Sikhs began addressing Guru Hargobind with a royal title. According to Dr. Kanwarjit Singh,

> Guru Hargobind maintained a regular army, of which he himself
> was the supreme commander. He used to hold courts at Akal Takht.
> He was called *Sacha Padshah* — the true King — by his follow-
> ers.[32]

Cunningham further reports, "[The Gurus came] to be regarded by their
followers as '*Sacha Padshahs*' or 'veritable kings,' meaning, perhaps, that
they governed by just influence and not by the force of arms, or that they
guided men to salvation while others controlled their worldly actions."[33]
Indeed, even the Mughals recognized the royal authority assumed by the
Gurus. The earliest evidence of this came from Jahangir's own writings in
which he worried that Guru Arjun was "in the garb of *Pir* [saint] and *Sheikh*
[king]."

Guru Arjun taught that royalty is obtained by service, not lineage.
Thus, Guru Hargobind's followers recognized his nobility and voluntarily
acknowledged him as their legitimate ruler — the "true King." At the Akal
Takht, writes Gurmit Singh, "Guru Hargobind sat like a king and administered justice to the Sikhs. He wore a turban with a royal aigrette."[34] Ballad-
eers filled his court, including Muslim singers Nath Mal and Abdullah Mir,
who composed songs about how he was a superior ruler to Jahangir.

> The Guru bound two swords: one of *miri* and one of *piri*. One of
> grandeur and one of sovereignty; one for rule and one for protec-
> tion of the sovereign. Your turban is far more elegant than that of
> Emperor Jahangir.[35]

The Guru's reputation as a king spread beyond Punjab. While traveling in Kashmir in the 1620s, Guru Hargobind reportedly encountered Swami Samarth Ramdas of Maharashtra. Confused by the Guru's appearance,
Ramdas said to him, "You are wearing arms and keeping an army and horses. You have yourself called *Sacha Padshah* — a true King. What sort of
a *sadhu* (saint) are you?" The Guru replied, "Internally a hermit and exter-
nally a prince; arms mean protection for the poor and destruction for the
tyrant."[36]

Thus, under the leadership of the Guru, the lowest of the low took up
arms, mounted horses, and trained for war — rights they were historically

denied by caste laws. The *Panth*, which had been preparing for this moment since its genesis, was now ready to make war. As Edward Thornton observes, Guru Arjun "having fallen a victim to the persecution of the Muhammadans, his successor, Hargobind, ordered his followers to arm and take vengeance on their persecutors."[37]

For the first time, the Mughals began marching armies against the flourishing Sikh Revolution. From 1628 to 1635, the Guru won five defensive battles against the aggressions of Emperor Shah Jahan (1592-1666). His leadership, writes Cunningham, "formed [the Sikhs] into a kind of separate state within the Empire."[38]

Fifth — The Sikh Revolution developed into a full-fledged rebellion against the Empire and the Brahman advisors who served it.

The power of the people turned the tide so swiftly that Emperor Jahangir was not only powerless to prevent the *Panth* from declaring independence and fielding an army, but soon after Guru Arjun's death, he even handed over Chandu to the *Mulnivasi*. Describing Chandu's fate, Fr. Xavier writes, "The guarantor tried to save himself, but he was imprisoned and killed."[39] Sikh traditions corroborate Xavier's account and testify that Chandu died in Sikh custody. Rebellion had taken such deep root that the Mughal was compelled to give up the Brahman.

For the rest of the 17th century, the Sikhs exerted themselves against the tyrants. Now armed and trained, the *Panth* was fit to fight pitched battles against any oppressor of any creed and so they began waging armed rebellion.

Brahmanism Creeps Into the Mughal Court — Meanwhile, the Mughal-Brahman nexus expanded. Like his father, Akbar, Jahangir surrounded himself with "Sanskrit thinkers." His son, Shah Jahan, pursued the same policy. As these Brahman collaborators swelled the ranks of the Mughal courts, the Emperors increasingly came under the influence of Brahmanical culture.

Twice annually, on their solar and lunar birthdays, members of the Imperial family participated in the *tuladan*, a weighing ceremony described by Islamic culture expert Father Michael Calabria as "the central ritual of the imperial Hindu kingdom in the eighth century." According to Fr. Calabria, "By offering his body weight in gold, silver, or other precious substances to Brahmans, the king asserted his power and glory."[40] British journalist Fergus Nicoll, documents one example in 1608.

Court astrologers, both Hindu and Muslim… advised the Emperor that the year… would be one of particular auspiciousness for Prince [Shah Jahan]. So, to celebrate his sixteenth birthday, they now cast a special horoscope…. So remarkable were their predictions that they urged the Emperor to break with tradition and grant [Shah Jahan] the unprecedented honor of an additional *Tuladan* weighing ceremony. This practice had been adopted by Khurram's liberal grandfather, the late Emperor Akbar. It was one of a number of ancient Hindu rituals — in which the ruler's weight in gold and precious stones was originally distributed to Brahman priests for the maintenance of temple precincts — appropriated by Akbar to enhance his own legitimacy in locally recognizable terms.[41]

Sir Thomas Roe, the English ambassador to the Mughal court, bears witness to another example in 1616. "This day was the birth of the king and solemnized as a great feast, wherein the king is weighed against some jewels, gold, silver, stuffs of gold [and] silver, silk, butter, rice, fruit, and many other things… which is given to the Brahmans," writes Roe in his journal.[42]

"The egg of superstition has burst," declared Guru Arjun. However, Jahangir, who ordered the Guru's execution, was enthralled by the "vast system of superstition" of the Brahmans. He was a devotee of the astrologers. As Pelsaert observes in 1626,

Some of the Brahmans are very ingenious…. They reckon eclipses very clearly, and they also do a great deal of fortune-telling. There are usually one or two such men with a great reputation in the city; indeed the present King generally kept one at Court…. The Brahmans have consequently secured a great reputation, and they have now acquired such influence over the great men, and then over all the Moslems, that they will not undertake a journey until they have enquired what day or hour is auspicious for the start; and when they return from a journey, or come to take up an appointment, they will not enter the city until the suitable day or hour has been predicted, and then they wait until the exact moment has arrived.[43]

In 1628, after the death of his father, Jahangir, Shah Jahan came to the throne. He had been under the tutelage of upper-caste Hindus since childhood. Moreover, he was trained in warfare by a Hindu. "At the age of eight,

[Shah Jahan] started additional musketry lessons, as well as swordsmanship, cavalry techniques, spear work, and wrestling — all under the watchful eye of Raja Salivahan, a trusted Hindu officer in [Jahangir's] personal militia," reports Nicoll.[44] In Shah Jahan's daily court sessions, Nicoll wrote, "Holy men of all faiths — ash-encrusted Hindu *sadhus*, Sufi mystics in white cotton robes — clustered into the royal presence, seeking to give blessings and receive alms."[45]

Meanwhile, the Gurus praised the Creator while rebelling against the Empire. In contrast, the "Sanskrit thinkers" in the Mughal courts sang hymns of praise to the Emperors. Two of the most notable of these flatterers were Pandit Jagannath and Chandar Bhan Brahman. Jagannath was in the service of Jahangir and Shah Jahan; Chandar Bhan was in the service of Akbar, Jahangir, Shah Jahan, and, eventually, his son Aurangzeb. While the Mughal throne switched hands, the Brahman hawks remained in the same roosts for generations.

Jagannath, writes Nicoll, was "one of the Emperor's favorite Sanskrit-language wordsmiths, a Hindu honored with the title *Mahakavirai*, 'Great Master of Verse.'"[46] According to Indian historian Dr. Malik Mohamed, "Shah Jahan honored Pandit Jagannath with the title '*Panditraja*.' The Emperor... was daily blessed by Pandit Jagannath with address as *Dillishwara-ba Jagdishwara* (The Lord of Delhi is the Lord of the Universe)."[47] As Nicoll reports, his strategy of flattery paid off.

> Sanskrit scholars like Pandit Jagannath, the Great Master of Verse, recited verses in honor of... Shah Jahan. One Sunday night in October 1634, encamped at Bhimar in Kashmir, the Emperor awarded the poet his weight in silver as prize money for a cycle of twelve literary masterpieces. Similar honors awaited favored Hindi poets, such as Hari Nath, who won an elephant, a horse, and twenty-five thousand rupees in January 1640.[48]

American historian Rajeev Kinra reports that Chandar Bhan "lived, worked, and thrived through part or all of the reigns of four different Muslim monarchs, at the peak of the Mughal Empire's power and global influence."[49] While Guru Hargobind made war with Emperor Shah Jahan, Chandar cheered the Mughal ruler's "victory and conquest" in the following paean:

Even though in this age adorned by the felicity and prosperity of His Most Exalted Majesty — the Sovereign of the Times, World Conqueror, and Treasure-Bestowing Emperor, who is bounteous as the sea, and the earthly shadow of the divine splendorous presence — a new social occasion takes place every day, and fabulous assemblies and festivals are arranged every month and every year; and from the six directions an amber-sweetened zephyr of victory and conquest wafts into nostrils eager for a whiff of its grace; and there is no way to measure or count the trappings of the court and the imperial apparatus of this eternal caliphate; and, if from the very beginning of this spring of Empire and fortune, the pen of narration were to commit to writing the details of the day-increasing festivities and freshness and verdancy of the garden of eternal spring in this stalwart Empire — the space of many volumes would be necessary.[50]

Imperial servants like Chandar and Jagannath, who groveled before the Mughals by comparing them to gods and proclaiming their Empire "eternal," typify the chasm between Brahmanism and the *Panth*. Incapable of speaking truth to power, Chandar praised the Emperor as "World Conqueror" and Jagannath praised him as "Lord of the Universe" instead of denouncing the injustice of his foreign occupation. As a consequence of the cheerful subservience of these Brahman courtiers, "the Mughal administration adopted a policy of tolerance towards Hindus and their places of worship."[51]

Through rituals like *Tuladan,* the Mughals subsidized the "vast system of superstition" and helped to perpetuate the exploitation and oppression of Brahmanism. By embracing the false creeds and crooked politics which Guru Nanak condemned, Brahmans secured their superior position in society and facilitated the foreign rule of the Mughals by enslaving the masses. Furthermore, due to their policy of obsequiousness, "the upper-caste Hindus emerged as the greatest beneficiaries of the Mughal-Sikh conflict, and rather developed a vested interest in it both for keeping their positions and carrying on their war against Sikhism."[52]

The Sikh Gurus, however, had no interest in scheming for political favor by coddling and flattering tyrants. They were not interested in lining their pockets at the expense of the starving, half-naked, and ignorant. Instead, they pursued a full-scale sociopolitical revolution to secure for the masses the human rights of equality and liberty.

Guru Tegh Bahadur (1621-1675) — The Empire's attempt to crush the *Panth* reached new heights under the ninth Guru, Tegh Bahadur. Originally named Tyag Mal, the Guru was renamed *Tegh Bahadur* (brave swordsman) by his father, Guru Hargobind, after proving himself on the battlefield against Shah Jahan. Like his grandfather, Guru Arjun, the ninth Guru was destined to sacrifice his life.

After the death of his father in 1644, Tegh Bahadur endured near Amritsar for twenty years before becoming Guru. During that time, his nephew Guru Har Rai (1630-1661) and then his grandnephew Guru Har Krishan (1656-1664) stewarded the *Panth* and *Granth*.

Following the first Sikh battles with the Mughals, the two groups exchanged armed conflict for a tense truce. "Although Guru Har Rai was a man of peace, he never dissolved the armed Sikh warriors who earlier were exerted by his grandfather," explains Sikh historian Sardar Harjeet Singh. "He always encouraged the military spirit of the Sikhs, but he never himself indulged in any direct political and armed controversy with the Mughal Empire."[53] The seventh steward of Begampura, reported Macauliffe, "had been forbidden by his grandfather, Guru Hargobind, to engage in warfare."[54] As Sikh historian Dr. Harbans Singh states, "Since militarism for its own sake was not their object, the Sikhs preserved the truce as long as they were left alone."[55]

Since the origins of Guru Nanak's *Panth*, the movement always gained the most traction in times of peace. Yet, as the revolution vigorously undermined exploitive and tyrannical sociopolitical systems, it was a miracle that the *Panth* successfully avoided extended armed conflict for so long. The Sikhs were certainly the last to want war.

Under the guidance of Guru Har Rai and Guru Har Krishan, the patrons of the warm shop enjoyed a window of respite from the hounding they endured during the stewardship of Guru Arjun and Guru Hargobind. Meanwhile, however, the Mughals maintained hawk-eyed surveillance on the growing movement. In his 1723 composition, *Ibratnama*, Mughal historian Muhammad Qasim Lahauri writes,

In old times in a particular year, there was a dervish by the name of Nanak, clothed in Reality, rooted in Knowledge, endowed with spiritual perfections, rising above physical repute and name.... Some generations after him, Har Rai came into the world [and became his successor]. Group upon group of people bent their necks to follow and obey him, and glorified him through a thousand ways of giving him respect and honour.[56]

The simple-hearted who flocked to the *Panth* found equality and liberty, but because most were from low-born backgrounds, they were deprived of education and basic human needs. To successfully transform them from "worms" into free people, the movement needed time to develop deeper roots. The institution designed by the Gurus needed infrastructure, which Tegh Bahadur was deputed to develop before stepping into the public eye as Guru. Traveling extensively, the future Guru reached out to the *Mulnivasi* throughout Bihar, Haryana, Punjab, Uttarakhand, and Uttar Pradesh.

Sikh historian Surjit Singh reports, "He was deeply concerned and took keen interest in social and political changes that were taking place, as an artist watches a drama in which he is to play a hero's part."[57] The most significant sociopolitical change Tegh Bahadur observed before becoming Guru was a *coup d'état* in Delhi.

When Emperor Shah Jahan became sick in 1657, reports Dr. Audrey Truschke, his "four sons believed their father was on the brink of death, so they seized the opportunity created by this power vacuum to determine — according to time-honored Mughal practices of force and trickery — who would be crowned the next Emperor." Aurangzeb (1618-1707) made war on his brothers, emerged triumphant, then "executed two of his brothers, [drove] out the third, and locked away his recovered father."[58]

In the midst of this ruthless power struggle, none of the ruling elite gave a thought to the needs of the common people. As the Mughal throne switched from Shah Jahan to Aurangzeb, the masses continued to live as "worms." In the words of Abraham Eraly,

> Behind the shimmering imperial facade, there was another scene, another life — people in mud hovels, their lives barely distinct from those of animals, wretched, half-naked, half-starved, and from whom every drop of sap had been wrung out by their predatory masters, Muslim as well as Hindu. Only chieftains and amirs fattened....
>
> Under Shah Jahan, over a quarter of the gross national product of the Empire was appropriated by just 655 individuals, while the bulk of the approximately 120 million people of India lived on

a dead level of poverty. Famine swept the land every few years, devouring hundreds of thousands of men, and in its wake came, always and inevitably, pestilence, devouring several hundreds of thousands more. In Mughal India, the contrast between legend and reality was grotesque.[59]

Despite the prevailing culture of violence, Aurangzeb's *coup* was so cold-blooded that at least one individual at the court was outraged enough to take a stand. As Truschke explains, "Overthrowing one's reigning father was considered abhorrent. The chief *qazi* (Muslim judge) of the Mughal Empire refused to endorse Aurangzeb's ascension."[60] So the Emperor hired a more subservient *qazi*.

In contrast, the Brahmans remained obsessed with self-aggrandizement. For instance, the royal secretary, Chandar Bhan, felt no hesitation in endorsing the usurping prince. Despite previously praising Shah Jahan as "the earthly shadow of the divine splendorous presence," he applauded Aurangzeb in a letter to the new Emperor.

May your felicitous and propitious accession, which is like the onset of springtime in a garden of wealth and fortune, and likewise the cause of the opening of the gates of the hopes and desires of the world and its inhabitants, bring happiness and blessings: upon the throne of *khilafat* and governance and the seat of kingship and universal rule that is the asylum of kings of the seven climes and the refuge of rulers on the face of the earth; upon Your Royal Majesty the sovereign Emperor of the universe, the *qibla* of the world and its people, the clarion blast of whose conquest and governance has been broadcast to all four quadrants of the world, and the seed of whose justice and beneficence has been planted in all six directions of the universe; and to all of your sympathizers, well-wishers, relations, and those who pray for the good of your daily increasing Empire.[61]

As it had been since the beginning of foreign occupation, collaboration between Mughals and Brahmans remained crucial for both to maintain their stranglehold on political and social power. "To the end, Aurangzeb depended on non-Muslim courtiers," write American historians Barbara Metcalf and Thomas Metcalf. "More than a quarter of the *mansab* holders [bureaucrats], along with his leading general, were Hindus."[62] In fact, according to Eraly, the co-rule of the combined Mughal-Brahman elite actually expanded during Aurangzeb's reign.

> Aurangzeb continued to employ Hindus in high offices.... In the second half of his reign, their percentage was higher than ever before under the Mughals — in the rank of commanders of 5000 and above, it was 32.9 percent under Aurangzeb as against fourteen percent under Akbar; among all officers of the rank of 500 and above, it was 31.6 percent under Aurangzeb as against 22.5 percent under Akbar. A Brahman, Raghunath, served for a while as Aurangzeb's acting revenue minister, one of the highest offices in the Empire.[63]

Like Chandar Bhan, Raghunath flourished in the Mughal court. "Raghunath Ray... had supported Aurangzeb's effort to win the throne during the war of succession," writes Rajeev Kinra.[64] Truschke reports, "Raghunath joined a group of administrators who pledged loyalty to Aurangzeb."[65] In the early years of Aurangzeb's reign, he appointed Raghunath as Chief Finance Minister. As Truschke writes, "This high position mirrored Akbar's appointment of Todar Mal as his top finance minister one hundred years earlier." Furthermore, François Bernier, a French physician who worked in Aurangzeb's court and knew Raghunath, noted that "the Raja Ragnat... acts as Vizier [Prime Minister]."[66]

Thus, under Aurangzeb, Brahmans collaborating with the Mughals were invested with the highest powers in the Empire. His reign was more beneficial to the upper-caste elite than the reigns of any of the previous Emperors. According to Kinra, "Chandar Bhan continued to serve Aurangzeb for nearly a decade following the war of succession, and, in Raghunath's case, it was Aurangzeb who gave him the highest promotion of all."[67]

Aurangzeb's most pressing goal was, in the words of Chandar, "daily increasing" the Empire. Truschke explains, "He expanded the Mughal Empire to its greatest extent, subsuming most of the Indian subcontinent under a single Imperial power for the first time in human history."[68] Above all, his legacy was one of territorial conquest and fierce intolerance towards all threats to his political power.

The Emperor waged war on Muslim kingdoms in the south, on a Buddhist territory in Bengal, and on a Hindu kingdom in Assam. "A major focus of Aurangzeb's reign was warfare directed against other Muslims," write the Metcalfs.[69] "His reign was nearly as hard on Muslims as it was on Hindus," reveals Eraly.[70] Offering further details on the brutality of this warlord, Truschke writes,

> Throughout his reign, Aurangzeb crushed rebellions, waged cold-blooded wars of expansion, and oversaw merciless sieges.... Aurangzeb was not unusual in his time in turning to violence, including of a gruesome variety, as a standard political tactic. For Aurangzeb, State violence was not only permissible but necessary and even just.... One poignant example of Aurangzeb's violence that sits ill with many today concerns Tegh Bahadur.[71]

Tegh Bahadur became Guru in 1664. As Lahauri notes, "After [Guru Har Rai], Guru Tegh Bahadur... rose further in status."[72] The Guru began touring Punjab and, writes Surjit Singh, soon decided to "build a new settlement" and "buy a suitable piece of land for the purpose."[73]

In 1665, he laid the foundation stone of a village, naming it Chak Nanaki after his mother. As the village grew, it became the City of Anandpur Sahib. Guru Tegh Bahadur's plan was for this new settlement to serve as the future site of the culmination of Guru Nanak's mission to uplift the "lowest of the low" as well as the fulfillment of Guru Hargobind's doctrine of *miri/piri* when his successor, Guru Gobind Singh, issued a call for the Sikhs to form a new body in 1699.

From 1664 to 1668, Guru Tegh Bahadur traveled widely throughout India to spread the message of the *Adi Granth*. "In the 1660s, a young Sikh Guru, Tegh Bahadur, began a vigorous missionary campaign across northern India from the Punjab to Assam," explains British historian Francis Robinson.[74] Surjit Singh notes, "The Guru undertook tours to strengthen the links with the *sangats* [congregations] functioning in the eastern regions of the country whom he had personally observed during his earlier tour in Uttar Pradesh and Bihar."[75] He also toured Assam, Bengal, and Tripura. According to Punjabi historian Mohindar Pal Kohli, the Guru took specific measures to improve the physical as well as spiritual wellbeing of the downtrodden.

> The Guru caused many tanks and wells to be dug for public use, preached to the people, quite irrespective of caste and creed, to ab-

stain from violence and thieving, to live in peace with their neighbors, and love all human beings. These measures, coupled with his
saintliness, greatly contributed to their welfare as well as moral
spiritual awakening. They began to flock to him for comfort and
solace and for worldly as well as spiritual advancement, and to
embrace his faith voluntarily.[76]

As Guru Tegh Bahadur traversed the vast lands of the Indian subcontinent, his teachings and his concern for social welfare captivated the
simple-hearted. The Guru was laying the groundwork for a greater calling
which his son would carry out. The warm shop which disturbed Aurangzeb's
grandfather, Jahangir, was more heavily trafficked by the "simple-hearted"
than ever before. "Large numbers of Jats, the largest cultivating group of the
region, were converted, as were some Muslims," writes Robinson. "Aurangzeb did not approve."[77] Not only was traffic flowing, but the "simple-hearted" flocking to this shop were now armed. Consequently, the grandson of
Jahangir sought to destroy the grandson of Guru Arjun.

Writing in 1904, Scottish historian William Irvine explains, "One of
this Guru's crimes, in the Emperor's eyes, may have been the style of address adopted by his disciples, who had begun to call their leader *Sacha
Padshah* or the True King."[78] Like his predecessors, Guru Tegh Bahadur
followed "God's path" by seeking the company of the "low born." He fulfilled the teaching of Guru Arjun: "He who deems himself as of the lowly,
shall be esteemed as the highest of the high." Aurangzeb's arrogance dis-
tanced the people, who were instead drawn to Guru Tegh Bahadur's humility. His followers, who realized that a ruler is only legitimate if he has the
voluntary consent of the governed, identified the Guru as their "true king."

Furthermore, the Sikhs were developing a totally separate society. For
instance, they were creating their own economic system — a closed econo-
my in which the community was becoming self-sufficient. Writing in 1788,
Lieutenant Colonel James Browne of the British East India Company explains,

> His followers conceived a… veneration for him, and used among
> themselves to call him *the true King*; he, on his part, whatever he
> received in presents, or offerings, from his disciples or the Sikhs
> in general, he laid out in provisions, which he publicly distributed
> to all who chose to receive them; this brought great numbers to

participate of his bounty.[79]

Instead of being dependent on the Central State for their sustenance, the Sikhs were becoming independent by learning to provide for themselves. This did not escape the attention of the ruling elites, however, who were keenly aware of the Guru's strident message and his swift organization of the *Panth*. The rapid growth of the Sikhs and the economic support they voluntarily showered upon their Guru aroused the envy of the Mughals. According to Lahauri,

> Because of the effect of the attention and pleasing ways of acceptance of that accepted one, the inclinations of the people and the flow of worldly things [towards him], such as petty items and valuables, money and goods, elephants and horses, did not decrease. Instead of himself [doing so], his followers from time to time claimed sovereignty for him.... [Aurangzeb], owing to his own passionate nature and regard for royal power, did not like such meaningless tumult.[80]

Guru Tegh Bahadur's followers "claimed sovereignty for him," notes Lahauri, proving the Mughals understood he was being called *Sacha Padshah*. "This title was readily capable of a twofold interpretation," explains Irvine. "It might be applied as the occasion served in a spiritual or a literal sense. Its use was extremely likely to provoke the mistrust of a ruler even less suspicious by nature than [Aurangzeb]."[81]

In his 1707 memoir, *Tarikh-i Dilkusha*, Bhimsen Saxena (an upper-caste Hindu general in Aurangzeb's service) substantiates Irvine's conclusion.

> Nanak wrote books in the praise and assertion of the unity of God. Gradually, it happened that in every country he appointed deputies, so that they might guide people to his religion. Now it has been seen and heard that no country, city, township, and village is without people believing in him.... Many took to the path of rebellion, such as Tegh Bahadur, by name, who lived in the mountains near Sirhind; he got himself called King (*Padshah*), and a large body of people gathered around him.[82]

Although the liberated Sikhs bore arms as the right of free people, they did not wage an armed rebellion. "Thousands of people… swarmed round the Guru, but they cannot be taken as soldiers of revolt," reports Surjit Singh. "No contemporary record shows that there was any outbreak of revolt on the part of the Sikhs, although under the impact of the Guru's preachings, the process of mass awakening had set in."[83]

The masses were behaving independently. Guru Arjun was viewed by Jahangir as garbed in the attire of both a saint and a king. His son, Guru Hargobind, established an official doctrine of unity between *miri* and *piri* — a harmony between spiritual and kingly powers. Sikhs were, as many have worded it, saints *and* soldiers. They embraced a doctrine of the universal nobility of the common person. The doctrine envisioned a person who, because he himself can be both priest *and* king, need not be subjugated to the whims of anyone else who assumes those titles to dictate to others. In short, the Sikhs practiced peace through strength. This disturbed tyrants.

The expansion of the Sikh population to every "country, city, township, and village," as well as their identification of Guru Tegh Bahadur as "king," convinced Bhimsen that they were on the "path to rebellion." As a result of his perception, the Mughal-Brahman alliance confronted the Sikhs. Writing in 1768, Father François Xavier Wendel (a Jesuit priest living, like Fr. Jerome Xavier, in the Mughal court) explains, "A number of devotees incorporated themselves into this sect and made so much of this Guru… that this king… asked him to explain himself."[84] Soon, this led to troubling times for the Sikhs.

Meanwhile, a different kind of trouble was brewing. For generations, Sikh philosophy had influenced and inspired some Brahmans throughout the northwest of the subcontinent. One Brahman clan, the Chhibbers, had followed the *Panth* since the days of Guru Nanak. They had disavowed caste, become Sikhs, and worked tirelessly for centuries to uproot Brahmanism. Their descendants served many of the Gurus as secretaries, administrators, and warriors. In 1621, Praga Das died fighting alongside Guru Hargobind in a skirmish with the Mughals. His grandsons, Mati Das and Sati Das, "were in charge of [Guru Tegh Bahadur's] bodyguards and correspondence respectively."[85]

Further to the north, in the hills of Jammu and the valley of Kashmir, lived another group of Brahmans who also had a friendly but more recent relationship with the Sikhs. Known as the Kashmiri *Pandits*, their relationship with the *Panth* began in the 1620s when Guru Hargobind was traveling in Kashmir. In 1660, when Guru Har Rai also travelled in Kashmir, he was "in the company of Sikhs such as... Aru Ram, father of Kirpa Ram Datt, who later led to the presence of Guru Tegh Bahadur a group of Kashmiri *Pandits* driven to dire distress by State persecution."[86]

The first Imperial attempts to convert the *Pandits* began with Aurangzeb's father in the mid-1600s. According to Eraly, "In Kashmir, where Muslims and Hindus often intermarried, Shah Jahan decreed that if a Hindu had a Muslim wife, he could keep her only if he became a Muslim; otherwise, he was to be fined and his wife separated."[87]

Forced conversion of Kashmiris became a dominant policy under ruling officials in the 1670s. "During the 49 years of Aurangzeb's reign, Kashmir was administered by no less than 14 governors sent from Delhi," writes Kashmiri historian P. N. K. Bamzai. "Most of them were broadminded and efficient.... There were, however, some exceptions."[88] Bamzai elaborates,

> Iftikar Khan, a Governor of Aurangzeb, was using force to convert the *Pandits* in Kashmir to Islam.... About 500 *Pandits* proceeded to Anandpur Sahib where Guru Tegh Bahadur was living. They told him about the atrocities committed on them by Aurangzeb's governor, Iftikar Khan, in Kashmir.... [He] advised the crowd of *Pandits* to go to Aurangzeb and tell him straightaway that they, together with all the Brahmans in Kashmir, were quite ready to embrace Islam if Tegh Bahadur, who was the Chief Guru of the Hindus, would first be converted.[89]

Facing such persecution, the *Pandits* turned to Guru Tegh Bahadur for assistance. Led by Kirpa Ram Datt, they presented their case for his consideration.

In light of the historical relationship, and following Guru Nanak's example of being an equal opportunity activist for all oppressed peoples, Guru Tegh Bahadur was willing to sacrifice everything to relieve the suffering of the *Pandits* from Kashmir — whether or not they wore "holy threads." The Guru understood that absolute commitment to the spiritual principles of equality and compassion took precedence over everything else. He recognized, as Bhagat Farid taught, that "the Lord Eternal in all abides." Serving as the Steward of Begampura, Guru Tegh Bahadur applied the Golden Rule that all *Mulnivasi* will live by in the "heavenly city."

Why would the persecuted Kashmiri *Pandits* approach the Guru, who was in rebellion against the Empire, instead of the "Sanskrit thinkers" who were favored by the Empire? Many high-caste personalities clearly held positions of power and influence in the Mughal courts. Birbal led armies, Chandu incited the execution of Guru Arjun, and Chandar ingratiated himself as a secretary in the Imperial courts — not to mention Todar Mal, Bhagwant Das, Jagannath, Raghunath, Bhimsen, and others.

The *Pandits* were illuminated by the message of the Gurus in the early 1600s, but developed an enmity with the Brahmans in the mid-1300s. British author Walter Roper Lawrence explains the reason for the rift, which dated back to when Raja Sehdev ruled Kashmir.

> The Kashmiri *Pandits* will not intermarry with the Brahmans of India. It is said that, in Raja Sehdev's time, a Musalman in the disguise of a Pandit mixed with the Kashmiri Brahmans and learnt their Sanskrit lore. On this being discovered, the *Pandits*, in order to guard against similar frauds, decided to have no intercourse with foreign Brahmans.[90]

The two communities, therefore, treated each other as outcastes. Their bitter rivalry meant all avenues of interaction were closed. They shared no exchange of *roti* (bread) or *beti* (daughter).

Furthermore, since the mid-1400s, the Kashmiri *Pandits* had drifted far from the doctrines of Brahmanism. Some became Sikhs. Others intermarried with Muslims. While many "Sanskrit thinkers" entered the Mughal courts and influenced the Emperors to adopt aspects of Brahmanical culture, the *Pandits* of Kashmir instead embraced Islamic culture. According to Dr. Malik Mohamed,

> During the rule of Sultan Zayn al-Abidin, the Kashmiri *Pandits*… took up the study of Persian…. [They were] the only group of Brahmans who took to the Muslim culture…. Steeped in Persian intellectualism, some of them adopted the externals of the Muslim way of life, while others combined it with erudition in Sanskrit and the study of their own religion.[91]

Although the *Pandits* of Kashmir had voluntarily taken to the Muslim culture, they had not necessarily accepted the Islamic religion. Yet, despite their acceptance of Muslim culture, they were still treated as slaves by the Mughals occupying Delhi. The Kashmiri *Pandits* were, in many ways, now identified with the masses toiling in the fields. The situation of the Brahmans at the court in Delhi, however, is best described by African-American activist Malcolm X. Contrasting the behavior of slaves living in the master's house in Delhi with those in the field, Malcolm labels the former as "House Negroes" who self-identify with the master.

> During slavery, he was called 'Uncle Tom.' He was the House Negro. And during slavery you had two Negroes. You had the House Negro and the Field Negro.
>
> The House Negro usually lived close to his master.... And he lived in his master's house....
>
> Whenever that House Negro identified himself, he always identified himself in the same sense that his master identified himself....
>
> You had another Negro out in the field. The House Negro was in the minority. The masses — the Field Negroes were the masses. They were in the majority....
>
> If someone came to the House Negro and said, 'Let's go, let's separate,' naturally that Uncle Tom would say, 'Go where? What could I do without boss? Where would I live? How would I dress? Who would look out for me?' That's the House Negro. But if you went to the Field Negro and said, 'Let's go, let's separate,' he wouldn't even ask you where or how. He'd say, 'Yes, let's go.'[92]

Therefore, three factors brought the Kashmiri *Pandits* to the door of the Guru for help. First, a centuries-old rift prevented them from appealing to the Brahmans while a flourishing relationship with the Sikhs drew them to the Guru. Second, the Brahmans were comfortable working as "House Negroes" in the courts of the Mughals and would have no interest to help, anyways, because it would have jeopardized their positions. Third, the Brahmans, who benefited as co-rulers living the master's house in Delhi, would rather have seen the whole of Kashmir converted to Islam than see Sikh ideology spread amongst the *Mulnivasi*.

In contrast, Guru Tegh Bahadur stood ready to protect the freedom of religion of all people. Refusing to sell his principles at any price, the Guru stood shoulder-to-shoulder with the enslaved masses as he urged them to seek freedom.

Amidst this confluence of events — as the *Panth* flourished, the *Mulni-*

vasi and others hailed the Guru as *Sacha Padshah*, and the Kashmiri *Pandits* sought relief from oppression — Aurangzeb summoned the Guru.

In July 1675, Guru Tegh Bahadur set out for Delhi accompanied by three of his most trusted advisors — Mati Das, Sati Das, and Bhai Dyala. A war veteran who probably anticipated diplomatic dialogue with the Emperor, he began the journey of his own volition. Bhimsen, however, who thought the Guru was on "the path of rebellion," states, "When the news was conveyed to His Majesty Emperor [Aurangzeb], it was ordered that he should be brought to the Court." Consequently, despite setting out voluntarily for the court, the Sikh delegation was arrested on the way and taken to Delhi in chains.

Father Wendel reports that, upon their arrival in Delhi, "Having made Tegh Bahadur come to his presence… [Aurangzeb] questioned him a great deal about his conduct and way of living."[93] Lahauri, who documented Aurangzeb's knowledge that the Sikhs ascribed sovereignty to Guru Tegh Bahadur, continues, "Owing to what has been written above, he came under [the Emperor's] wrath and saw himself condemned to death."[94] According to Wendel, "Tegh Bahadur had, in the end, to choose either to renounce the doctrine and become a Musalman or confirm it by the death to which he had been condemned."[95] Imprisoned and facing death, the Guru writes,

ਬਲੁ ਛੁਟਕਿਓ ਬੰਧਨ ਪਰੇ ਕਛੂ ਨ ਹੋਤ ਉਪਾਇ ॥
ਕਹੁ ਨਾਨਕ ਅਬ ਓਟ ਹਰਿ ਗਜ ਜਿਉ ਹੋਹੁ ਸਹਾਇ ॥
ਬਲੁ ਹੋਆ ਬੰਧਨ ਛੁਟੇ ਸਭੁ ਕਿਛੁ ਹੋਤ ਉਪਾਇ ॥
ਨਾਨਕ ਸਭੁ ਕਿਛੁ ਤੁਮਰੈ ਹਾਥ ਮੈ ਤੁਮ ਹੀ ਹੋਤ ਸਹਾਇ ॥
ਸੰਗ ਸਖਾ ਸਭਿ ਤਜਿ ਗਏ ਕੋਊ ਨ ਨਿਬਹਿਓ ਸਾਥਿ ॥
ਕਹੁ ਨਾਨਕ ਇਹ ਬਿਪਤਿ ਮੈ ਟੇਕ ਏਕ ਰਘੁਨਾਥ ॥

My strength is exhausted, and I am in bondage;
I cannot do anything at all.
Says Nanak, now, the Lord is my Support;
He will help me, as He did the elephant.
My strength has been restored,
and my bonds have been broken; now, I can do everything.
Nanak: everything is in Your hands, Lord;
You are my Helper and Support.
My associates and companions have all deserted me;
no one remains with me.

Says Nanak, in this tragedy, the Lord alone is my Support.[96]

Guru Tegh Bahadur was condemned to death. First, however, Mati Das, Sati Das, and Bhai Dyala faced the same fate. Yet even when offered life if they renounced the Sikh doctrines and adopted Islam, the three all refused to convert. According to Sikh historians, Mati was sawed in half, Sati was burned alive, and Dyala was boiled alive. Thus, in their courageous deaths, they confirmed their membership in the family of the *Mulnivasi.*

Next came the Guru's execution. When he was ordered to convert, reports Wendel, the Guru "did not hesitate to refuse, graciously giving his head and arousing by his example his disciples to do as much in their turn."[97] On November 11, 1675, writes British historian James Talboys Wheeler, "The ninth guru was beheaded in the Imperial palace of Delhi in the presence of Aurangzeb and his courtiers."[98] According to Macauliffe, "The Emperor ordered the Guru's body to be quartered and the parts thereof to be suspended at the four gates of the city."[99] Thus, Guru Tegh Bahadur became the second martyred Guru.

Guru Tegh Bahadur is fondly remembered as Srishat di Chadar, meaning "Protector of Humanity." The Guru, who mobilized Sikhs across the whole of northern India, worked for the welfare of the downtrodden, and was welcomed by his followers as *Sacha Padsha*, thus earned recognition as the guardian of the whole region. Consequently, in his 1711 composition, *Sri Gursobha*, Chandra Sain Sainapati makes statements "suggestive of a general principle, the freedom of human conscience, upheld by Guru Tegh Bahadur, who became a protector of 'the honor of the world.'"[100]

As the Guru protected "the honor of the world," his advancement of the *miri/piri* doctrine appears to have aroused the Mughal-Brahman alliance to act against him for the same reasons it acted against his grandfather, Guru Arjun.

"The popular story… that Tegh Bahadur was protesting against the forced conversion of Kashmiri Brahmans is not elaborated in the earliest sources on the execution," reports Truschke. Writing in 1788, Browne states, "Aurangzeb seems on this, as well as on many other occasions, to have made religion a veil to cover his political tyranny; the real motive of this cruelty to Tegh Bahadur was most probably resentment for his having allowed his followers to call him *the true King*."[101] Thus, concludes Truschke, "The Mughal State executed Tegh Bahadur in 1675 for causing unrest in the Punjab."[102] According to Eraly, both political and religious factors led to the Guru's martyrdom.

> The Sikhs had by the mid-seventeenth century transformed them-
> selves… into a political community. Their guru was as much a
> monarch as a spiritual head, and was therefore a potential threat
> to the Mughal authority. Political as well as religious consider-
> ations therefore induced Aurangzeb to bear down on the Sikhs.
> This drove Tegh Bahadur, the Sikh guru, into rebellion, but he was
> arrested, tortured, and beheaded.[103]

The eyes of the double-headed hawk — one head adorned with the turban of a Mughal and the other marked with the *tilak* of a Brahman — never
left the entrance of the warm shop. Under Guru Tegh Bahadur's auspices,
as the shop grew warm with traffic from all across northern India, the ruling
elites recognized this vibrant force's threat to their power. With so much
to lose if the flow of traffic continued to increase, the upper-caste and the
conquerors continued to collaboratively suppress the freedom movement at
any cost.

Nevertheless, the Guru's execution failed to disrupt the Sikh Revolution. By killing Guru Tegh Bahadur, the elites demonstrated that he was, in
fact, a King. A *just* King. A *true* King. He was a King who set the people
free. His people were, as Bhimsen suggested, on the path to rebellion. After
being so long enslaved, they were saying, "Let's go, let's separate."

Under the command of Guru Tegh Bahadur's son and successor, Guru
Gobind Singh, the warm shop burgeoned into a powerhouse as he led the
way towards full independence.

Yet, as the shop's traffic grew heavier, the persecution always grew in
tandem. From Guru Nanak, who called Babur a tyrant and was briefly imprisoned, to Guru Arjun, who was tortured to death after Jahangir confessed
to keeping the shop under surveillance "for three or four generations." From
Guru Hargobind, who was imprisoned and waged war with Shah Jahan, to
Guru Tegh Bahadur, who was beheaded by Aurangzeb. Thus, as Guru Gobind Singh began stewarding the *Panth* and *Granth*, it was destined for him
to sacrifice not only his own life, but also the lives of all his children.

Guru Gobind Singh (1666-1708) — By the advent of Guru Gobind
Singh, the masses in the field were flocking to align themselves with this
community whose leaders were sacrificing their lives to resist and destroy
the power of slave-masters.

After 500 years of *Shabad* history developed by the Bhagats and the Gurus, formation of the *Adi Granth*, and construction of Harmandir Sahib and Akal Takht, the next stage in the struggle to secure human dignity was to establish national status for the participants in the Sikh Revolution. Guru Gobind Singh did this by uniting *Panth* and *Granth* in a body called the *Khalsa* (sovereign) which could enrich the world at large.

In 1699, Guru Gobind Singh stood before tens of thousands of his followers who had traveled from far and wide to assemble at Anandpur Sahib, the city originally planned by his father in 1665. Speaking to the assembly, he began by calling for five followers to volunteer their heads in sacrifice. He took the first volunteer inside his tent and returned, alone, carrying a sword covered in blood. He requested another volunteer and repeated this process until, at last, he returned with all five, alive but now dressed as kings in turbans.

The five came from diverse castes and far-flung geographical regions. One was from Delhi, one from Gujarat, one from Karnataka, one from Lahore, and one from Orissa. Four of them were originally members of the oppressed classes. Now, however, the differences and divisions of their old identities were to be abandoned as the Guru stripped them of their caste names and baptized them all as "Singh" (lion). Instead of "worms" these men were to be lions.

"From now on, you have become casteless," declared the Guru. In a single statement, he upheld the equality of men and women, the shared humanity of all people, the plight of the poor, and the distinctiveness of the Sikh religion.

> No ritual, either Hindu or Muslim, will you perform and believe in superstition of no kind, but only in one God who is the Master and the Protector of all, the only Creator and Destroyer. In your new order, the lowest will rank with the highest and each will be to the other a brother.... Women shall be equal of men in every way.... Serve the poor without distinction of caste, color, country, or creed. My *Khalsa* shall always defend the poor.[104]

Then the Guru bowed, submitted himself to the five, and asked them to similarly anoint him a "Singh." He had so much faith in the commitment of the *Khalsa* that he surrendered himself to the institution. The Sikhs, by this point in history, were so infused with the principles of the *Adi Granth* that any number the Guru called for — whether five or five thousand — would have willingly answered the call.

After the five volunteered their heads and were anointed as "Singhs," many others stepped forth to accept the call of the *Khalsa*. According to Dr. Gopal Singh, "about 80,000 Sikhs were baptized in a similar way within a few days."[105] Among them was Kirpa Ram Datt, who led the delegation of Kashmiri *Pandits* in 1675. He bowed and became Kirpa Singh.[106] The high born humbled themselves while the low born were uplifted. Thus, these many individuals of vastly varied backgrounds stood united as all equally human.

"Gobind exclaimed that the lowly should be raised, and that hereafter the despised should dwell next to himself," writes Cunningham. In 1499, Guru Nanak declared that God's path required seeking the company of the low born. Occurring exactly 200 years after Guru Nanak began his mission, the establishment of the *Khalsa* was a graduation ceremony of *summa cum laude* students. As Cunningham states, "It was reserved for Nanak to perceive the true principles of reform, and to lay those broad foundations which enabled his successor Gobind to fire the minds of his countrymen with a new nationality, and to give practical effect to the doctrine that the lowest is equal with the highest, in race as in creed, in political rights as in religious hopes."[107]

With their minds fired by a new nationality, the five Singhs and those who joined them now dedicated their lives to liberating humanity. Freed from their own chains, they devoted their heads to the mission of annihilating dehumanizing systems and ushering in Begampura. Since then, this extraordinary torch of liberty has been passed on to the *Mulnivasi* so that the oppressed can learn to represent themselves, stop being victimized, and seize control of their own destinies.

Speaking to the assembly, Guru Gobind Singh proclaimed the universal equality of all people, declaring, "Someone is Hindu and someone a Muslim, then someone is Shia, and someone a Sunni, but all the human beings, as a species, are recognized as one and the same."[108] His declaration has since been summarized as "recognize the whole human race as one." In longer remarks (which are recorded in Mughal historian Ghulam Muhi-uddin's 1723 *Fatuhat-namah-i-Samadi*), the Guru exhorts,

Embrace one creed and follow one path, rising above all differences of the religions as now practiced. Let the four Hindu castes, who have different rules for their guidance, abandon them all, adopt the one form of adoration, and become brothers. Let no one deem himself superior to another. Let none pay heed to the Ganges, and other places of pilgrimage which are spoken of with reverence in the *Shastras*, or adore incarnations such as Ram, Krishna, Brahma, and Durga, but believe in Guru Nanak and the other Sikh Gurus. Let men of the four castes receive my baptism, eat out of one dish, and feel no disgust or contempt for one another.[109]

In short, Guru Gobind Singh introduced what is now known as the "*Nash* Doctrine." Also called the Five Freedoms, this doctrine liberates people from being shackled by slavery to artificial social and spiritual constraints. As Harinder Singh explains, "Initiated Sikhs renounced their previous occupations (*krit nash*) to work for *Akal-Purakh* (Creative Personality); severed their family ties (*kul nash*) to become the family of the Guru; rejected their earlier creeds (*dharm nash*) for the *Khalsa*; replaced karma (*karam nash*) with the Grace; and stopped superstitions (*bharam nash*) for belief in Ik Oankar (One Force)."[110]

Guru Gobind Singh's establishment of the *Khalsa* expanded Guru Arjun's concept of the nobility of the common person. In his 1841 book, *Sri Gur Panth Parkash*, Sikh historian Rattan Singh Bhangoo explains, "The *Khalsa* must be as autonomous and self-respecting.... Never submitting to the sovereignty of anyone else, except the sovereignty and autonomy of God alone."[111] Writing in 1933, Kapur Singh explains, "The *Khalsa* [is] a sovereign... owing allegiance to no earthly person or powers. One God Almighty, the Timeless, is your only Sovereign to whom you owe allegiance, and He alone is entitled to your devotion and worship."[112] Consequently, as Kapur Singh further substantiates, Sikhs are "uncompromisingly anti-totalitarian."

Sikhism attaches such high significance to the worth of the individual that it is uncompromisingly anti-totalitarian, opposed to all universal busybodies, whether of political Islam, welfarism, or *sarvodaya* of the secular Hindu by State coercion. It is from this teaching of Sikhism that the Sikh concern with polities and sociopolitical life arises, and the commandment, "Though shalt not submit to slavery," is also grounded in this teaching, and this teaching has far-reaching political and social implications, as it has constituted the basic impulse of the Sikh history throughout the past centuries.[113]

In defense of this empowerment of the individual, Guru Gobind Singh taught the emancipated masses how to defend themselves. "From people weak as straw and reeds, he would turn them into men of steel," writes Bhangoo.[114] Defying caste restrictions prohibiting Shudras and Ati-Shudras from carrying arms or riding on saddled horses, the Guru determined "to break, at once, those rules by which the Hindus had been so long chained; to arm, in short, the whole population of the country."[115] Lt. Col. John Malcolm elaborates,

> The great points... by which Guru Gobind has separated his followers forever from the Hindus are those which have been before stated. The destruction of the distinction of castes, the admission of proselytes [converts], and the rendering the pursuit of arms not only admissible, but the religious duty of all his followers; whereas, among the Hindus, agreeable to the *Dharmashastras* [Hindu scriptures, such as *Manusmriti*, dealing with caste duties]... carrying arms on all occasions, as an occupation, is only lawful to the Kshatriya or military tribe.[116]

As a warrior, the Guru led by example. Sangat Singh observes that he "fought against tyranny in all its denominations and did not mince words in calling a spade a spade, be it a Hindu or a Muslim oppressor."[117] From 1689 to 1705, the Guru waged war against the systemic aggression of tyrants, leading armies first against the high-caste Hill Rajas who colluded with the Mughals. "The Rajas," writes historian Zahiruddin Faruki, "being defeated and disgraced in several actions, applied to the Court of Aurangzeb for aid against Guru Gobind."[118] Aurangzeb joined the war against the Sikhs. According to Thornton, "Guru Gobind, at the head of his followers... gained repeated victories over the armies of the Mughal Emperors."[119]

As Guru Gobind Singh continued to move the caravan of freedom forward, he eventually suffered significant setbacks and paid a heavy personal price. In 1704, he lost all of his sons. The two eldest, Ajit (age 17) and Jujhar (age 13), died in battle. The two youngest, Zorowar (age 8) and Fateh (age 5), were executed by the Mughals.

Concerning the fate of the youngest, Thornton explains that, when the

Guru's forces were overpowered, he "was obliged to flee."[120] According to Sangat Singh, "The Guru entrusted his mother and his two younger sons to a Sikh." As they were led away to safety, they "met Gangu... a Kashmiri Brahman, once an employee in the Guru's household." Gangu reportedly offered to provide the Guru's family safe passage, took them to his home, stripped them of their valuables, and turned them over to the Mughals. Bamzai reports, "The children were taken to Sirhind and there, 'by order of the Emperor Aurangzeb, were buried alive.'"[121]

Nevertheless, Bamzai continues, "This tragedy did not dampen the spirit of the Guru, who continued to give fight to the forces of the decaying Mughal Empire." Oral tradition records that, speaking to the *Khalsa* about his loss, Guru Gobind Singh states, "Although four of my sons have joined Waheguru, many thousands of my sons are still alive." Despite enduring the death of his sons, as well as many other horrific trials and tribulations, he preserved the lives of thousands by resolutely standing in the gap between the oppressors and the oppressed.

In a 1705 letter to Aurangzeb, Guru Gobind Singh reveals defense of the oppressed as his motivation. He warns the Emperor, "Stop harming and tormenting people on the advice of your courtiers." Referencing his battles against those who collaborated with the Mughals, he states, "I am also the annihilator of the Hill Rajas, the idol worshippers." Aurangzeb's tyrannies were a violation of his own religion, asserted the Guru. He writes, "You neither follow the teachings of Islam nor [do] you understand its meaning." Implying the Emperor was a bully, the Guru concludes, "Aurangzeb! Stop torturing the weak and the timid with your military might."[122]

Like Guru Nanak, Guru Gobind Singh was determined to resist false creeds and crooked politics. In Cunningham's words: "In the heart of a powerful Empire, he set himself to the task of subverting it, and from the midst of social degradation and religious corruption, he called up simplicity of manners, singleness of purpose, and enthusiasm of desire."[123] The *Panth* grew stronger, more unified, and more resilient as it opposed this depraved culture. "Under Guru Gobind, the tenth and last of the old Sikh pontiffs, the Sikhs were transformed by persecution from a brotherhood of saints into an army of warriors," writes James Wheeler.[124]

The Guru defended the rights of the *Mulnivasi* until his dying breath, which came when, in Nanded, Maharashtra, "his life was cut short... by an assassin in 1708 AD."[125] Thus, Guru Gobind Singh became the third martyred Guru. In a testament to the sacrifices he made in his relentless pursuit of freedom for the *Mulnivasi*, the liberated *Khalsa* fondly remember Guru Gobind Singh as *Pita* (father).

Before his death, Guru Gobind Singh updated and bestowed the Guruship on the *Adi Granth*, the collected writings of his predecessors and the Bhagats who inspired them. The *Khalsa*, with the *Guru Granth* as its guide, accepted as its general Banda Singh Bahadur, who was deputed by the Guru carry on the mission.

Banda Singh Bahadur (1670-1716) — In 1708, Banda travelled from Maharashtra to Punjab and issued a call to arms. As he raised an army, "partly because the peasants were struggling against the excessive land tax of the Mughals, he had considerable success."[126] According to Irvine, "Soon he had forty thousand armed men gathered round him, recruited chiefly from the lower caste Hindus."[127]

In Banda's first military engagement, the Sikh general "turned his attention to the town of Sirhind and its governor, who had bricked up the two younger sons of Guru Gobind Singh."[128] He consequently vanquished Sirhind and executed the governor. From 1709 to 1715, the "brave but ferocious leader" led a peasant revolt against the Mughals.

Thereafter, Banda began instituting national policies. "He struck coins as a mark of Sikh sovereignty," explains Sangat Singh. "He abolished Zamindari — the institution of absentee landlordism — and made tillers of the soil the proprietors. That was applicable to tillers of all classes, whether Sikh, Hindu, or Muslim."[129]

The elimination of caste practices was such a central part of the rebellion that even contemporary Mughal historians took note. In his 1724 composition, *Tazkirat us-Salatin Chaghta*, Muhammad Hadi Kamwar Khan writes, "A large number of persons belonging to the class of sweepers and tanners, and the community of *banjaras* [nomads] and others of base and lowly castes, assembled around him and became his disciples."[130] In his 1734 composition, *Mirat-i Waridat*, Muhammad Shafi Warid describes Banda's "habits and manners."

He laid down that, of Hindus and Muslims, whoever enrolled among his Sikhs, should be one body and take their meal together so that the distinction in honor between the lowly and the well born was entirely removed and all achieved mutual unison, acting together. A sweeper of spittle sat with a raja of great status, and they felt no hostility to each other. He thus initiated numerous innovations and strange practices and put them into effect....

If a lowly sweeper or cobbler (*chamar*), more impure than whom there is no caste (*qaum*) in Hindustan, went to attend on that rebel, he would be appointed to govern his own town and would return with an order (*sanad*) of office of government in his hand.... Such is the power of the Almighty that, in the twinkling of an eye, He can put such a lowly person in authority over a whole world of the high born in such a manner that so many thousands of persons who had displayed bravery in so many manly contests became helpless and lost even the courage to speak in front of that single man.[131]

Banda Singh Bahadur's rebellion outlasted two Emperors before it was finally crushed by the third Emperor. Fighting first against Aurangzeb's son, Bahadur Shah (1643-1712), then against Jahandar Shah (1661-1713), and finally against Farrukhsiyar (1685-1719), the rebels animated the centuries-old struggle for human dignity like never before.

As Banda's rebellion became a people's revolution, the Brahmans and Mughals deepened their alliance. As Farrukhsiyar fought the Sikhs, "he co-opted upper-caste Hindus — Khatris, Brahmans, and Banias — into the system of administration and widened the schism between this section of the Hindus and the Sikhs." According to Sangat Singh,

The rise of the *Khalsa*, mainly taking converts from the low and middle class Hindus, in the process making them self assertive and militant, had made the upper class of Hindus — mainly Brahmans, and clannish hill-rulers, etc., rabidly anti-Sikh. This alignment was widened in Farrukhsiyar's period to include sections of Khatris and Banias, the moneyed and business classes, who thought it advisable to align with the Mughal administration. Faced by a rising tide of Sikh militancy, the administration thought it prudent to follow a religious tolerance towards the Hindus as against systematic persecution of the Sikhs. This, at times, led to a collaboration between the upper-caste Hindus and the Mughal administration. It must be understood that a section of Punjabi or North Indian Hindus was not reconciled to the emergence of the *Khalsa*, which struck at the roots of the Brahmanical culture.[132]

Banda, reports Thornton, "overran the whole district of Sirhind and threatened to conquer all Hindustan until, being defeated in a decisive engagement, he was made prisoner."[133] In December 1715, he lost a battle at Gurdaspur, Punjab. Captured along with hundreds of other Sikhs, he was taken to Delhi and executed on June 9, 1716 — a few days after the 110th anniversary of Guru Arjun's martyrdom.

Accounts of his imprisonment, torture, and execution are given by many sources, including British and Mughal eyewitnesses. Writing in 1724, Khan provides a triumphant account.

> The order was issued... to bring that doomed crew, in a manner suitable for this base gang, to the Imperial Presence.... That chief of heretics [was] placed in an iron cage, along with his principal men and companions, [who were] made to wear wooden-hats and to appear strange and ridiculous. To see this doomed crewed, so many people gathered from the city and suburbs that it was difficult to move in the roads and streets, and hard to breathe. The above-mentioned rebel... [was] handed over to the *Mir Atish* [general of artillery] Ibrahimuddin Khan to be incarcerated.... His three-year-old son, his wife, and his son's nurse were handed over to... the Harem. Six hundred and ninety-four persons from amongst his followers were handed over to Sarbarah Khan, the *Kotwal* [Chief of Police], so that every day a party from amongst them might be killed by the sword by the executioners....
>
> Sarbarah Khan, *Kotwal*, had a hundred persons of this sect beheaded every day.... The *Kotwal*, and Ibrahimuddin, the *Mir Atish*, had the doomed rebel executed with much torture along with his three-year-old son.... Thus the world was cleansed of the presence of that polluted one.[134]

Agents of the British East Company, writing from Delhi in March 1716, not only offer a more somber eyewitness account of the gory spectacle, but also express clear admiration for the resolve of the rebels.

> Some days ago, they entered the city laden with fetters, his whole attendants which were left alive being about seven hundred and eighty... besides about two thousand heads stuck upon poles, being those who died in battle. He was carried into the presence of

the King and, from thence, to a close prison. He, at present, has his life prolonged along with most of his [clerks] in the hope to get an account of his treasure in the several parts of the Kingdom, and of those that assisted him, when afterwards he will be executed. For the rest, there are 100 each day beheaded. It is not a little remarkable with what patience they undergo their fate, and to the last it has not been found that one apostatized from his new formed religion.[135]

Elphinstone concurs, noting that the Sikhs "died with the utmost firmness, disdaining every offer to save their lives at the expense of their religion."[136] However, while his followers were all beheaded, Banda Singh Bahadur was set aside for an even crueler death. In his 1841 *History of India*, Elphinstone documents Banda's execution.

He was exhibited in an iron cage, clad in a robe of cloth of gold, and a scarlet turban; an executioner stood behind him with a drawn sword; around him were the heads of his followers on pikes, and even a dead cat was stuck on a similar weapon to indicate the extirpation of everything belonging to him. He was then given a dagger and ordered to stab his infant son; and, on his refusing, the child was butchered before his eyes and its heart thrown in his face. He was, at last, torn to pieces with hot pincers and died with unshaken constancy, glorying in having been raised up by God to be a scourge to the iniquities and oppressions of the age.[137]

Persecuted, martyred, and overpowered in war, the Sikhs still refused to yield. The sacrifices of the Bhagats and the Gurus, the teachings of the *Guru Granth*, the creation of the *Khalsa*, and the progression of those once treated as "worms" into saints, warriors, and leaders had made an irrevocable impact on India. By the 1800s, Sikhs existed in all regions of the subcontinent. Throughout the land, they entirely opposed Brahmanism as they consistently practiced a distinct way of life separate from Hindus or Muslims.

"They are not confined to the Punjab only," writes Mughal historian Gulam Ali Khan Naqavi in 1808. "In the whole of Hindustan, from Shahjahanabad [Delhi] to Calcutta, Hyderabad, and Chennai, groups after groups are found to belong to this sect; but most of them are market people and only a few are well-born."[138] In 1765, Afghan historian Qazi Nur Muhammad recognizes them as a unique people.

> If you are not conversant with their religion, I [should] tell your honour that the Sikhs are the disciples of a Guru.... The ways and practices of these people are derived from Nanak, who showed to the Sikhs a separate path. His [last] successor was Gobind Singh, from whom they received the title "Singh." They are not from amongst the Hindus.... [They] have a distinct religion of their own.... They have not learnt to have fear of anyone.[139]

The "separate path" — the *Panth* — particularly entailed abolition of caste, which Naqavi acknowledges, writing, "Their leaders of high dignity are mostly from the lower classes, such as carpenters, shoemakers, and Jats.... The number of Sikhs in the Punjab has reached millions since yogurt-sellers, confectioners, fodder-venders, grain-sellers, barbers, [and] washermen... saying *Waheguru di Fateh* [Victory is God's], inter-dine with each other."[140]

The revolutionary social changes produced by the Gurus in their mission to liberate the downtrodden were widely observed by Europeans who traveled to India as early as 1751 (in Fr. Wendel's case), a mere 35 years after Banda's death.

Writing in 1812, British Lt. Col. John Malcolm remarked that, as a result of the "institutions and usages" established by the Gurus, the Sikhs, "by the complete abolition of all distinction of castes, destroyed, at one blow, a system of civil polity that, from being interwoven with the religion of a weak and bigot race, fixed the rule of its priests upon a basis that had withstood the shock of ages."[141] Thus, he argued, the Sikhs succeeded in developing an ideology — and a lifestyle — of liberation in contrast to the Brahmanical caste system which was designed solely to subjugate the masses. As Malcolm explains,

> Though the code of the Hindus was calculated to preserve a vast community in tranquility and obedience to its rulers, it had the natural effect of making the country in which it was established an easy conquest to every powerful foreign invader; and it appears to have been the contemplation of this effect that made Guru Gobind resolve on the abolition of caste as a necessary and indispens-

able prelude to any attempt to arm the original population of India against their foreign tyrants. He called upon all Hindus to break those chains in which prejudice and bigotry had bound them.... His religious doctrine was meant to be popular, and it promised equality. The invidious appellations of Brahman, Kshatriya, Vaishya, and Shudra were abolished.[142]

Thus, observed Malcolm, the Sikh religion was entirely distinct from Brahmanism because, among other things, it rejected the foundational Brahmanical doctrine of caste. "It is impossible to reconcile the religion and usages which Gobind has established with the belief of the Hindus," he writes. Expounding on the profound social impact of Sikhism, he states,

Wherever the religion of Guru Gobind prevails, the institutions of Brahma must fall. The admission of proselytes, the abolition of the distinctions of caste... the form of religious worship, and the general devotion of all Singhs to arms are ordinances altogether irreconcilable with Hindu mythology and have rendered the religion of the Sikhs as obnoxious to the Brahmans, and higher tribes of the Hindus, as it is popular with the lower orders of that numerous class of mankind.[143]

Malcolm's conclusions were shared by other European visitors. "The prejudices of the Hindus... were shocked by the abolition of the distinction of castes," writes British Major William Thorn in 1806.[144] John Griffith, who served as Governor of Bombay, writes in 1794, "The Sikhs receive proselytes of almost every caste, a point in which they differ most materially from the Hindus."[145] In 1787, Swiss mercenary Colonel Antoine-Louis Henri Polier remarks, "All that came, [although] from the lowest and most abject castes, were received, contrary to the Hindu customs, which admit no change of caste, and even Musalmen were in the number of converts."[146] In 1768, Fr. Wendel provides some of the earliest observations, writing,

[Sikhs] have no regard to caste distinctions.... Anyone could become Sikh.... All Sikhs were fit for anything.... Hence this strange confusion and mixture of persons of all castes and extractions among the Sikhs of today, a thing so abominable and, until then, unknown to the gentilism of Indostan.... Hindus and Muhammadans, most of the lowest extraction and the most cursed in Indostan, are welcomed. There is no rank or definition among them…. There are Sikhs in small or large number throughout all of Indostan.[147]

From the martyrdom of Guru Arjun after he completed Harmandir Sahib and compiled the *Adi Granth* to the formation of a community in which caste was stripped away and every person was royal, the *Panth* rose from the ashes to become a pillar of fire purifying India of social division, inequality, and hatred. The thirst of the downtrodden was quenched by the life-giving river of liberty flowing from the souls of the self-sacrificing saints who struggled for centuries to achieve emancipation. Once treated as "worms," they now stood tall and dignified, perceiving the path to royalty as a certainty.

Liberation had become possible for the simple-hearted people who were captivated by Guru Arjun's "ways and manners." They flocked to the warm shop opened generations earlier by Guru Nanak, whose doctrines overthrew the complex-hearted. As Puran Singh writes,

Guru Nanak is seen busy destroying the strongholds of Brahmanical superstition, with a persistent determination. And lo! He has cleared the ruins away and built on their sites a towered and thousand-pillared temple of song for all peoples and nations of the earth to gather in and worship. Guru Nanak offers to the simple folk the cup of nectar to taste.[148]

The simple-hearted were energized as their parched throats tasted the nectar of liberty served freely at the warm shop of the Gurus. Transformed of their own accord, they demanded power, they gave themselves power, and they became powerful. Through their own efforts, they achieved success. It was something they did all by themselves. The basic human dignity the *Mulnivasi* secured represented a resounding victory. It represented the power of the people, by the people, for the people. Finally, the sons and daughters of the soil were able to fill their lungs with the fresh air of the earth upon which they were placed.

Citations

1 *Granth.* 1105.

2 The canon of Hindu scripture is vast and open. Scholars typically differentiate between

the *Srutis* (which include the four Vedas) and the *Smritis* (which were written after the Vedas). Because they all share similar affirmations of *Varnashrama Dharma*, and for the sake of clarity, we are comfortable referring to the canon as, simply, the *Shastras*.

3 Smith, Brian K. *Classifying the Universe: The Ancient Indian* Varna *System and the Origins of Caste*. New York: Oxford University Press. 1994. 27.

4 Griffith, Ralph T.H. (tr.). *Rig Veda*. 1896. Santa Cruz: Evinity Publishing, Inc. 2009. Hymn 10.90, Verse 12.

5 Smith. *Classifying*. 8-9.

6 Elphinstone, Mountstuart. *The History of India* (Vol. 1). London: John Murray. 1843. 20-23.

7 Muller, F. Max and George Bühler (eds.). *The Sacred Books of the East: The Laws of Manu*, Vol. 25. Oxford: Clarendon Press. 1886. Chapter 1, Verses 99-101.

8 Smith. *Classifying*. 34.

9 Ibid., 28-29.

10 Ibid., 32.

11 Muller. *Manu*. Chapter 1, Verse 91.

12 Ibid., Chapter 11, Verse 181.

13 Dubois, Jean A. *Hindu Manners, Customs and Ceremonies*. Henry K. Beauchamp (tr.). 1897. Oxford: Clarendon Press. 1906. 15.

14 Smith. *Classifying*. 5.

15 Ibid., 15.

16 Ibid., 34.

17 Ibid., 34.

18 Manucci, Niccolao. *Storia do Mogul or Mogul India: 1653-1708*. William Irvine (tr.). London: John Murray. 1907. 7.

19 Ibid., 35-36.

20 Pelsaert. *India*. 64.

21 Mayo, Katherine. *Slaves of the Gods*. New York: Harcourt, Brace and Company, Inc. 1929. 150.

22 Rawat. *Studies*. 143.

23 Grewal. *Persian Sources*. 66.

24 Singh. *Struggles*. 26.

25 Ibid., 24-25.

26 Singh, Kapur. "The Golden Temple: Its Theo-Political Status." 1960. Sikh Research Institute. April 25, 2016. Full text available at http://www.sikhri.org/the_golden_temple_its_theo_political_status.

27 Ibid., 25.

28 Ibid., 68.

29 Grewal. *Persian Sources*. 66.

30 Elphinstone. *History*. 526.

31 Grewal. *Persian Sources*. 69.

32 Singh, Kanwarjit. *Political Philosophy of the Sikh Gurus*. New Delhi: Atlantic Publishers & Distributors. 1989. 8.

33 Cunningham. *History*. 66.

34 Singh. *Struggles*. 26.

35 Nahal, Tarlochan Singh. *Miri and Piri: Religion and Politics in Sikhism with Special*

Reference to the Sikh Struggle (1947-1999). Paper presented at International Sikh Conference. 2000. Vancouver, British Columbia.

36 Singh, Kanwarjit. *Political Philosophy*. 2.

37 Thornton. *Gazetteer*. 911.

38 Cunningham. *History*. 57

39 Madra. *Sicques*. 7.

40 Kollar, Nathan R. and Muhammad Shafiq (eds.). *Poverty & Wealth in Judaism, Christianity, & Islam*. Rochester: Palgrave Macmillan. 2016. 36.

41 Nicoll. *Shah Jahan*. 15.

42 Roe, Thomas. *The Embassy of Sir Thomas Roe to the Court of the Great Mogul, 1615-1619 as Narrated in His Journal and Correspondence*, Vol. 1. William Foster (ed.). London: Redford Press. 1899. 252.

43 Pelsaert. *India*. 77.

44 Nicoll. *Shah Jahan*. 30.

45 Ibid., 202.

46 Ibid., 187.

47 Mohamad, Malik. *The Foundations of Composite Culture in India*. Delhi: Aakar Books. 2007. 294.

48 Nicoll. *Shah Jahan*. 202-203.

49 Kinra, Rajeev. *Writing Self*. 2.

50 Ibid., 66

51 Singh. *History*. 87.

52 Ibid., 87-88.

53 Singh, Sardar Harjeet. *Faith and Philosophy of Sikhism*. Delhi: Kalpaz Publications. 2009.

54 Macauliffe. *Religion* (vol. 4). 296.

55 Singh, Harbans. *The Heritage of the Sikhs*. New York: Asia Publishing House. 1964. 35.

56 Grewal. *Persian Sources*. 111-112.

57 Gandhi, Surjit Singh. *History of Sikh Gurus Retold: 1606-1708 CE*. New Delhi: Atlantic Publishers & Distributors. 2007. 621.

58 Truschke, Audrey. *Aurangzeb: The Life and Legacy of India's Most Controversial King*. Ebook. Stanford: Stanford University Press, 2017.

59 Eraly. *Mughal*. 520.

60 Truschke. *Aurangzeb*. Ebook.

61 Kinra. *Writing Self*. 54.

62 Metcalf, Barbara D. and Thomas R. Metcalf. *A Concise History of Modern India*. 2001. Cambridge: Cambridge University Press. 2012. 22-23.

63 Eraly. *Mughal*. 401.

64 Kinra. *Writing Self*. 53.

65 Truschke. *Aurangzeb*. Ebook.

66 Bernier. *Travels*. 391.

67 Eraly. *Mughal*. 82.

68 Truschke. *Aurangzeb*. Ebook.

69 Metcalf. *History*. 21.

70 Eraly. *Mughal*. 407.

71 Truschke. *Aurangzeb*. Ebook.

72 Grewal. *Persian Sources*. 112.

73 Gandhi. *Gurus*. 628.

74 Robinson, Francis. *The Mughal Emperors And The Islamic Dynasties of India, Iran and Central Asia, 1206-1925*. New York: Thames & Hudson, Inc. 2007. 161.

75 Gandhi. *Gurus*. 629.

76 Kohli, Mohindar Pal. *Guru Tegh Bahadur: Testimony of Conscience*. New Delhi: Sahitya Akademi. 1992. 23.

77 Robinson. *Mughal*. 161.

78 Irvine, William. *Later Mughals: 1707-1720*, Vol. 1. London: Luzac & Co. 1922. 79.

79 Browne, James. *India Tracts: Containing a Description of the Jungle Terry Districts, Their Revenues, Trade, and Government: With a Plan for the Improvement of Them; Also An History of the Origin and Progress of the Sicks*. London: Logographic Press. 1788. 2-3.

80 Grewal. *Persian Sources*. 112.

81 Irvine. *Mughals*. 78.

82 Grewal. *Persian Sources*. 105.

83 Gandhi, Surjit Singh. *History of the Sikh Gurus (A Comprehensive Study)*. Delhi: Gur Das Kapur & Sons (P) Ltd. 1978. 380.

84 Madra. *Sicques*. 14-15.

85 Gupta, Hari Ram. *History of the Sikhs*, Vol. 1. New Delhi: Munshiram Manoharlal. 1978.

86 Gandhi. *History*. 574.

87 Eraly. *Mughal*. 314.

88 Bamzai, P.N.K. *Culture and Political History of Kashmir: Medieval Kashmir* (vol. 2). New Delhi: M. D. Publications Pvt Ltd. 1994. 412.

89 Bamzai, P.N.K. *Culture and Political History of Kashmir: Modern Kashmir* (vol. 3). New Delhi: M. D. Publications Pvt Ltd. 1994. 615.

90 Lawrence, Walter R. *The Valley of Kashmir*. London: Oxford University Press. 1895. 304-305.

91 Mohamed. *Foundations*. 317.

92 X, Malcolm. "The Race Problem." African Students Association and NAACP Campus Chapter. Michigan State University, East Lansing, Michigan. 23 January 1963.

93 Madra. *Sicques*. 15.

94 Grewal. *Persian Sources*. 111-113.

95 Madra. *Sicques*. 15.

96 *Granth*. 1429.

97 Madra. *Sicques*. 15.

98 Wheeler, J. Talboys. *India Under British Rule From the Foundation of the East India Company*. London: Macmillan and Co. 1886. 156.

99 Macauliffe. *Religion* (vol. 1). xlix.

100 Grewal. *Persian Sources*. 40.

101 Browne. *India*. 4.

102 Truschke. *Aurangzeb*. Ebook.

103 Eraly. *Mughal*. 407.

104 Singh. *Sikhs*. 66.

105 Singh, Gopal. *The Religion of the Sikhs*. 1971. New Delhi: Allied Publishers Private Limited. 1981. 24.

106 In 1705, Kirpa Singh died fighting the Mughals alongside Guru Gobind Singh.

107 Cunningham. *History*. 69.

108 *Dasam Granth*. Akal Ustat. 50.

109 Singh. *Struggles*. 32-33.

110 Singh, Harinder. "Nash Doctrine: Five Freedoms of Vaisakhi 1699." Sikh Research Institute. April 16, 2017. Full text available at http://www.sikhri.org/nash_doctrine_five_freedoms_of_vaisakhi_1699.

111 Bhangoo, Rattan Singh. *Sri Gur Panth Prakash* (vol. 1). Kulwant Singh (tr.). Chandigarh: Institute of Sikh Studies. 2006. 35.

112 Singh, Kapur. *Sikhism: An Oecumenical Religion*. Gurtej Singh (ed.). Chandigarh: Institute of Sikh Studies. 1993. 78.

113 Ibid., 39.

114 Bhangoo. 3.4

115 Malcolm. *Sketch*. 47.

116 Ibid., 141-142.

117 Singh. *Sikhs*. 80.

118 Faruki, Zahiruddin. *Aurangzeb & His Times*. Bombay: D.B. Taraporevala Sons & Co. 1935. 256.

119 Thornton. *Gazetteer*. 911-912.

120 Ibid., 912.

121 Bamzai. *Kashmir* (vol. 3). 617.

122 Singh, Guru Gobind. *Zafarnama*. Jasbir Singh (tr.). 1705. Full text available at zafarnama.com.

123 Cunningham. *History*. 65.

124 Wheeler. *India*. 156.

125 Bamzai. *Kashmir* (vol. 3). 617.

126 Kuiper, Kathleen (ed.). *Understanding India: The Culture of India*. New York: Britannica Educational Publishing. 2011. 134.

127 Irvine. *Mughals*. 94.

128 Kuiper. *India*. 134.

129 Singh. *Sikhs*. 84.

130 Grewal. *Persian Sources*. 143.

131 Ibid., 161-162.

132 Ibid., 81.

133 Thornton. *Gazetteer*. 912.

134 Grewal. *Persian Sources*. 153-154.

135 Madra. *Sicques*. 47.

136 Elphinstone. *History* (vol. 2). 538.

137 Ibid., 539.

138 Grewal. *Persian Sources*. 215.

139 Ibid., 209

140 Ibid., 214-215.

141 Malcolm. *Sketch*. 148-149.

142 Ibid., 149-150.

143 Ibid., 151.

144 Thorn, William. *Memoir of the War in India*. London: Military Library. 1818. 489

145 Madra. *Sicques*. 163.
146 Ibid., 77.
147 Ibid., 16.
148 Singh. *Spirit* (vol. 2, p. ii). 168.

Harmandir Sahib & Akal Takht

Akal Takht Damage After June 1984 Attack

Guru Nanak Gurdwara, Baghdad, Iraq
(Commemorates Guru Nanak's Visit)

Guru Nanak Shahi, Dhaka, Bangladesh
(Commemorates Guru Nanak's and Guru Tegh Bahadur's Visits)

Gurdwara Guru Nanak Dham, Rameswaram, Tamil Nadu
(Commemorates Guru Nanak's Visit)

Gurdwara Pathar Sahib, Phey, Jammu and Kashmir
(Commemorates Guru Nanak's Visit)

Gurdwara Kartarpur Sahib, Kartarpur, Pakistan
(A town established by Guru Nanak)

Hazur Sahib, Nanded, Maharashtra
(Commemorates Guru Gobind Singh's Martyrdom Site)

**Gurdwara Dera Sahib, Lahore, Pakistan
(Commemorates Guru Arjun's Martyrdom Site)**

Guru Nanak Khalsa College, Mumbai, Maharashtra
Founded by Dr. Ambedkar: "To instill the idea of 'Service to Humanity'
in the young Khalsaites; maximize their civic and sensitivity quotient and
uphold the Ambedkarian ideal by making education accessible to students
of the lower socio–economic strata."

**Gurdwara Sahib
Bhagat Ravidas Jeo,
New Delhi**

**Gurdwara Sahib
Bhagat Kabir Jeo, Maghar,
Uttar Pradesh**

**Gurdwara Sahib
Bhagat Namdev Jeo,
Ghuman, Punjab**

**Gurdwara Sahib
Baba Sheik Farid Jeo,
Faridkot, Punjab**

Honorable Dr. B.R. Ambedkar
with Honorable E. V. Ramasamy

Honorable Jyotirao Phule

Silver Coins Struck by Banda Singh Bahadur in 1712

THE UNIVERSAL MESSAGE OF GURU GRANTH SAHIB, COMPRISING THE NOBLE SOULS OF:

BHAGAT JAI DEV	BHAGAT FARID
BHAGAT SADHANA	BHAGAT NAM DEV
BHAGAT BENI	BHAGAT RAMANAND
BHAGAT KABIR	BHAGAT DHANNA
BHAGAT SAIN	BHAGAT RAVIDAS
BHAGAT PIPA	GURU NANAK
BHAI MARDANA	BHAGAT BHIKAN
BHAGAT TRILOCHAN	GURU ANGAD
BHAGAT PARMANAND	GURU AMAR DAS
BHAGAT SURDAS	BABA SUNDER
GURU RAM DAS	BHAI SATTA
GURU ARJUN	BHATT KALSAHAR
BHAI BALWAND	BHATT BHALH
BHATT BHAL'S	BHATT GAYAND
BHATT BHIKA	BHATT JALAP
BHATT HARBANS	BHATT MATHURA
BHATT KIRAT	BHATT SALH
BHATT NALH	GURU TEGH BAHADUR

GURU GOBIND SINGH, WHO INVESTED AUTHORITY OF THE LIVING GURU TO SRI GURU GRANTH SAHIB JI IN 1708, THUS BLENDING ALL NOBLE SOULS INTO

ONE SOVEREIGN GURU

— 4 —
Maharaja Ranjit Singh's Sikh Empire

After Banda's death, the *Panth* continued to preserve and practice the teachings of the *Guru Granth* despite extreme persecution. Under Aurangzeb, the Mughal Empire reached its apex as it spread across almost the entire Indian subcontinent. After the Emperor's death in 1707, however, the Empire quickly crumbled as his successors were overwhelmed by internal disputes and external wars.

After executing Banda in 1716, Emperor Farrukhsiyar died in April 1719. The Empire then endured a succession of three new Emperors in the space of four months. Finally, Muhammad Shah (1702-1748) assumed the throne of Delhi in September 1719.

Muhammad Shah's reign was marked by repeated defeats by indigenous and foreign powers as well as the defection of a number of Mughal governors who transformed the provinces they governed into independent kingdoms.

In 1738, Persian Emperor Nader Shah (1698-1747) invaded India. The following year, he pillaged Delhi. From 1747 to 1769, Afghan Emperor Ahmad Shah Durrani (1722-1772) repeatedly invaded and plundered India.

Britannica Educational Publishing records this account: "The ruler of Afghanistan, Ahmad Shah Durrani, led a series of nine invasions of the Punjab that eventually brought Mughal power in the region to an end. In rural areas, the Sikhs took advantage of the weakening of Mughal control to form several groups later known as *Misls*. Beginning as warrior bands, the emergent *Misls*… gradually established their authority over quite extensive areas."[1] As the mighty Mughal Empire grew increasingly unstable, *Misls* (autonomous but allied armed bands) waged guerrilla war against the Mughals as well as against Persian and Afghan invaders.

Sikhs were crucial in preventing Durrani from gaining a foothold in India, but the Afghan-Sikh conflict was particularly costly. Durrani's forces perpetrated the *Chhota Ghallughara* (Lesser Massacre) in 1746 and the

Vadda Ghallughara (Greater Massacre) in 1762, slaughtering tens of thousands of Sikh men, women, and children. Thrice — in 1757, 1762, and 1764 — the Afghans destroyed Harmandir Sahib.

While the Sikhs resisted the invasion of Persians and Afghans through Punjab, the British East India Company — under the charter of the British Empire — swiftly expanded throughout all other areas of India. In 1757, the British obtained a decisive foothold when they established their first colony in Bengal. Thereafter, the Company's armies conquered territories in Bihar, Karnataka, Maharashtra, Orissa, Tamil Nadu, Uttar Pradesh, and elsewhere. Thus, the British became such a dominant power in the subcontinent that, by the dawn of the 19th-century, the Mughal Empire was a British protectorate.

The Rise and Fall of the Sikh Empire (1801-1849) — While the Mughal Empire declined and the rest of the Indian subcontinent fell under British occupation, a different series of events unfolded in Punjab. Political independence began taking root with the people's rebellion led by Banda, which was one the world's first genuine democratic revolutions. Subsequently, in the face of rising persecution, the Sikhs reorganized into the groups which became known as *Misls*, and, by about 1744, banded together as a confederacy.

During the Sikh Confederacy, the principles of *Guru Granth* took deeper root in Punjabi society. In 1784, British statesman Richard Joseph Sullivan offered his opinion of the Sikhs after traveling in India. "They are now composed of all castes," observes Sullivan. "The Sikhs have a high notion of the equality of mankind. They carry this so far that the lowest among them pay no sort of respect to the highest. They never rise to salute each other or bend the head." Moreover, he explains, they had risen in political power.

> From small beginnings… the Sikhs have risen to such an alarming degree of consequence that they now possess an extent of dominion computed at eight hundred miles in length and four hundred miles in breadth; its capital Lahore…. The influence and almost irresistible force of the Sikhs have for some years past alarmed the powers of Hindustan. In a word, the Sikhs and their relatives have every appearance of being one day or other a very formidable power in Hindustan.[2]

Despite the long history of conflict with the Mughals and even the recent horrors suffered at the hands of Durrani, the Sikhs lived in harmony with the Muslim commoners. "Their cities abound with Muhammadan artificers and tradesmen, who are most liberally encouraged," reports Sullivan. "Even many Afghan families have hereditary estates in their dominions, which they allow them quietly to possess."[3]

In 1801, the confederacy was replaced by the Sikh Empire as the *Misls* gave way to the military might of Maharaja Ranjit Singh (1780-1839).

Punjab was finally free from foreign rule, a crowning achievement for the Sikh Revolution. However, consolidation of political power in the hands of a single ruler ultimately resulted in a victory for Brahmanism and led to the downfall of the Sikh Empire.

During the Maharaja's reign, Western observers testify that the common people maintained a commitment to the principles of equality and liberty propagated by the Gurus. In 1833, the first American Christian missionaries arrived in Punjab. The wife of Reverend William Reed explains their choice of destination, writing that the Sikhs "are less superstitious than the Hindus, more open to conviction, in a great degree free from the evils of caste, and more desirous of education."[4] Reverend John C. Lowrie, also writing in 1833, elaborates,

> The people north of the Sutlej, in the territory of Lahore, are under the influence of Ranjit Singh, long the most formidable enemy of the British, but in friendship at present. They are all one people on both sides of the Sutlej, called Seiks or Sikhs; speaking the same language, the Punjabi; having the same religion and the same customs.... They are described as more free from prejudice, from the influence of Brahmans, and from caste, than any other people in India. Indeed, the Seik religion is quite distinct.[5]

Although short-lived, the political entity of the Sikh Empire gave the masses room to breathe freely as they found relief from the deprivations of both the caste system and foreign occupation. The Empire briefly provided the people a peaceful environment in which to realize and establish their distinct identity. The sociopolitical situation even won the praise of the British Government.

The government of Ranjit Singh seems in many respects to have been better than the contemporary governments of neighboring independent Native States.... Oppression beyond the customary degree was punished, the country from the Indus to the Sutlej enjoyed peace, and the comparatively mild system of government, such as it was, no doubt was popular.[6]

Yet it was not to last. According to Sangat Singh, the Sikh Empire "contained within itself the seeds of its destruction."

Upheaval soon resulted as the Sikh Empire swiftly fell prey to the false creeds and crooked politics against which the Gurus fought. In particular, the rise of a hereditary monarchy contradicted the concept of the nobility of the common person which Guru Nanak, Guru Arjun, and Guru Gobind Singh all taught. Cunningham clarifies, "Ranjit Singh never arrogated to himself the title or the powers of despot or tyrant."[7] Yet not all Sikhs were comfortable with the rule of a Maharaja. According to Malcolm, many considered it a "usurpation which they deemed subversive of the commonwealth of their constitution."[8]

One of those who was uncomfortable with the hereditary monarchy was General Hari Singh Nalwa, Commander-in-Chief of the Empire's army. He rebukes Ranjit Singh, telling him,

This State belongs not to an individual, but to the *Khalsa* commonwealth. It is by the sacrifices of a whole people over a century, blessed by the Guru's Grace, that we have won an Empire. Let them choose who shall lead them by consensus.[9]

The downfall of the Sikh Empire began when Ranjit "passed on the levers of power to the hands of Dogras."[10] A British Government report adds, "Much of the trouble, too, that befell the Sikh Government after Ranjit Singh's death may be traced to the inordinate power he had permitted his favorites to acquire.... Foremost in influence and ability of the favorites were the three Dogra brothers from Jammu: Gulab Singh, Dhian Singh, and Suchet Singh."[11]

The Dogras, descendants of the Hill Rajas against whom Guru Gobind Singh made war, eventually "usurped to themselves the whole of the functions of government."[12] In 1818, Dhian became Prime Minister. The territory of Jammu was controlled by the Sikh Empire and, in 1822, Gulab was appointed as Raja of Jammu. "Scarcely any affair of importance was undertaken by Ranjit that was not entrusted to one of them," observes Lt. Col. Henry Steinbach, a German mercenary who served in the Sikh military.[13] In their positions of power, the Dogras directly caused the downfall of the Sikh Empire. As Puran Singh reports, "Under Maharaja Ranjit Singh... the Hindu and the Brahman ministers proved traitors."[14]

Ranjit Singh reigned until June 27, 1839, when he died in his sleep. The circumstances of his funeral reveal just how completely this monarch departed from the teachings of the Gurus. He took many wives and, in the pattern of the Mughal Emperors, contracted marriages with several Hindu *ranis* (princesses). At Ranjit's funeral, his family followed the Hindu custom of *sati* against which the Gurus taught. Steinbach, who witnessed the ceremony, writes,

> Four of his favorite queens, together with seven female slaves, having, in conformity with the horrible practice of the country, expressed their intention of burning themselves upon his funeral pile, preparations were immediately made for the solemnity....
>
> The body of the Maharaja having been placed upon the pile, his queens seated themselves around it, when the whole were covered over with a canopy of the most costly Kashmir shawls. The Maharaja Kharak Singh then taking a lighted torch in his hand, pronounced a short prayer, set fire to the pile, and in an instant the whole mass, being composed of very ignitible material, was in flames. The noise from the tom toms (drums) and shouts of the spectators immediately drowned any exclamation from the wretched victims.[15]

Immediately afterwards, the kingdom fell into complete disarray as it was overwhelmed by political intrigues, cloak and dagger schemes, murders, *coups d'état*, and civil war. At the center of it all were the Dogras. Steinbach reports, "For a long time after the death of Ranjit, their paramount influence over public affairs, added to their prodigious wealth, enabled them almost to hold the destinies of the Punjab in their own hands. They were, however, more feared than liked."[16]

Succeeding Ranjit, Kharak Singh (his oldest son) became Maharaja. Dhian remained Prime Minister, but Kharak turned to another for counsel — "Chet Singh, a man of low birth."[17] According to Steinbach, "Dhian Singh, although still nominally Prime Minister, found his authority virtually annulled. Revenge for the loss of power took possession of his thoughts, and he soon found an opportunity of carrying his intentions into effect."[18] The Dogra brothers secretly schemed with Kharak's son, Nau Nihal, and convinced him to depose his father. In October, the conspirators staged a *coup*. "The privacy of the Maharaja's household was rudely violated by the prince and minister at daybreak on the 8th of October 1839, and Chet Singh was awakened from his slumbers to be put to death, within a few paces of his terrified master," reports Cunningham.[19]

Nau Nihal imprisoned his father and became Maharaja. The deposed Kharak died, "not without suspicion of poison," on November 5, 1840.[20] The following day, Nau Nihal died under mysterious circumstances, as Cunningham indicates.

> He had performed the last rites at the funeral pyre of his father, and he was passing under a covered gateway… when a portion of the structure fell… and so seriously injured the prince that he became senseless at the time and expired during the night. It is not positively known that the [Dogras] thus designed to remove Nau Nihal Singh; but it is difficult to acquit them of the crime, and it is certain that they were capable of committing it…. It is equally certain that the prince was compassing their degradation, and, perhaps, their destruction.[21]

Civil war followed. In January 1841, Sher Singh (a son of Ranjit) emerged triumphant and was proclaimed Maharaja by Dhian who, according to Sangat Singh had "virtually emerged as the King-maker, and firmed up his grip over the *Darbar* [court]."[22] However, after ascending to the throne amidst this wave of treachery, "Sher Singh principally feared his own chiefs and subjects." Cunningham continues, explaining, "He felt uneasy under the jealous domination of Dhian Singh…. During the summer of 1843, Dhian Singh perceived that his influence over the Maharaja was fairly on the wane."[23]

The Dogras orchestrated another *coup*, convincing some of Sher's advisors to betray him. On September 15, 1843, they murdered Sher and his son, Pratap. The plot backfired on Dhian, however, as the king-slayers simultaneously betrayed and murdered the Dogra Prime Minister.

Consequently, the five-year-old Duleep (the youngest son of Ranjit) assumed the throne. The Sikh Empire soon crumbled as the British made war with the Sikhs. Once again, the role of the Dogras was treachery.

In 1845, while the Empire was led by a boy king, the British declared war on the Sikhs. With no one else to turn to during the war, explains Cunningham, Gulab was "spontaneously hailed as minister and leader."[24] According to Shah Mohammad, a Punjabi poet living in Amritsar during the war, Gulab had the majority of the Sikhs "removed from the army, thus weakening the *Khalsa* beyond retrieval."[25]

Within two years, British forces overwhelmed the Sikhs and occupied Lahore. "Gulab Singh had been appointed [minister] by the chiefs and people when danger pressed them, and he had been formally treated with as minister by the English," writes Cunningham. Meanwhile, the army "readily assented to the requisition of the [Maharaja's] court that Gulab Singh, their chosen minister, should have full powers to treat with the English."[26] In response, Gulab negotiated the Empire's surrender with representatives of Henry Hardinge, the British Governor-General of India.

Mohammad suggests that Gulab "was serving none but himself." He welcomed the British with open arms. "Raja Gulab Singh paid obeisance to the [Governor-General] with all obsequiousness," writes Mohammad. "He brought him into Lahore, holding him by the arm. [He said:] 'O Sahib! Have mercy on us.'"[27] According to Cunningham, "The overtures of the Raja... were all made in the hope of assuring to himself a virtual viceroyalty over the whole dominion of Lahore."[28] He failed to achieve that specific goal, but Gulab's sycophantic self-interest did cost Punjab its independence.

Under the March 1846 treaty he negotiated, large portions of the Empire's territory were ceded to the British, most of the Sikh army was disbanded, and their arms were seized. Under a subsequent December 1846 treaty, a permanent British garrison was established at Lahore and the whole administration of the country was transferred to a Council of Regency, which was allowed to act only "under the control and guidance" of a British agent who took up residence at the court.

In short, the Sikh Empire became a vassal state of the British East India Company. "In this way, the *Feringhee* [foreigners]... stationed their own contingents in Lahore," explains Mohammad. "The country now passed into the hands of Company functionaries."[29]

While negotiating the March 1846 Treaty of Lahore, the Dogra minister did not neglect to consider his own future. "Gulab... suddenly perplexed the Governor-General by asking what *he* was to get for all he had done to bring about a speedy peace and to render the army an easy prey," states

Cunningham. He asserts the treaty was composed "to appease Gulab Singh in a manner agreeable to the Raja." Under Hardinge's auspices, "Kashmir and the hill states... were cut off from the Punjab Proper and transferred to Gulab Singh as a separate sovereign."[30] Even the treaty records that it was crafted to satisfy Raja Gulab's desires.

> In consideration of the services rendered by Raja Gulab Singh of Jammu to the Lahore State towards procuring the restoration of the relations of amity between the Lahore and British Governments, the Maharaja hereby agrees to recognize the independent sovereignty of Raja Gulab Singh in such territories and districts in the hills as may be made over to the said Raja Gulab Singh by separate agreement between himself and the British Government.[31]

Having thus betrayed the Sikh Empire in exchange for lining his own pockets, the Hill Raja fled north. Mohammad reports, "After getting Kashmir in the bargain, Gulab Singh repaired forthwith to Jammu." So he became the Maharaja of Jammu and Kashmir.

The Sikhs and British waged war again in 1848. Yet the damage was already done. The Sikh Empire was the youngest of the independent nations of the Indian subcontinent, and the last bastion against the complete foreign occupation of the subcontinent by the British. Yet, in 1849, it was finally absorbed into the territory of the British East India Company.

Establishment of a political State led by the Sikhs was a fleeting experiment which was short-circuited when Ranjit created a hereditary monarchy (in contradiction to the Gurus' teachings) and relinquished power to Brahman bureaucrats (the very same ruling elites who conspired with the Mughals to kill Guru Arjun).[32] Soon, history took another wild turn as the British absorbed the Indian subcontinent into its colonial domains.

Citations

1 Kuiper, Kathleen (ed.) *Understanding India: The Culture of India*. New York: Britannica Educational Publishing. 2011. 135.
2 Sullivan, Richard Joseph. *An analysis of the political history of India. In which is considered, the present situation of the East, and the connection of its several powers with the Empire of Great Britain*. 1779. London: T. Beckett. 1784. 206-207.
3 Ibid., 202-203.
4 Swift, E.P. *The Foreign Missionary Chronicle: Containing a Particular Account of the Proceedings of the Western Foreign Missionary Society and a General View of the Trans-*

actions of Other Similar Institutions (Volumes 1 and 2). Pittsburgh: Christian Herald. 1834. 207.

5 Ibid., 201.

6 British Indian Empire. *Report on the Administration of Punjab and Its Dependencies for 1901-1902*. Lahore: Punjab Government Press. 1902. 17.

7 Cunningham. *History*. 168.

8 Malcolm. *Sketch*. 110.

9 Singh. *Sikhs*. 107.

10 Ibid., 108.

11 British. *Report*. 17.

12 Cunningham. *History*. 223.

13 Steinbach, Henry. *The Punjab: Being a Brief Account of the Country of the Sikhs*. London: Smith, Elder, & Co. 1845. 20.

14 Singh, Puran. *Open Letter to Sir John Simon*. October 21, 1928. Full text available at globalsikhstudies.com and archive.org.

15 Steinbach. *Punjab*. 17-19.

16 Ibid. 20.

17 British. *Report*. 17.

18 Steinbach. *Punjab*. 21.

19 Cunningham. *History*. 225.

20 British Indian Empire. *The Imperial Gazetteer of India* (vol. 20). Oxford: Clarendon Press. 1908. 272.

21 Cunningham. *History*. 231.

22 Singh. *Sikhs*. 113.

23 Cunningham. *History*. 255.

24 Ibid., 304.

25 Mohammed, Shah. *The First Punjab War: Shah Mohammed's Jangnama*. P. K. Nijhawan (ed. and tr.). Amritsar: Singh Brothers, 2001. 247.

26 Cunningham. *History*. 316-17.

27 Mohammed. *War*. 247.

28 Cunningham. *History*. 318.

29 Mohammed. *War*. 251-252.

30 Cunningham. *History*. 318-319.

31 Ibid., 400.

32 One may contrast the behavior of the Dogra family as bureaucrats under the Sikh Empire with the behavior of the Das family as bureaucrats under the Sikh Gurus. On one hand, the Gurus did not relinquish all power into the hands of the bureaucrats; on the other hand, the Das family repeatedly proved their devotion to the *Panth* and *Granth* by laying down their own lives to defend it. The Gurus understood that, because caste is a fraud, a person should be judged by the content of their character and not the caste with which they may have been associated.

Dr. Ambedkar's Warning:
"There is Great Danger of Things Going Wrong"

In 1858, the British Empire revoked the East India Company's charter, took over all its territories, administrative apparatus, and armed forces, and instituted direct Crown Rule over the Indian subcontinent, thereby establishing the British Raj.

Foreign rule switched from the hands of the Mughals to the British, yet Brahmanism persisted as the underlying sociopolitical structure. On one hand, the British Raj raised the hopes of some *Mulnivasi* when many British identified Brahmanism, denounced it, and partially acknowledged the significance of the *Panth*. On the other hand, the foreign occupiers needed the counsels of Brahmans to subvert and destroy popular uprisings against imperial rule.

Under imperial rule, the *Mulnivasi* found a little freedom to break some caste restrictions by, for instance, championing women's education and publicly expanding efforts to socially uplift the lowest of the low. Yet the basic liberties of the common people still faced restrictions reminiscent of the Mughal era. The British Raj restricted human rights to freedom of assembly, speech, and the press; *habeas corpus* and trial by jury; the keeping and carrying of arms; ownership of property — to name a few.

Sikhs Under the British Raj — In particular, the British interfered with management of religious institutions and, as a result, many *Gurdwaras* fell under total control of Brahmanical elements. Loss of Sikh control of Sikh institutions traced back to the days of the Mughals. "In the early eighteenth century, with the large-scale Muslim persecution of Sikhs, first by the Mughals and then by the Afghan invaders, taking charge of Sikh places of worship became a hazardous enterprise," reports Singaporean historian Dr. Tan Tai Yong. The Sikhs "were forced to flee into exile," and in their absence, *de facto* Hindus "subsequently filled the positions of *granthi* (scripture reader) and *mahant* (manager) in most of the important Sikh *Gurdwaras*." As a result, explains Yong,

> Legal ownership of these estates [was] conferred on the manager.... The office of the *mahant* soon became not only an influential post but an extremely lucrative one as well. Gradually, the *mahants* gained complete control over the temples, converting *Gurdwara* lands and revenue into their personal possessions, and leaving the congregation virtually powerless to exercise any influence on the ways they conducted the affairs of the temple. Without having to account for their conduct to the congregation, the *mahants* turned the Sikh temples into their private properties, and, in some cases, Hindu practices and idol worship soon found their way into the *Gurdwara*.[1]

The system was entrenched by Maharaja Ranjit Singh and embraced by the British. "The English, right from the annexation of Punjab, regarded the Sikh shrines as fulcrums of power and authority," writes Sangat Singh. "The British followed the precedent of Ranjit Singh since 1825 in appointing a manager for the Golden Temple, Amritsar, to justify their appointing a manager of the shrine." With administrative control of Harmandir Sahib, they pursued the same policy as Emperor Jahangir's *pandits* and *qazis*, attempting to expunge all practices objectionable to the ruling elite. As with Guru Arjun, they objected to the content of the *Granth* itself. To this end, they banned "singing of *gurbani*" (the *Shabads* of the *Granth*) and "performance of *katha*, discourse over Guru's words, as that could have political overtones."[2]

In response to this and other issues, Sikhs initiated the Singh Sabha Movement in 1873. Their goal was to reform Sikhism by removing outside influences and returning control of Sikh institutions to the *Panth*. Prominent stalwarts of the Movement like Giani Ditt Singh and Gurmukh Singh challenged elitism in Sikhism as another version of Brahmanism.

Simultaneously, in 1875, Swami Dayanand Saraswati founded the Arya Samaj, a Hindu reform movement which cloned aspects of Sikhism. Yet Saraswati's attempted movement eliminated the soul of the *Panth*. He openly criticized Guru Nanak for his lack of Brahmanical influence. As Saraswati alleges, "The aim of Nanak was, no doubt, good; but he did not possess any learning.... He was quite ignorant of the Vedas and the *Shastras* and of

Sanskrit."[3] When Saraswati and Giani Ditt Singh engaged in public debate, Singh thoroughly defeated the Swami. This intellectual victory led to some respite from the rising anti-Sikh campaign launched by the Arya Samaj.

Singh Sabha agitated for decades until, finally, "the Sikh reformers succeeded in 'cleansing' the Golden Temple of Brahman priests, idols, and Hindu rituals."[4] Energized by this victory, they led a broader movement to remove all *mahants* and restore democratic control of the *Gurdwaras* to the Sikh people. According to Indian historian V. K. Agnihotri,

> The Gurdwara Reform Movement launched an agitation for freeing the *Gurdwaras* from these corrupt *mahants* and for handing over the *Gurdwaras* to a representative body of Sikhs. Under the growing pressure of… the *Gurdwara* agitators, the *Gurdwaras* came under control of an elected committee known as the Shiromani Gurdwara Parbandhak Committee in November 1920. The movement for liberation of the *Gurdwaras* soon turned into the Akali Movement.[5]

Meanwhile, outside of Punjab, the struggle for human dignity spread as great *Mulnivasi* leaders arose to further challenge Brahmanism. However, as they fought for the liberation of the masses by opposing unjust and oppressive social orders, they largely discarded political means. Instead, they began to educate, agitate, and organize on a social level.

Jyotirao Phule (1827-1890) — In Maharashtra, Jyotirao Phule worked in partnership with his wife, Savitribai, as they championed education. Together, they founded a school for girls, with Savitribai as its first teacher, and continued to open more schools for *Mulnivasi* children. Notably, Phule conceived the name "Dalit" (broken) to describe the Ati-Shudras.

According to a biographical sketch, "Phule was firm in his belief that the emancipation of the women, Shudras, and Ati-Shudras could be achieved only through the total annihilation of the Brahmanical culture system."[6] Insisting on the urgency and primacy of "the education of the masses," Phule declares, "Let there be schools for the Shudras in every village; but away with all Brahman schoolmasters!" Moreover, he affirms the universal equality of all people.

> All men and women are, by birth, independent and are entitled to enjoy all due human rights…. Our Creator has graciously be-

stowed all human rights on all men and women, without any distinction. No particular man or a group has any right to oppress any human being.[7]

In his 1873 book, *Slavery*, he explained how the caste system brainwashes members of society by producing a colonial mentality wherein the degraded feel incapable of surviving without those who degrade them. Describing the synergy between the oppressor and the oppressed, he writes,

How far the Brahmans have succeeded in their endeavors to enslave the minds of the Shudra and Ati-Shudra, those of them who have come to know the true state of matters know well.... The Brahman had, at last, so contrived to entwine himself round the Shudra in every large or small undertaking, in every domestic or public business, that the latter is by custom quite unable to transact any concern of moment without his aid.... The Shudra, on the other hand, is so far reconciled to the Brahman yoke that, like the American slave, he would resist any attempt that may be made for his deliverance and fight even against his benefactor.[8]

According to Phule, *Manusmriti* was one of the foundations of the caste system; it was also a reason for the abject ignorance of the masses. He famously states, "Without education, wisdom was lost; without wisdom, morals were lost; without morals, development was lost; without development, wealth was lost; without wealth, the Shudras were ruined; so much has happened through lack of education." In his 1881 book, *The Whipcord of the Cultivators*, he further elaborates,

When the original Arya Bhat-Brahman regime was started in this country, they forbade knowledge to the Shudras and so have been able to loot them at will for thousands of years. Evidence for this will be found in such self-interested literature of theirs as the *Manusmriti*.... The Aryan Brahmans, in order to give them all kinds of harassment, made many selfish and tyrannous "laws." Among them some written points can be found in pitiless and partisan books such as Manu's.... It was their cunning ancestors like Manu who established the fabrication of casteism in the filthy books of the *Dharmashastras*.

Periyar (1879-1973) — In Tamil Nadu, E.V. Ramasamy (more commonly called "Periyar") agitated for rationalism, self-respect, women's rights, and against caste. He asks, "If our people do not consent to bring about reforms in caste, religion, habits, and customs, in what other way can freedom, excellence, and self-respect be ushered in?"[9] Devoting himself to the eradication of caste and proclaiming the equality of all, he states,

> No man is inferior to me. Similarly, none is superior to me. This means that each one should live free and equal. To create this condition, caste should be eradicated.[10]

Periyar conceived a separate identity — "Dravidian" — for the indigenous people of southern India. Calling *Manusmriti* "the weapon of the highest caste," he notes that it is used "to render injustice to all Dravidians." Further explaining the significance of the text, he writes, "So far as the Hindus are concerned, where there is a problem to be decided, the *Dharmashastras* are deemed to be the main basic rock of determination. Of all, the Manu code is the most important one."[11]

Consequently, Periyar organized public burnings of *Manusmriti*. Denouncing the *Shastras*, he insisted people simply abandon observance of caste. As he asks, "Should we still be frightened of false Hindu codifications (*Shastras*) and useless traditions? Why not our people divest themselves of the subjugation imposed on the basis of birth?" The outcome of caste practice, Periyar warns, was a perverted society which retarded the development of individuals and handicapped their ability to progress or succeed.

> The caste system has perverted our ideas about human conduct. The principle of different codes of conduct for each caste based on birth and life, led in accordance with it for centuries, have spoiled the Hindu mentality almost beyond repair, and destroyed the idea of uniformity in conduct. Graded inequality has got so much into the Hindu blood that general intelligence is warped and refused to mend even after English education and higher standards of living.[12]

Periyar put his principles into action in 1924 when he took a leading role in an agitation against untouchability organized in Vaikom, Kerala. "In Vaikom, you have a temple with four entrances on the four sides, leading to four streets around the temple," writes Periyar. "There was a law that the low-caste Untouchables… should not enter those roads. If an Untouchable had to go to the other side of the temple, he had to go two or three furlongs away from the temple and walk about a mile to reach the other side."

Challenging the caste-based law, Periyar and others began repeatedly courting arrest by passing over the streets. The demand for the right to freedom of movement within all parts of the city quickly gained support from other communities. Keralan attorney George Joseph, a Christian, took a leading role. Furthermore, as Periyar reports, "The news reached Punjab." About 30 Punjabis traveled to join the agitation. "They offered 2000 rupees as donation and consented to meet the catering expenses for the volunteers."[13] Muslims also joined. With Periyar at the head, the movement developed into one of the most unified in South Asian history.

Dr. Bhim Rao Ambedkar (1891-1956) — In Maharashtra, Dr. Bhim Rao Ambedkar organized a movement for the annihilation of caste.

Born as an Ati-Shudra, the trajectory of his life was the exception to the rule of suffering typically experienced by other Ati-Shudras. Educated as an economist in New York and London, he became heavily involved in the movement for independence from the British Empire. After independence, he chaired the Drafting Committee for the Constituent Assembly of India and became the country's first Law Minister. Dr. Ambedkar was devoted to liberating the *Mulnivasi* and spent his professional life organizing, educating, and agitating for them.

In 1927, he organized mass public burnings of *Manusmriti*. The book, as he explains, is "a divine Code which lays down the rules which govern the religious, ritualistic, and social life of the Hindus in minute detail and which must be regarded as the Bible of the Hindus and containing the philosophy of Hinduism." Analyzing *Manusmriti* from the perspective of a Dalit, Dr. Ambedkar concludes, "There is no code of laws more infamous regarding social rights than the Laws of Manu. Any instance from anywhere of social injustice must pale before it."[14]

As Ambedkar reasons, however, the other *Shastras* also enshrine caste. "The Philosophy of Hinduism will be the same whether one takes the *Manusmriti* as its Gospel or whether one takes the *Vedas* and the *Bhagavad Gita* as the gospel of Hinduism." In *Philosophy of Hinduism*, Ambedkar further elaborates on what led him to that conclusion.

In Hinduism, inequality is a religious doctrine adopted and conscientiously preached as a sacred dogma. It is an official creed and nobody is ashamed to profess it openly. Inequality for the Hindus is a divinely prescribed way of life as a religious doctrine.... As a prescribed way of life, it has become incarnate in Hindu Society and is shaped and moulded by it in its thoughts and in its doings. Indeed, inequality is the Soul of Hinduism.[15]

Initially, he hoped to eradicate the caste system by reforming Hinduism to allow equal treatment of Ati-Shudras. However, such efforts proved fruitless. Eventually, he realized efforts at reformation were doomed to failure because the practice of untouchability does not stem from a correctable defect in Hinduism. Rather, it is a direct result of the orthodox practices of that religion. The hierarchical nature of the caste system makes it intrinsically incompatible with a philosophy of equal treatment. Consequently, Ambedkar announced to an assembly of approximately 10,000 Ati-Shudras in Pune, Maharashtra in 1935, "I solemnly assure you that I will not die a Hindu."

In his monumental May 15, 1936 speech, "The Annihilation of Caste," Dr. Ambedkar explains that Hinduism is inseparable from caste.

Religion compels the Hindus to treat isolation and segregation of castes as a virtue. Religion does not compel the non-Hindu to take the same attitude towards caste. If Hindus wish to break caste, their religion will come in their way.... The Hindus observe caste not because they are inhuman or wrong-headed. They observe caste because they are deeply religious. People are not wrong in observing caste. In my view, what is wrong is their religion, which has inculcated this notion of caste. If this is correct, then obviously the enemy you must grapple with is not the people who observe caste but the *Shastras* which teach them this religion of caste.[16]

Having recognized that caste is intrinsic to Hinduism, Ambedkar concluded it was necessary to consciously reject the Hindu religion in order to escape the caste system. Reforms were incapable of annihilating caste from a belief system — Hinduism — which was founded on the practice. Thus, in his speech on May 31, 1936 to the Bombay Presidency Conversion Convention, he reasons,

Caste is a state of mind. It is a disease of the mind. The teachings of the Hindu religion are the root cause of this disease. We practice casteism, we observe untouchability, because we are asked to do it by the Hindu religion in which we live.... So long as we remain in a religion which teaches man to treat man as a leper, the sense of discrimination on account of caste, which is deeply rooted in our minds, cannot go. For annihilating castes and untouchability from among the Untouchables, change of religion is the only antidote.[17]

Dr. Ambedkar followed the example of the Bhagats and the Gurus by formally renouncing Hinduism. Guru Nanak said, "There is neither Hindu nor Muslim." Guru Arjun said, "We are neither Hindus nor Muslims." Likewise, Dr. Ambedkar decided the path to liberation from the shackles of caste required a deliberate act of conversion to another religion.

Initially, Dr. Ambedkar planned to become a Sikh. He reached out to Sikh leaders in Amritsar and worked with them to found Guru Nanak Khalsa College in Mumbai. The college opened in 1937 with the mission, "To instill the idea of 'Service to Humanity' in the young Khalsaites, maximize their civic and sensitivity quotient, and uphold the Ambedkarian ideal by making education accessible to students of the lower socio–economic strata."[18]

Dr. Ambedkar delayed his conversion for decades, however, and only changed his faith two months before his death. At a gathering in Nagpur of approximately 500,000 Ati-Shudras, he converted to Buddhism on October 14, 1956. Although his conversion aligned him with the oldest indigenous religion of India, he also credited the youngest indigenous religion. In 1936, speaking to an audience of Sikhs, he says,

I have made up my mind that I will go away from the Hindu fold. My decision is firm. There are many people who will have their says in regard to the Depressed Classes, but this much is certain that when that day comes for them to decide which religion to embrace, Sikhism will demand the best of our attention. It is not a mere sentiment that I am uttering. I am not here to please you. It is because of two reasons that Sikhism will demand our best consideration. Firstly, that Sikhism can be a spiritual home for any people who want peace with honor. The *Guru Granth Sahib* can be a good spiritual guide for myself, and I hope that what is good for me may be considered good for the rest of my brethren. We are disgusted with the social and religious inequality of the Hindus. The *Guru Granth Sahib* depicts a casteless society....

The Depressed Classes will certainly take note of the fact that Sikh brethren in the thousands have assembled here to consider the problem of the depressed classes.[19]

In the 21st century, the membership of the two indigenous religions of India constitutes a total of three percent of the population. Sikhism is approximately two percent; Buddhism is approximately one percent. The size of these two religions, which both introduced doctrines of equality and liberty to India, is a grave issue requiring deep introspection by their adherents.

One reason they have failed to thrive in modern India may be found in the philosophy of the most famous icon of the independent nation.

Mohandas Gandhi (1869-1948) — Although Dr. Ambedkar devoted his life to liberating victims of Brahmanism, it is Brahmanical preacher Mohandas Gandhi who is internationally acknowledged as the "Father of the Nation."

Educated as an attorney in London, Gandhi spent the first 21 years of his professional life as a political activist in colonial South Africa, where he initiated a caste-like system of racial segregation shortly before apartheid. Returning to India in 1915, he assumed leadership of the Indian National Congress (INC) party in 1924 and became a dominant figure in India's struggle for independence.

Throughout his life, Gandhi presented himself as a *Sanatani* (orthodox) Hindu. As such, he vigorously promoted the practice of *varna* (caste). As Indian political scientist Aakash Singh Rathore explains, "Gandhi remained attached to an idealized version of the *varna* system, a system against which Ambedkar was inalterably and profoundly opposed, and, indeed, intent on completely 'annihilating.'"[20]

Writing in 1920, for example, Gandhi declares, "I believe that one acquires one's caste by birth. One who is born in a Brahman family dies a Brahman.... The prohibition as to dining with or marrying a person of another *varna* or another religion is an essential protective fence for its culture put up by Hinduism."[21]

Defending caste as the salvation of Hinduism, Gandhi insists that social status is and should remain based on heredity. While claiming caste has nothing to do with "inferiority," he simultaneously argues that a Brahman who "misbehaves" will be "degraded" by being reincarnated within a "lower division." In other words, according to Gandhi, the punishment for a "misbehaving" Brahman is the "degradation" of that Brahman to a "lower division" in the supposed next life. Yet, at the same time, he insists caste is not a system of inequality. He proclaims,

> I believe that caste has saved Hinduism from disintegration.... I am certainly against any attempt at destroying the fundamental divisions. The caste system is not based on inequality, there is no question of inferiority.... The law of heredity is an eternal law and any attempt to alter that law must lead us, as it has before led, to utter confusion. I can see very great use in considering a Brahman to be always a Brahman throughout his life.... Nature will, without any possibility of mistake, adjust the balance by degrading a Brahman, if he misbehaves himself, by reincarnating him in a lower division, and translating one who lives the life of a Brahman in his present incarnation to Brahmanhood in his next.... I am prepared to defend, as I have always done, the division of Hindus into four castes.[22]

In short, he endorsed the basic Brahmanical doctrine that the goal of life is to fulfill one's *Varnashrama Dharma* (caste duties) in order to achieve good *karma*, reincarnate, and move up (or avoid falling down) the hierarchical ladder of caste. Social mobility, from his perspective, is only achievable in a hypothetical "next life" — and only if one fulfills their *dharma* in this life.

Thus, in 1927, Gandhi termed *Varnashrama* an "immutable law of nature." Insisting that a person must remain in the *varna* into which they are born, he clarifies, "*Varna* means pre-determination of the choice of man's profession. The law of *varna* is that a man shall follow the profession of his ancestors for earning his livelihood."[23] Applying his logic to Shudras, he further claims, "A Shudra has as much right to knowledge as a Brahman, but he falls from his estate if he tries to gain his livelihood through teaching.... He who changes profession from time to time for the sake of gaining wealth degrades himself and falls from *varna*."[24]

According to Gandhi, accepting one's *dharma* — which, in the case of Shudras, means serving the top three castes — is a sign of "humility." As he argues, "*Varnashrama Dharma*, to my mind, is a law which, however much you and I may deny, cannot be abrogated. To admit the working of that law is to free ourselves for the only pursuit in life for which we are born. *Varnashrama Dharma* is humility."[25] Consequently, Gandhi concludes that the low-castes should accept their place, stating, "[A Shudra] may not be called a Brahman in this birth. And it is a good thing for him not to arrogate a *varna* to which he is not born. It is a sign of true humility…. The law of *varna* is nothing if not by birth."[26]

Ultimately, Gandhi confessed that the underlying philosophy of the Hindu religion is Brahmanism. "I do say Brahmanism is the culmination of other *varnas*, just as the head is the culmination of the body," he writes.[27] "Brahmanism is synonymous with Hinduism."[28] Furthermore, in 1933, revealing that the very foundation of Hinduism is caste, Gandhi declares,

The caste system, in my opinion, has a scientific basis. Reason does not revolt against it…. Caste creates a social and moral restraint — I can find no reason for their abolition. To abolish caste is to demolish Hinduism. There is nothing to fight against the *Varnasharma*. I don't believe the caste system to be an odious and vicious dogma…. There is nothing sinful about it.[29]

From 1895 to 1948, Gandhi consistently championed the caste system. He held to the authority of *Manusmriti* throughout his entire life. In 1895, he writes, "The Institutes of Manu have always been noted for their justice and precision."[30] Again, in 1905, he writes, "The tenfold law, as laid down by Manu, gives some of the qualities needed for the discipline of the mind and reaching the highest Truth."[31] In 1934, he writes, "I hold *Manusmriti* as part of the *Shastras*…. I hold *Manusmriti* as a religious book because of the lofty teachings contained in it."[32] Shortly before his death in 1948, he praised the text for teaching restraint, stating, "According to Manu, men and women should both understand their own limits."[33]

Gandhi's staunch support for the caste system would have been enough to put him at odds with the Sikh community, but he went further by specifically condemning core Sikh practices.

The institution of *langar* (communal dining) was established to destroy the segregation of caste. Yet, in 1924, Gandhi campaigned against establishment of a langar hall by Sikhs who were supporting the Vaikom agitation against untouchability. He writes, "So far as the Sikh kitchen is concerned, it is a menace whether the Sikhs may be regarded as Hindus or non-Hindus.... It compromises the self-respect of the Kerala people."[34] Sikhs stood firmly upon the founding principles of the Panth by aligning with Ati-Shudras. Yet, writes Gandhi, "The Vaikom satyagraha is, I fear crossing the limits. I do hope that the Sikh free kitchen will be withdrawn."[35]

Guru Gobind Singh taught his followers to recognize "the whole human race as one," founded the *Khalsa*, and lost his four sons in an epic struggle to stop the Mughal-Brahman nexus from "torturing the weak and the timid." Yet, in 1925, Gandhi dismissed the Guru as "a misguided patriot."[36]

The Sikhs began to arm themselves after the Brahmans and Mughals conspired to murder Guru Arjun. Under Gurus Hargobind and Gobind Singh, they rode to war to defend the emancipation of the downtrodden. This offended Gandhi who, in 1942, insists, "I do not like the wearing of *kirpan* or the like by human beings as part of their religion."[37] Although the Sikhs prevented extermination of the powerless by sacrificing themselves in battles with the Mughals, the Persians, and the Afghans, Gandhi argues, "The Sikhs should learn to die without killing and then the history of the Punjab would be completely changed."[38]

Summarizing his opinion of the *Panth* and *Granth* united in the *Khalsa*, Gandhi said, "My belief about the Sikh Gurus is… that they were all Hindus."[39] Guru Nanak and Guru Arjun both explicitly proclaimed the Sikhs as a separate people — neither Hindu nor Muslim — and yet Gandhi directly contradicts that fact, claiming, "Even Guru Nanak never said that he was not a Hindu nor did any other Guru." A host of European and Mughal writers specifically identified the Sikhs as distinct from Hindus, but that made no difference to Gandhi. He insists the *Guru Granth* was derived directly from the Hindu *Shastras*:

> To me there is no difference between Sikhism and Hinduism. I have read the *Granth Sahib*. What it contains is also contained in the Vedic *dharma*…. The *Granth Sahib* of the Sikhs is actually based on the Hindu scriptures.[40]

Repeating these claims in December 1947, Gandhi asserts, "The same is true of the teachings of Guru Gobind Singh. What he taught is also to be found in the Hindu scriptures." In fact, not only did he repeatedly insist that Sikhs are Hindus, but he also asserted the success of Hinduism depended on assimilating *every other religion*, stating,

It cannot be said that Sikhism, Hinduism, Buddhism and Jainism are separate religions. All these four faiths and their offshoots are one. Hinduism is an ocean into which all the rivers run. It can absorb Islam and Christianity and all the other religions and only then can it become an ocean. Otherwise it remains merely a stream along which large ships cannot ply.[41]

Dr. Ambedkar's Warning — Of all the major religions present in the Indian subcontinent, Hinduism is the most predominant by virtue of its imposition of the caste system. It is also the most diverse in its practices. "There is no place in India which does not possess certain customs and practices of its own, and it would be impossible to give descriptions of them all," writes French missionary Jean-Antoine Dubois in 1816. Hindus can be found worshipping different gods, acknowledging a host of scriptures, and preaching often contradictory ideas about the meaning and morality of life. Yet the Hindu religion does possess a single unifying doctrine — caste. Despite the diversity of Hindu practices, Dubois continues, "Caste constitutions are the same everywhere."[42]

In 1947, the Indian subcontinent achieved independence and the British left. The Republic of India, formally established in 1950, is the most diverse country in the world. It has 29 states and seven union territories. It recognizes 22 official languages and 122 major mother tongues. A region which had historically consisted of dozens of separate nation-states, it was left artificially united by colonial occupation.

Like Hinduism, the political entity of independent India contains so many contrasting elements that it seems to have no natural claim to internal unity. In the words of Abraham Eraly:

The Republic of India... is today only a union of nations, not a nation-state. Nor has India ever been a nation-state in its long history, because we have never had the basic elements — common history, religion, language, culture, and ethnicity — essential to forge national unity. In fact, India has no stronger basis for national unity than Europe has — it has less basis, really, because of its greater diversity.

In short, the concept of an "Indian" is a legal construct. As Eraly enquires, "What defines an Indian today? Certainly not any ethnic, linguistic, cultural or historical distinctiveness." He further explains, "There came into existence, for short periods, a couple of pan-Indian Empires, like those of the Mauryas and the Mughals, but these were established by conquest, and not by any national integrative process." While the majority of the subcontinent is now united as the "Republic of India," as Eraly notes, "Even the political unity that India enjoys today is the result of conquest, the British one."

As a political entity, however, independent India does possess one universally defining feature. India's characteristics, thus, are similar to those of Hinduism — infinite diversity united by one specific singularity. The single common element of the Indian subcontinent is the domination of Brahmanism.

Historically, Brahmanism provided a sense of *territorial unity* by imposing upon the masses a system of *social disunity*. Thus, the universally shared element which prevails throughout the subcontinent is an *enforced division* which segregates even the people groups which would otherwise share elements such as common history, religion, language, culture, or ethnicity. As Eraly clarifies,

> A peculiar aspect of Indian history is that, not only was there no pan-Indian nationalist sentiment, but even the linguistically- and culturally-cohesive communities in India — the Tamils, for instance — did not consider themselves as one people. What prevented this was our caste system — our loyalty was to our caste, not to the larger society, certainly not to the State. The State was transient; the caste permanent.[43]

Thus, the single defining element of the Indian subcontinent is Brahmanism. What defines Brahmanism? A belief in the superiority of the Brahman caste. What defines a Hindu? Segregation by caste. What defines an Indian? A shared subjugation by the caste system.

Just as caste is the single defining doctrine of Hinduism, caste subjugation is the single defining element of an Indian — not of the naturally occurring and distinct identities of a Punjabi, a Tamil, a Kashmiri, or a Maharashtran, but of the legal construct of an "Indian."

Yet it was this single common element — the predominance of Brahmanism over the Indian subcontinent — which the Bhagats and the Gurus specifically sought to eliminate. In its place, they sought to institute the commonality of universal human dignity and the equality and right to liberty that commonality entails. Standing in the way of that goal, though, was the man who claimed, "To abolish caste is to demolish Hinduism."

Just as caste subjugation is the single defining element of an Indian, the single defining figure of the Indian State is Mohandas Gandhi. His picture is displayed in every government office in the Republic of India. All visiting foreign dignitaries pay homage at his official memorial, Raj Ghat. Furthermore, he is commemorated as the "Father of the Nation."

However, the reason that Gandhi remains the defining figure of the Indian State in the eyes of the international community is because the State sponsors his promotion as its figurehead. He is India's leading propaganda tool. In a 1955 British Broadcasting Corporation interview, Dr. Ambedkar exposes the State's promotion of Gandhi.

> Gandhi has already vanished from the memory of the people in this country. His memory is kept up because the Congress Party annually gives a holiday, either on his birthday or on some other day connected with some event in his life, and has a celebration every year going on for several days in a week. Naturally, peoples' memory is revived, but if these artificial respirations were not given, I think Gandhi would be long gone.[44]

Just as the Republic of India is inseparable from Gandhi (thanks to the tireless propagandizing of the Indian State), Gandhism is inseparable from Brahmanism. Writing in 1945, Dr. Ambedkar explains how Gandhi's philosophy preserved the same unjust social order against which the Sikh Revolution struggled,

> Gandhism is a paradox. It stands for freedom from foreign domination, which means the destruction of the existing political structure of the country. At the same time, it seeks to maintain intact a social structure which permits the domination of one class by another on a hereditary basis which means a perpetual domination of one class by another....
>
> Gandhism is simply another form of *Sanatanism* which is the ancient name for militant orthodox Hinduism. What is there in Gandhism which is not to be found in orthodox Hinduism? There is caste in Hinduism, there is caste in Gandhism. Hinduism believes

in the law of hereditary profession, so does Gandhism. Hinduism enjoins cow-worship. So does Gandhism. Hinduism upholds the law of karma, predestination of man's condition in this world, so does Gandhism. Hinduism accepts the authority of the *Shastras*. So does Gandhism. Hinduism believes in avatar or incarnations of God. So does Gandhism. Hinduism believes in idols, so does Gandhism. All that Gandhism has done is to find a philosophic justification for Hinduism and its dogmas. Hinduism is bald in the sense that it is just a set of rules which bear on their face the appearance of a crude and cruel system. Gandhism supplies the philosophy which smoothens its surface and gives it the appearance of decency and respectability and so alters it and embellishes it as to make it even attractive.[45]

In short, Gandhism represents a reinvigorated Hindu orthodoxy. It reaffirms all the false creeds and crooked politics condemned by Guru Nanak. In particular, it affirms the *Shastras* and endorses the practice of the caste system.

It is no surprise, then, that Gandhi and Ambedkar were bitter enemies. In 1955, the champion of the *Mulnivasi* discussed his previous interactions with the "Father of the Nation."

As I met Mr. Gandhi in the capacity of an opponent, I've a feeling that I know him better than most other people because he opened his real fangs to me. I could see the inside of the man, while others who generally went there saw nothing of him except the external appearance which he had put up as a Mahatma.... He was never a Mahatma and I refuse to call him Mahatma. I've never in my life called him Mahatma. He doesn't deserve that title, not even from the point of view of his morality.[46]

Gandhi and Ambedkar were clearly opposing personalities — according to Ambedkar himself. They were enemies. Furthermore, explains Ambedkar, their enmity was premised on Gandhi's support for the doctrine of Brahmanism. "You will see him the more orthodox man, supporting the caste system (the *Varnashrama Dharma*) and all the orthodox dogmas that have kept India down through the ages," says Ambedkar. Noting that Gandhi only spoke against aspects of caste practice for the sake of political expedience, Ambedkar continues,

> Gandhi was absolutely an orthodox Hindu. He was never a reform-
> er.... All this talk about untouchability was just for the purpose of
> making the Untouchables drawn into the Congress. That was one
> thing. Secondly, he wanted that Untouchables would not oppose
> his movement of *swaraj*. I don't think beyond that he had any real
> motive of uplift.[47]

Unfortunately, as the result of deliberate State propaganda, it was Gandhi whose legacy prevailed in independent India.

Pan-Indian Empires never existed except as a result of conquest. Among those conquerors were the British, the Mughals, and possibly also, long before them, the Aryans. The conquering Aryans reputedly invented and imposed the Brahmanical doctrines of caste which became the basis for Hinduism. Gandhi suggests that, "Aryanism would have been a better descriptive word than Hinduism."[48]

As Gandhi also states, "Brahmanism is synonymous with Hinduism." Over the centuries, Brahmanism infiltrated the entire Indian subcontinent and became the only defining element of "India" as a unified whole. Thus, when India finally threw off the yoke of foreign rule, it reverted to the hegemony of Brahmanism.

Because of the looming threat of a Brahman hegemony, Dr. Ambedkar recognized the danger that India might become a country with *swaraj* (independence) but without *azadi* (freedom). In other words, the Republic of India, although *independent*, might not actually be *free*. As Ambedkar explains in 1948, "Democracy in India is only a top-dressing on an Indian soil which is essentially undemocratic."[49]

Although Ambedkar chaired the drafting committee for India's constitution, he was deeply dissatisfied with the finished product. On November 25, 1949, the day before the Constituent Assembly approved the document, he delivered his final remarks to the assembly. Because of the social disunity created by caste, he warned, an independent Indian nation faced possibly insurmountable challenges.

> It is quite possible for this newborn democracy to retain its form
> but give place to dictatorship in fact....
> On the social plane, we have in India a society based on the

principle of graded inequality.... I am of [the] opinion that, in be-
lieving that we are a nation, we are cherishing a great delusion.
How can people divided into several thousands of castes be a nation? The sooner we realize that we are not as yet a nation in the
social and psychological sense of the word, the better for us....
In India, there are castes. The castes are anti-national. In the first
place because they bring about separation in social life. They are
anti-national also because they generate jealousy and antipathy between caste and caste. But we must overcome all these difficulties
if we wish to become a nation in reality. For fraternity can be a fact
only when there is a nation. Without fraternity, equality and liberty
will be no deeper than coats of paint....

By independence, we have lost the excuse of blaming the British for anything going wrong. If hereafter things go wrong, we will
have nobody to blame except ourselves. There is great danger of
things going wrong.[50]

Citations

1 Yong, Tan Tai. *The Garrison State: The Military, Government, and Society in Colonial Punjab, 1849-1947*. New Delhi: Sage Publications. 2005. 195.

2 Singh. *Sikhs.* 124.

3 Saraswati, Maharishi Swami Dayanand. *The Satyartha Prakasha.* 1975. New Delhi: Sarvadeshik Arya Pratinidhi Sabha. 1984. 443.

4 Agnihotri, V. K. (ed.). *Indian History with Objective Questions and Historical Maps.* 1981. New Delhi: Allied Publishers Private Limited. 2010. C-171.

5 Ibid., C-172.

6 Mugali, Shiladhar Yallappa and Priyadarshini Sharanappa Amadihal. "Mahatma Jyotirao Phule's Views on Upliftment of Women as Reflected in Sarvajanik Stayadharma." Proceedings of the Indian History Congress (vol. 69). 2008. 691.

7 Phule, Jyotirao. *Collected Works: The Book of the True Faith* (vol. 2). 1991. 33-34.

8 Phule, Jyotirao. *Slavery: In This Civilized British Government Under the Cloak of Brahmanism.* 1873. Full text available at velivada.com. Preface.

9 Ramasamy, E.V. *Collected Works of Periyar E.V.R.* K. Veeramani (ed.). Vepery: The Periyar Self-Respect Propaganda Institution. 2014. Ebook.

10 Ibid.

11 Ibid.

12 Ibid.

13 Ibid.

14 Ambedkar, Bhim Rao. *Dr. Babasaheb Ambedkar: Writings and Speeches* (vol. 3). Vasant Moon (ed.). Bombay: Education Department, Government of Maharashtra. 1987. 70.

15 Ibid., 66.

16 Ambedkar, Bhim Rao. *Dr. Babasaheb Ambedkar: Writings and Speeches* (vol. 1). Vasant

Moon (ed.). Bombay: Education Department, Government of Maharashtra. 1979. 25-96.

17 Ambedkar, Bhim Rao. *Thoughts of Dr. Baba Saheb Ambedkar*. Y.D. Sontakke (ed.). New Delhi: Samyak Prakashan. 2004. 241.

18 Guru Nanak Khalsa College of Arts, Science & Commerce. gnkhalsa.edu.in. Vision.

19 *Gurdwara Gazette*. 1936. 19.

20 Pföstl, Eva (ed.). *Between Ethics and Politics: Gandhi Today*. New Delhi: Routledge. 2014. 165.

21 Gandhi, Mohandas. *The Collected Works of Mahatma Gandhi*. 100 Volumes. Delhi: Publications Division, Ministry of Information and Broadcasting, Government of India. 1958-1994. Vol. 22, 314-315.

22 Ibid., 67-78.

23 Ibid., Vol. 40. 481.

24 Ibid., 482 & 484.

25 Ibid., 122.

26 Ibid., 484-485.

27 Ibid., 485.

28 Ibid., 487.

29 Pföstl. *Gandhi*. 166.

30 Gandhi. *Collected Works*. Vol. 1, 196.

31 Ibid., Vol. 4, 230.

32 Ibid., Vol. 63, 355.

33 Ibid., Vol. 98, 154.

34 Ibid., Vol 28, 11.

35 Ibid., Vol. 27, 362.

36 Ibid., Vol 31, 142.

37 Ibid., Vol. 83, 52.

38 Ibid., Vol. 95, 205.

39 Ibid., Vol. 83, 74-75.

40 Ibid., Vol. 98, 378 & 402.

41 Ibid., Vol. 97, 465.

42 Dubois. *Hindu*. 11.

43 Eraly, Abraham. "Just A Legal Indian." *Outlook*. August 20, 2001.

44 Ambedkar, Bhim Rao. "Mohandas Karamchand Gandhi: Memories of the Mahatma, by Bhimrao Ramji Ambedkar." Francis Watson (int.). British Broadcasting Corporation Sound Archive. February 26, 1955.

45 Ambedkar, Bhim Rao. *What Congress and Gandhi Have Done to the Untouchables?* 1945. Delhi: Gautam Book Centre. 2009. 279 & 284.

46 Ambedkar. *Memories*. BBC.

47 Ibid.

48 Gandhi. *Collected Works*. Vol. 4, 200.

49 Constituent Assembly of India Debates (Proceedings). 1946-1950. Vol. 7, November 4, 1948.

50 Ibid., Vol. 11, November 25, 1949.

— 6 —
Independent India:
Bleeding the Sons and Daughters of the Soil

How has this history impacted the ground realities of modern India? Through the blood of the martyred Sikh Gurus, the efforts of the Bhagats, and the compilation of their message in the *Guru Granth*, the foundations were laid for the downtrodden to progress from "worms" to free people. In the struggle for human dignity, Banda Singh Bahadur took up the torch from Guru Gobind Singh. After him, others pursued a similar mission, including Dr. Ambedkar, who credited the *Guru Granth* as his guide.

The result was a powerful community, deeply rooted in the Indian subcontinent, which abandoned the crippling practice of caste in favor of love and equality.

In the 21st century, however, the complex-hearted are still attempting to suppress the *Mulnivasi*. In the 21st century, the battle-lines in the struggle for human dignity have expanded. The religious doctrines of Brahmanism are now politicized as *Hindutva,* a hegemonic ideology "which holds non-Hindus as foreign to India."[1] According to *Hindutva*, all inhabitants of the Indian subcontinent are Hindus (regardless of their personal religious preference), Indian culture is defined exclusively by Hindu values, and India is a nation solely for Hindu people.

In 1941, before India even attained independence, Swami Dharma Theertha warned about the rise of *Hindutva*. The details of his description *perfectly* capture the reality of the situation in modern India.

There is rising in the country a Hindu nationalism which is a travesty of all true progress. This creed is being fostered by distinguished scholars and propagated both within and without the country with pride and religious fervor. It is marked by such claims as these: the Hindu civilization is the best in the world, Hindu religion is the highest glory of man, Hindu institutions are the models of righteousness. Hindu nationalism is peculiarly its own and unlike those of other nations. The parading of these stupendous claims and exhibition of self-esteem is only a prelude to a justification of all the evils and wickedness of caste and priestcraft as the unique contributions of Hindu culture.[2]

The supremacist ideology of *Hindutva* is the platform of the Bharatiya Janata Party (BJP), the chief competitor to Gandhi's Indian National Congress (INC). Since 2014, India has been under BJP rule. Hindu nationalism is flourishing. As Prime Minister Narendra Modi said before taking office in May 2014, "My identity is of a *Hindutvawadi*."[3]

In practice, however, both major political parties are Hindu entities led by elites who wield power to suppress and enslave the masses. Both the BJP and the INC have orchestrated genocides of minorities — Christians, Muslims, and Sikhs — with impunity. Dr. Ambedkar prophetically warns, "There is great danger of things going wrong." They have, indeed, gone *very* wrong.

No longer subjugated by foreign rule or constrained by the need to align with occupiers, India's Brahmanical elites are able to act unilaterally. Independence has empowered Brahmanism to firmly plant its roots. In independent India, Brahmanism continues to target anyone who threatens the sacredness of the caste system. In the spirit of Gandhi, the *Hindutva* movement believes that "Hinduism is an ocean into which all the rivers run." It seeks to "become an ocean" by absorbing "all the other religions."

Standing on the shoulders of the Bhagats and Gurus, champions of emancipation have moved the caravan forward since Banda's death in 1716. The flame of liberty has not died. The blaze has spread throughout India, from the far north to the deep south, but the struggle continues. Many have stoked the furnace. Nevertheless, the fire has not yet become the furnace necessary to burn away all the dross and refine the gold of India. Instead, independent India has embraced all the false creeds and crooked politics against which the saints of freedom fought.

Since gaining independence in 1947, India has become a tyranny. "This was the first time since the violent extermination of Buddhism under the auspices of Adi Shankaracharya that a homogenized caste-Hindu state came into being from North to South and East to West, thanks to the legacy of British imperialism," writes Sangat Singh.[4] India gained *swaraj*, but without *azadi*. While the simple-hearted, who endured the degradations of Brahmanism, continue to flock to ideologies of liberation, independent

India's rulers forcibly impose Hindu hegemony. As Dr. Ambedkar warned, the newborn democracy became a *de facto* dictatorship.

India escaped the oppression of foreign occupation, but exchanged it for Brahman-Raj. From Delhi, the Indian Central Government projects force as though it were a colonial power. As Arundhati Roy notes in 2016, independent India's military is employed almost exclusively to subjugate Indian citizens.

> There has not been a single day since Independence in 1947 when the Indian Army and other security forces have not been deployed *within* India's borders against what are meant to be their "own" people — in Kashmir, Nagaland, Manipur, Mizoram, Assam, Junagadh, Hyderabad, Goa, Punjab, Telangana, West Bengal, and now Chhattisgarh, Orissa, and Jharkhand.
>
> Tens of thousands of people have lost their lives in conflicts in these places. An even greater number have been brutally tortured, leaving many of them crippled for life.... If you take a hard look at the list of places within India's current borders in which its security forces have been deployed, an extraordinary fact emerges — the populations in those places are mostly Muslim, Christian, Adivasi, Sikh, and Dalit. What we are being asked to salute obediently and unthinkingly is a reflexively dominant-caste Hindu state that nails together its territory with military might.[5]

"Emergency" Provisions — Besides holding its territory together with military might, the Indian Central Government has used dictatorial powers granted by the Constitution to compel the states to submit to its will.

In particular, the Centre has relied upon "Emergency" provisions contained within Articles 352, 356, and 365 of the Indian Constitution. Article 352 allows the President to declare a national "Emergency," suspend the "Fundamental Rights" protected by the Constitution, and institute martial law. Articles 356 and 365 allow the Centre to dissolve democratically-elected state governments, suspend state elections, and indefinitely institute "President's Rule" directly from Delhi.

In debates over the Constitution in 1949, several members of the Constituent Assembly warned against these "Emergency" provisions. "As regards over-centralization, I need only point to the emergency powers," notes Muhammad Saadulla of Assam. He further states,

Article 352 refers to the proclamation of an emergency by the President of the Union. Well, this proclamation can be had, according to Article 356, for failure of the constitutional machinery in a Province... and, according to Article 365, for failure to comply with directions issued by the Union.... Instead of breathing an atmosphere of independence, freedom, and liberty, we will be subject to the utmost interference from the Centre and the president which is bound to go against the very peace, tranquillity, and contentment of the people.[6]

P. T. Chacko of Travancore (later Kerala) specifically denounced Article 365, which allows President's Rule "where any State has failed to comply with or to give effect to any directions given in the exercise of the executive power of the Union."[7] Warning that "extraordinary powers are vested in the Centre," Chacko states,

Article 365 makes Indian States almost complete vassals. For a moment, I am constrained to think of the long struggle for freedom in which the peoples of the Indian States took no little part. There are people in the States who have given up even their lives in the freedom struggle. There are many of us who have made smaller sacrifices also. What is the final outcome of all these struggles? In the place of the foreign imperialism, we are now having an Indian imperialism.[8]

Furthermore, Hukam Singh of Punjab explains, "There are other provisions... which may provide an ambitious politician an opportunity to assume dictatorial powers while professedly acting within the strict letter of the settled Constitution." As one of two Sikh representatives to the Constituent Assembly, he ultimately refused to sign the Constitution, asserting,

We have not guarded against the emergence of dictators.... The common man has been squeezed out of politics and the President has been enthroned as the Great Mughal to rule from Delhi with enough splendor and grandeur.... The discontent and dissatisfaction is sure to grow without any economic solution of difficulties of the masses. This shall consequently facilitate the development of administration into a fascist State.[9]

Constituent Assembly members from entirely separate regions — Assam in the far northeast, Kerala in the deep south, and Punjab in the northwest — all shared identical concerns about the totalitarian tendencies of these constitutional provisions. Their warnings were prophetic.

Since 1950, when the Constitution went into effect, the Centre has imposed "President's Rule" in 26 of 29 states and two of seven territories — most commonly in Manipur (10 times), Uttar Pradesh (9 times), Punjab (8 times), Bihar (8 times), and Jammu and Kashmir (7 times).

In 1975, Dr. Ambedkar's warning of a "dictatorship in fact" became a reality when Prime Minister Indira Gandhi (INC) emerged as one. Convicted of electoral fraud by the Allahabad High Court, she faced loss of her seat in Parliament, which would have also forced her out of her role as Prime Minister. In response, she convinced President Fakhruddin Ali Ahmed to declare a National Emergency.

From June 1975 to March 1977, Gandhi suspended elections and arbitrarily arrested, tortured, and indefinitely detained her political opponents. In the words of American scientist Dr. Robert Zubrin, "Prime Minister Gandhi declared a state of National Emergency and assumed dictatorial power."[10] American economist Dr. Murray Rothbard, writing in July 1975, describes India as "the most dramatic" of the world's "burgeoning dictatorships." As he observes,

> The most dramatic, of course, is the brutal takeover of India by Mrs. Indira Gandhi, jailing thousands of political opponents and imposing a drastic censorship on the press. Ever since World War II, the *New York Times* and the rest of the Establishment press have trumpeted the glories and virtues of India as the "world's largest democracy"; massive amounts of foreign aid have been pumped into India by the U.S. on the strength of this rosy view of the Indian subcontinent. At the very least, the Establishment press, standing there with egg on its face, will have to mute its paeans to Indian "democracy" in the future. Predictably, American press reaction has been far more in sorrow than in anger, and replete with pitiful hopes that Mrs. Gandhi will revert to democracy soon.
>
> But Indian "democracy," let alone Indian liberty, has been a sham and a mockery from the beginning. Even in political form, India has suffered from its inception under the one-party rule of the Congress party, with other opposing political groupings shunted to

the periphery to preserve democratic camouflage. More important, the Indian polity is one of the most thoroughly rotten in the world: a collectivist mass of Statist activities, controls, subsidies, taxes, and monopolies, all superimposed upon a frozen caste system that governs in the rural villages in which most Indians continue to live. Considering this unholy mess, the savaging of the opposition by Mrs. Gandhi comes, not as a sudden and inexplicable act, as Americans tend to see it, but as merely the last link in a chain of Statist despotism fastened upon that blighted land. When we discard the myths propagated by the American Establishment, we see that, rather than a source of wonder, Mrs. Gandhi's takeover becomes all too explicable.[11]

S. K. Ghosh, a retired Inspector General of Police who lived through the Emergency, describes specific details of some of the atrocities committed by the State.

Legal institutions were paralysed and the press was gagged. Politically motivated raids were conducted and houses of political opponents were searched indiscriminately. Law enforcement officials made arrests, held prisoners incommunicado, made searches without warrants, and prosecuted anyone whose political thinking did not conform to the ruling party's ideology.[12]

Seizing the opportunity to advance a Brahmanical agenda during the Emergency, Gandhi instituted a program of mass forced sterilization. "Both the British colonial administrators and the high-caste Brahmans who succeeded them in power following independence in 1947 looked upon the 'teeming masses' of [India's] lower classes with fear and disdain," writes Zubrin. Thus, under the guise of population control, Gandhi's government went to work sterilizing anyone considered "unworthy" to reproduce. According to Zubrin, "Ruling upper-caste Hindus… focused the population control effort on getting rid of lower-caste Untouchables and Muslims."

In 1976 alone, over eight million Indians were sterilized by the "fascist state" about which Hukam Singh warned. As Zubrin explains,

Overt coercion became the rule: sterilization was a condition for land allotments, water, electricity, ration cards, medical care, pay raises, and rickshaw licenses. Policemen were given quotas to nab individuals for sterilization. Demolition squads were sent into slums to bulldoze houses — sometimes whole neighborhoods — so that armed police platoons could drag off their flushed-out occupants to forced-sterilization camps. In Delhi alone, 700,000 people were driven from their homes. Many of those who escaped the immediate roundup were denied new housing until they accepted sterilization.[13]

Sangat Singh notes that, in response to the Emergency, "by and large, the people in hushed tones took it casually." Yet not all citizens reacted passively.

"When Prime Minister Gandhi declared a State of Emergency on June 26, 1975 — suspending fundamental rights, imposing press censorship and arresting hundreds of opposition party leaders — Sikhs were among her most outspoken critics," reports American human rights researcher Patricia Gossman.[14] Among the most prominent of those critics were Sikh political party Shiromani Akali Dal (SAD), Sikh university Damdami Taksal, and Taksal leader Kartar Singh Bhindranwale.

On June 30, 1975, SAD leaders met at Harmandir Sahib and Akal Takht and passed a resolution to oppose "the fascist tendency of the Congress."[15] Meanwhile, the Taksal, a traveling university founded by Guru Gobind Singh, organized dozens of peaceful protests all around Punjab. "During the Emergency years, Damdami Taksal was like a thorn in the side of the Indian government because its head protested Emergency measures," explains American anthropologist Cynthia Mahmood.[16] "140,000 persons were detained without trial during the Emergency and, of them, 60,000 were Sikhs," notes Sangat Singh. "The anti-Emergency agitation from the Golden Temple complex, with volunteers offering prayers at Akal Takht before offering themselves for arrest, was taken as a serious and personal affront by Indira."[17]

Sikh resistance to the Emergency was so resolute, principled, and exceptional that the community even garnered respect from members of Gandhi's own family. Indian politician Vijay Laxmi Pandit, the aunt of Indira Gandhi, states,

Punjab which had always been in the forefront of resistance to oppression, kept its colors flying during the Emergency also. It was in Punjab and Punjab alone that a large scale resistance was organised against it. The worst thing that happened during the Emergency was that a brave nation was frightened into submission and nobody spoke except in hushed tones.[18]

Ethnic Cleansing and Genocide of Minorities — Aside from deploying the military against the citizenry and dissolving democratically-elected governments to institute dictatorial rule from Delhi, the Indian State has also sponsored ethnic cleansing and genocide of minorities, atrocities which have been orchestrated by both the BJP and the INC.

Several instances of acute violence wherein pogroms yielded body counts passing into the thousands qualify as genocide under the definition agreed upon by the United Nations in 1948, which states,

> Genocide means any of the following committed with intent to destroy, in whole or in part, a national, ethnical, racial, or religious group, as such:
>
> (a) Killing members of the group;
> (b) Causing serious bodily or mental harm to members of the group;
> (c) Deliberately inflicting on the group conditions of life calculated to bring about its physical destruction in whole or in part.[19]

Acts of genocide have garnered vast international attention. Meanwhile, chronic and more "silent" killings — conducted systematically, in secret, and rarely attracting notice on the world stage — rise to the level of ethnic cleansing. As reported by the United Nations,

> "Ethnic cleansing" is a purposeful policy designed by one ethnic or religious group to remove by violent and terror-inspiring means the civilian population of another ethnic or religious group from certain geographic areas.[20]

The chronic patterns of violence burst forth into acute incidents, bleeding together into one. Between the acute and the chronic, smaller scale pogroms which kill dozens, scores, or hundreds occur with regularity. Thus, Indian minorities, as a civilian population, are the targets of a ceaseless, low-intensity war which sometimes rises to red-hot intensity.

In June 1984, under leadership of Indira Gandhi, the Indian military laid siege to the Golden Temple complex at the same time that hundreds of thousands of Sikhs gathered to commemorate the anniversary of Guru Arjun's martyrdom. The siege's target was Jarnail Singh Bhindranwale, who succeeded Kartar Singh as Damdami Taksal head in 1977.

"The army's full assault, code-named Operation Bluestar, began in the early hours of June 4 and ended on June 6," writes Patricia Gossman. Using tanks and artillery, the Army bombarded the Akal Takht. After the attack, Gossman explains that the exact number of dead was impossible to determine because "the bodies of those killed were cremated en masse by the army and police."[21] In his book, *Reduced to Ashes,* Ram Narayan Kumar records a range of casualty figures,

> The soldiers were in a foul mood.... After the destruction of the Akal Takht, they drank and smoked openly inside the Temple complex and indiscriminately killed those they found inside. For them, every Sikh inside was a militant.... The eye-witnesses claim that "7,000 to 8,000 people were killed." Mark Tulley estimated that approximately 4,000 people might have died. Chand Joshi suggested 5,000 civilian deaths.[22]

"Four months after the 1984 attack, Prime Minister Indira Gandhi (INC) was assassinated by Sikh bodyguards," reports journalist Barbara Crossette.[23] From November 1st to 3rd, mobs in Delhi and other areas of India massacred Sikhs. According to Crossette, the dead numbered in "the thousands — officially 2,733, but, by some estimates, perhaps 5,000."[24] Tens of thousands were displaced and 50,000 of Delhi's nearly 400,000 Sikh residents fled the city permanently.[25]

"The Congress government in power at the time of the riots [was] responsible for not just allowing them to happen, but actively organizing the pogroms," states U.S. diplomat Robert Blake in a 2005 cable released by Wikileaks. "The mobs who targeted Sikh houses within mixed neighborhoods were clearly guided by electoral rolls or other government-supplied lists."[26]

The 1984 violence, especially the November genocide, haunts the Sikh community to this day. Impunity for the killers has been the only response. Nevertheless, the suffering inflicted on the community has gained international acknowledgement.

On the other side of the globe, the California State Assembly denounces the killings, proclaiming, "Government and law enforcement officials organized, participated in, and failed to intervene to prevent the killings through direct and indirect means." Furthermore, the Assembly states, "Individuals and organizations throughout the world, recognizing the need for justice, continue to demand prosecution of those responsible for the November 1984 anti-Sikh pogroms."[27] Meanwhile, the Legislative Assembly of Ontario declares it a genocide, stating, "We... condemn all forms of communal violence, hatred, hostility, prejudice, racism and intolerance in India and anywhere else in the world, including the 1984 Genocide perpetrated against the Sikhs throughout India."[28] Across North America, a number of city governments have passed similar proclamations.

Following the violence perpetrated by the INC government, various *Hindutva* groups affiliated with the BJP — sometimes led by BJP politicians — began orchestrating a series of riots and pogroms that grew in intensity from the late 1980s onward.

American political scientist Dr. Amrita Basu notes, "Numerous investigations have held Hindu nationalists responsible for extensive anti-Muslim violence in post-independence India.... They orchestrated campaigns that claimed 1,000 lives in Meerut (April-May 1987) and, following other campaigns, another 1,000 lives in Bhagalpur, Bihar (1989)."[29] These incidents, however, pale in comparison to what followed.

In December 1992, under leadership of Member of Parliament L. K. Advani (BJP), a mob acted on his long-standing demands that "the Babri Masjid, an old sixteenth-century mosque that stood on a disputed site in Ayodhya, be demolished and a Ram temple built in its place."[30] According to American political scientist Dr. Heather Gregg,

> An estimated 300,000 Hindu activists gathered in Ayodhya for a rally. The activists climbed the fences surrounding the site and, with pick axes, shovels, and their bare hands, destroyed the mosque in a matter of hours. The incident, broadcast across the country, ignited nationwide riots that left 1,700 to 3,000 dead and more than 5,500 injured.[31]

Most of the dead were Muslims. "There has been little justice for the victims... after the 1992 destruction of the Babri mosque," reports the U.S. State Department.[32] Yet there was no doubt about the BJP's culpability. In previous years, Advani called "for faithful Hindus throughout the country to make bricks and bring them to Ayodhya to rebuild the temple at the site of the Babri Mosque."[33] As historian Dr. Mark Juergensmeyer notes, "The day following the attack, Advani publicly took responsibility for the debacle."[34]

After the 1984 Sikh Genocide orchestrated by the INC, and the escalating violence in Meerut and Bhagalpur which preceded the Ayodhya conflict orchestrated by the BJP, attacks on minorities became a more silent but even deadlier affair as India's police and soldiers were used to quietly eradicate those perceived as troublesome. "Whether it's mass graves in Kashmir, mass cremations in Punjab, razing villages in Chhattisgarh, or rampant torture, India has refused to confront and redress atrocities perpetrated by its security forces," writes attorney Sukhman Dhami.[35] Human Rights Watch (HRW) notes, "Indian security forces commit human rights abuses with the knowledge that there is little chance of being held accountable."[36]

In 2011, HRW exposed one of those abuses. "Thousands of Kashmiris have been forcibly disappeared during the last two decades of violence, their whereabouts unknown."[37] In 2012, *The Guardian* reported the discovery of over 6,000 "unmarked and mass graves" in Kashmir.[38]

Attorney Jalil Andrabi investigated, documented, and publicized (to Amnesty International, HRW, and the United Nations) the disappearances and killings that led to many of these mass graves. Speaking in Delhi in 1996, he states,

It is really difficult to realize the real magnitude of atrocities committed on the people of Kashmir. According to some estimates, more than 40,000 people have been killed, which include all — old men and children, women, sick, and infirm. The youth of Kashmir have been mowed down. They are tortured in torture cells and, as a result of this, thousands of youth have been killed in police custody. These atrocities being committed on the people of Kashmir are not mere aberrations. These are part of deliberate and systematic State policy being perpetrated on Kashmir, which is aimed to silence the people.[39]

Similar crimes occurred during the same timeframe in Punjab, where the State implemented "the arbitrary detention, torture, extrajudicial execution, and enforced disappearance of thousands of Sikhs." HRW reported that, between 1984 and 1995, security forces targeted young Sikh men; police detained them, "often in the presence of witnesses, yet later denied having them in custody." Detainees were eliminated in "extrajudicial executions ending in secret cremations."[40]

Human rights activist Jaswant Singh Khalra investigated these disappearances. Speaking in Canada in 1995, he reveals his findings,

We were amazed that in Amritsar district's three cremation grounds, 6,017 bodies were clearly recorded as the dead bodies of Sikh youth between the ages of 15 and 35. And our brothers were not the only ones recorded in that list; women's dead bodies were also recorded. And we were amazed that the records included the bodies of the elderly.[41]

Indian security forces responded to exposure of their secret ethnic cleansing by murdering the whistleblowers. Andrabi was detained in March 1996 while Kashmir was under President's Rule and the INC was in power in Delhi. Khalra was detained in September 1996 while the INC ruled Punjab and an INC-dominated coalition was in power in Delhi. Like so many others, both men were disappeared by security forces, never to be seen again.

These simmering conflicts, in which thousands were silently killed while the brave souls who exposed the ethnic cleansing were picked up and quietly eliminated, were followed by an even more nightmarish incident. Speaking about *Hindutva*, American literary scholar Dr. Manisha Basu sets the scene: "One of the most grisly manifestations of this dangerous ideology was the genocidal cleansing of Muslim minorities in the western Indian state of Gujarat in February-March 2002."[42]

Days before the violence began in Gujarat, Advani — the self-professed architect of the Ayodhya conflict — became India's Deputy Prime Minister.

In February 2002, under leadership of Gujarati Chief Minister Narendra Modi (BJP), Hindus massacred Muslims throughout the state. From February 28 to March 2, reported Australian historian Dr. Eamon Murphy, "mobs began coordinated attacks: attackers arrived in trucks, dressed in saffron robes and khaki shorts, the uniform of Hindu nationalist groups." The pattern of attacks closely mirrored the 1984 Sikh Genocide. According to Murphy,

The mobs were armed with swords and other weapons and

explosives, gas cylinders which they used to set alight houses and businesses alike. They also had computer printouts obtained from government officials, listing the addresses of the homes of Muslims and their businesses. The attacks were carefully coordinated through the use of mobile phones. In numerous cases, Muslim businesses were looted and burnt down while neighboring Hindu businesses were left untouched.

Many attacks were made close to police stations and in view of the police but no attempts were made to stop the violence. Frantic calls by terrified men, women and children were answered by the police: "We have no orders to save you." In some instances, the police fired on Muslims who attempted to defend themselves. Police officers who tried to control the violence were later disciplined.[43]

The level of violence was beyond human comprehension. One central figure, a prominent Hindu nationalist named Babubhai Patel (known as Bajrangi), unashamedly states, "There was this pregnant woman. I slit her open." His declared motivation reflects his goal of ethnic cleansing. "We didn't spare anyone," says Bajrangi. "They shouldn't even be allowed to breed. I say that even today. Whoever they are — women, children, whoever — nothing to be done to them but cut them down, thrash them, slash them, burn the bastards."[44]

According to the U.S. State Department, "1,200-2,500 Muslims were killed across Gujarat by Hindu mobs, thousands of mosques and Muslim-owned businesses were looted or destroyed, and more than 100,000 people fled their homes. Christians were also victims in Gujarat, and many churches were destroyed."[45] Describing the violence, Amnesty International reports, "Muslim women were specifically targeted and several hundred women and girls were threatened, raped and killed; some were burned alive.... Some 2,000 people, mostly Muslims, were killed and many others were injured."[46]

"The violence in Gujarat, due to is very geographic scope and unbearable intensity, in fact marks the first example of ethnic cleansing targeting Muslims since India's Partition in 1947," writes French political scientist Christophe Jaffrelot. "The aim here was... to murder and run off those perceived as intruders."[47] He lays the blame at the feet of the ruling party, writing, "These riots also commit us to reconfirm the role of Hindu nationalist politicians." Jaffrelot adds, "[It was] the result of an organized pogrom with the approval of the State apparatus of Gujarat acting not only with the electoral agenda in mind, but also in view of a true ethnic cleansing."[48]

Just as in 1993, there was no doubt about the BJP's culpability in 2002. "The attacks were planned in advance and organized with extensive participation of the police and state government officials," said Smita Narula of HRW.[49] A BJP member of Gujarat's Legislative Assembly, Haresh Bhatt, was even caught on hidden camera bragging about his participation in the genocide. "[Modi] had given us three days to do whatever we could," says Bhatt. "After three days, he asked us to stop, and everything came to a halt.... We had three days and did what we had to do in those three days. Yes, he did what no other chief minister could have done."[50]

Nevertheless, as U.S. Consul General Michael Owen states in a 2006 cable released by Wikileaks, "The BJP leadership is convinced that Modi can appeal to wide segments of Indian voters outside of Gujarat, and that his role in the 2002 bloodshed will not necessarily damage his popularity."[51] Thus, despite orchestrating an atrocity that earned him the nickname "Butcher of Gujarat," Modi became the Prime Minister in 2014.

The central thread connecting all this violence — acute and chronic — is the consistent culpability of the State. Indian author Harsh Mander describes "a bloody trail of open State complicity in repeated traumatic bouts of ethnic cleansing and massacres." He sees the government's hand behind all of the largest-scale incidents. These "State-enabled carnages," writes Mander, occurred "in Delhi in 1984, Bhagalpur in 1989, Mumbai in 1993 and climaxed in Gujarat in 2002."[52] Regardless of which political party is in power, minorities suffer. Yet, despite international censure and recognition of State sponsorship, the answer to every one of these incidents has been largely the same — blanket immunity.

Torture — Besides internal military operations, dictatorship, ethnic cleansing, and genocide, the Indian State daily commits smaller-scale atrocities.

The Republic of India refuses to ratify the UN Convention Against Torture and it has no national law prohibiting torture. "The practice of torture is endemic in India," reports the Asian Human Rights Commission in 2010. "It is believed that torture, in its cognate and express forms, is practiced in every police station in the country."[53] In 2005, the International Committee of the Red Cross (ICRC) told U.S. Ambassador David Mulford that "New Delhi condones torture." The practice, revealed ICRC, is present in "all the branches of the security forces" and is "regular and widespread."[54]

"Oppression of minorities is still an untreated disease in the national bloodstream, and we must ask whether State-sponsored violence is necessarily a thing of the past," writes Dr. Rahuldeep Singh Gill.[55] Reports by the U.S. State Department indicate oppression and violence remain a terrifyingly present reality. "In 2015, religious tolerance deteriorated and religious freedom violations increased in India." Officials conclude,

> Minority communities, especially Christians, Muslims, and Sikhs, experienced numerous incidents of intimidation, harassment, and violence, largely at the hands of Hindu nationalist groups. Members of the ruling Bharatiya Janata Party (BJP) tacitly supported these groups and used religiously-divisive language to further inflame tensions. These issues, combined with longstanding problems of police bias and judicial inadequacies, have created a pervasive climate of impunity, where religious minority communities feel increasingly insecure, with no recourse when religiously-motivated crimes occur.[56]

Caste Pervades Modern Indian Society — The independent Indian State is bleeding the sons and daughters of the soil. Like the ancient rulers, it perpetuates systematic oppression designed to extinguish or subjugate any and all dissent. Above all other atrocities perpetrated in modern India, however, is the Brahmanical caste system.

The caste system prevails. The downtrodden still suffer the same ancient methods of subjugation, including dehumanization, segregation, and violence. The ancient prejudice still stands. The "vast system of superstition" has not been annihilated.

Instead of being rooted in a land occupied by the Mughals or British, caste today thrives in an independent India directly ruled by the elite members of the very same culture which invented and imposed the system. In 2007, Canadian philosopher Klaus Klostermaier offers details on the current status of the caste system.

> Every observer of Indian life will attest to the immense importance of caste and caste rules also in present, post-independence India. It is not true, as many outsiders believe, that the Constitution of the Republic of India abolished caste or even intended to do so. It merely abolished the notion of "outcaste" and made it a punishable offense to disadvantage a person because of such a status. Both

within political parties, professional groups, municipalities, in social and economic life, in education, and in government service, caste has remained an important part of life.[57]

In a 2009 report, International Dalit Solidarity Network (IDSN) reveals, "The caste system continues to exist, while the dominant castes wish to uphold their power and dominance."[58] In 2016, United Nations official Rita Izsák reports, "Violence against Dalits is reported to be widespread and driven by the effects of the caste system and the lack of justice for victims."[59] As HRW explains in 2014, "Police routinely fail to register and investigate complaints of crimes against Dalits when the perpetrators are of a dominant caste."[60]

"The shadow of caste and its stigma follows an individual from birth till death, affecting all aspects of life from education, housing, work, access to justice, and political participation," Izsák further warns. "We need not just legal and political responses but ways to change the mindset of individuals and the collective conscience of local communities."[61]

Confirming Izsák's conclusion, HRW states, "Political and rights movements have broken some caste barriers, but caste continues to be used to justify discriminatory, cruel, and inhuman treatment inflicted upon millions of Indians — especially in areas of rural India where caste-designation still dictates rigid roles and entitlements." Specifically, in day-to-day life, "Dalit communities are still denied access to community water sources, denied service by barbers, served tea in separate cups, barred from entering shops, excluded from temples, and prevented from taking part in community religious and ceremonial functions."[62]

While the practice of untouchability has been banned, enforcement of that ban is almost non-existent. Political and legal solutions have failed. The core problem is that the *Shastras* enshrine the doctrine of caste, especially in *Manusmriti* and *Rigveda*. Untouchability will exist as long as the *Shastras* exist. Mindsets and consciences cannot be changed so long as people continue to accept the teachings of these religious texts. As Dr. Ambedkar implores,

You must take the stand that Buddha took. You must take the stand which Guru Nanak took. You must not only discard the *Shastras*, you must deny their authority, as did Buddha and Nanak. You must have courage to tell the Hindus that what is wrong with them is their religion

— the religion which has produced in them this notion of the sacredness of caste.[63]

Further complicating the issue is that the mindsets of the oppressed often include an inbred inferiority complex produced by generations of dehumanizing doctrine and treatment. "Caste hierarchy and caste consciousness have been socially internalized through centuries," explains the IDSN. "It is not only the dominant powers, but also the Dalits themselves that maintain their subordination and self-suppression through acquired learning and socialization." Thus, as Phule cautions, it is possible that the oppressed person may "resist any attempt that may be made for his deliverance and fight even against his benefactor."

This inferiority complex is influenced by individual belief in the *Shastras*. Many of the *Mulnivasi*, despite suffering the deprivations dictated by those texts, unwittingly accept them and their teachings of the *karma* (fate) and *dharma* (duty) of the castes.

In his book, *East of Indus*, American scientist Dr. Gurnam Singh Sidhu Brard describes his upbringing in a post-independence India. According to his account, the oppressed classes were often brainwashed to accept oppression as their lot in life. Furthermore, even if they overcame their own insecurities and recognized their natural human dignity, their physical characteristics often make it impossible to prevent the surrounding culture from identifying them as "low-caste."

If you believed in *karma* and *dharma*, behaving according to your assigned caste role was your best course. Violating the role to which God had assigned you would get you in trouble with God as well as society. Even the low-caste men would say, "God has made these barriers; he could have given me birth in a raja's house if my *karma* allowed it." They pretended to believe in the sanctity of the caste system; but, if they had any choice, they might have discarded it instantly.

If a low-caste person went somewhere else to start a new life, other people would treat him as an unknown entity until they determined his caste. It was their *dharma* to not pollute and degrade themselves, even unknowingly. They would not hate the person, but until his caste was known, their interaction with him would be at the level necessary for labor or business transactions only.

Usually, they would be able to guess his caste because appearance was an indicator of caste. Castes were not made by God, but most likely what happened was that the tribes who at some ancient time fell into the lowest castes were those starting with a disadvantage in making war, in capabilities, and in knowledge. A low-caste person was usually obvious from his facial structure, skin color, mannerisms, clothing, and speech. In fact, the speech and accents of different castes was usually different even after they had lived and worked in the same place for generations. Each caste had its own section to live in, and the tones and accents of the low-caste speech were distinctive. Dark brown or black skin, together with a flat or wide nose, thick lips and coarse features, generally indicated lower caste, although there were always exceptions.[64]

If the oppressed reject the system, they are beaten by the oppressor for neglecting their *dharma* (duty). If the oppressor rejects the system, the brainwashed oppressed might insist that such oppression is his *karma* (fate). Like the enslaved Africans of past centuries, those who seek to escape may sometimes find an enemy in the "House Negro" who is comfortable in his slavery. Even those who escape to a different environment cannot find emancipation because their very appearance may betray their origins and force them back into the system of oppression.

The masses of India must realize that their value as individuals does not depend on gaining respect from proponents of caste. Nor does their liberation depend on the reformation of the Hindu religion. They do not need to first convince the "House Negro" to join them before they say, "Let's go, let's separate." Instead, the common people must begin to act as sovereign individuals by personally cultivating self-respect, exercising individual liberty, and allying with like-minded individuals who have shaken off the mental and spiritual shackles of Brahmanism.

The Bhagats and Gurus devoted — and sometimes sacrificed — their lives to empowering the common people to recognize their self-worth. Guru Arjun taught that a person "who has neither caste nor lineage" can still become "the king of the whole world, if his heart is imbued with the love of God." He was martyred for his work to liberate the downtrodden. Guru Gobind Singh instituted the *Khalsa* to unite people in a path of dignity and equality. Dr. Ambedkar pursued the annihilation of caste — a goal frustrated by India's *de facto* "Father of the Nation."

India Blocks Freedom of Religious Conversion — Ambedkar escaped the caste system by renouncing Hinduism. The Gurus likewise rejected the Hindu religion. As Arundhati Roy points out, "Over the previous centuries, in order to escape the scourge of caste, millions of Untouchables (I use this word only because Ambedkar used it too) had converted to Buddhism, Islam, Sikhism, and Christianity."[65] However, as the *Mulnivasi* consciously reject Hinduism and self-identify as non-Hindus, their exodus provokes the wrath of those who benefit from the Brahmanical caste. According to Dr. Rajkumar Hans, conversion by Dalits "amounts to a search for equality and human dignity that has been an anathema to Hinduism."[66]

Consequently, the exits are being blocked. The route of escape is being closed down. The masses are consistently denied the right to leave Hinduism for another religion.

Independent India has widely adopted "anti-conversion laws" which attempt to prevent people from converting. Nine states have passed these laws, including Arunachal Pradesh, Chhattisgarh, Gujarat, Himachal Pradesh, Jharkhand, Madhya Pradesh, Odisha, Rajasthan, and Tamil Nadu.

These laws generally require government permission to convert, establish waiting periods of up to 30 days before converting, and set prison sentences of up to five years for violation. Both the BJP and INC have backed anti-conversion legislation. Since the BJP took power in 2014, its leadership has repeatedly expressed interest in passing a national law.

In 2014, UN official Heiner Bielefeldt explained that anti-conversion legislation "is disrespect of freedom of religion or belief." The laws, he warns, place the State "in a position of being able to assess the genuineness of conversion." Moreover, they are biased in favor of Hindus. The laws are "applied in a discriminatory manner" and encourage unrestricted conversions to Hinduism — which are often organized under the auspices of State-affiliated entities who use access to government benefits as a form of blackmail to compel conversion.

Connecting anti-conversion laws to State-sponsored massacres, Bielefeldt concludes, "The acts of violence are part of a broader pattern of instigating fear into the minorities, sending them a message they don't belong to this country unless they either keep at the margins or turn to Hinduism."[67]

Citations

1 United States Commission on International Religious Freedom. *Annual Report: India*

Chapter. May 2010. 242.

2 Theertha. *History*. 261.

3 Sappenfield, Mark. "Obama's new India problem: What to do with Narendra Modi?" *The Christian Science Monitor*. May 18, 2014.

4 Singh. *Sikh*. 228.

5 Roy, Arundhati. "My Seditious Heart." *The Caravan*. May 1, 2016.

6 Constituent Assembly. November 21, 1949.

7 Constitution of India, 1950. Article 365.

8 Assembly. Nov. 21, 1949.

9 Ibid.

10 Zubrin, Robert. "The Population Control Holocaust." *The New Atlantis*. Number 35, Spring 2012. 33-54.

11 Rothbard, Murray. *The Libertarian Forum*. Volume VII, NO.7. July 1975.

12 Ghosh, S. K. *Torture and Rape in Police Custody: An Analysis*. New Delhi: Ashish Publishing House. 1993. 98.

13 Zubrin, Robert. "Population."

14 Gossman, Patricia. *Human Rights in India: Punjab in Crisis*. Human Rights Watch. 1991. 16.

15 Singh, Harinder. "The Emergency & The Sikhs." Sikh Research Institute. Full text available at http://www.sikhri.org/the_emergency_the_sikhs.

16 Mahmood, Cynthia Keppley. *Fighting for Faith and Nation: Dialogues With Sikh Militants*. Philadelphia: University of Pennsylvania Press. 1996. 54.

17 Singh. *Sikh*. 339-340.

18 Singh. "The Emergency."

19 United Nations. *"Convention on the Prevention and Punishment of the Crime of Genocide."* United Nations General Assembly. December 9, 1948. Article 2.

20 United Nations. *"Final Report of the Commission of Experts Established Pursuant to Security Council Resolution 780 (1992)."* United Nations Commission of Experts. 27 May 1994, section III.

21 Gossman. *Human Rights*. 21.

22 Kumar, Ram Narayan and Amrik Singh. *Reduced to Ashes: The Insurgency and Human Rights in Punjab*. Kathmandu: South Asia Forum for Human Rights. 2003. 38.

23 Crossette, Barbara. "India Uproots Thousands Living Near Sikh Temple." *The New York Times*. June 3, 1990.

24 Crossette, Barbara. "New Delhi Journal; The Sikh's Hour of Horror, Relived After 5 Years." *The New York Times*. September 7, 1989.

25 Kaur, Jaskaran. *Twenty Years of Impunity*. Ensaaf. October 2006. 4-5.

26 Embassy New Delhi. "Manmohan Singh a True Statesman in Reacting to Sikh Riot Report." Wikileaks Cable: 05NEWDELHI6310_a. August 12, 2005. Full text available at https://wikileaks.org/plusd/cables/05NEWDELHI6310_a.html.

27 California State Assembly. Concurrent Resolution No. 34, Chapter 36. "Relative to the November 1984 anti-Sikh pogroms." May 5, 2015.

28 Ontario Legislative Assembly. Private Members' Public Business, Ballot Item Number 47, Private Members' Notice of Motion Number 46. Ms. Malhi.

29 Basu, Amrita. *Violent Conjectures in Democratic India*. New York: Cambridge University Press. 2015. 2.

30 Roy, Arundhati. *Field Notes on Democracy: Listening to Grasshoppers.* Chicago: Haymarket Books. 2009. xvii.

31 Gregg, Heather Selma. *The Path to Salvation: Religious Violence from the Crusades to Jihad.* Lincoln: University of Nebraska Press. 2014. 67.

32 USCIRF 2010. *India Chapter.* 242.

33 Juergensmeyer, Mark. *The New Cold War? Religious Nationalism Confronts the Secular State.* Berkeley: University of California Press. 1993.

34 Bloom, Irene and J. Paul Martin and Wayne L. Proudfoot (eds.). *Religious Diversity and Human Rights.* New York: Columbia University Press, 1996. 251.

35 Dhami, Sukhman. "Confront India on Poor Human Rights Record." TheHill.com. January 26, 2015.

36 Kaur, Jaskaran. *Protecting the Killers: A Policy of Impunity in Punjab, India.* Human Rights Watch and Ensaaf. October 2007.

37 Human Rights Watch. *India: Investigate Unmarked Graves in Jammu and Kashmir.* August 24, 2011.

38 Scott-Clark, Cathy. "The mass graves of Kashmir." *The Guardian.* July 9, 2012.

39 Mathur, Shubh. *The Human Toll of the Kashmir Conflict: Grief and Courage in a South Asian Borderland.* New York: Palgrave MacMillan. 2016. 59.

40 Kaur. *Impunity.*

41 Khalra, Jaswant Singh. "Last International Speech — The Struggle for Truth." Ensaaf. April 1995.

42 Basu, Manisha. *The Rhetoric of Hindu India: Language and Urban Nationalism.* Delhi: Cambridge University Press. 2017. 35.

43 Jackson, Richard and Eamon Murphy and Scott Poynting (eds.). *Contemporary State Terrorism: Theory and Practice.* London: Routledge. 2010.

44 Goodman, Amy. "Explosive Report by Indian Magazine Exposes Those Responsible for 2002 Gujarat Massacre." Democracy Now! December 5, 2007.

45 USCIRF 2010. *India Chapter.* 246.

46 Amnesty International. *Report 2005: The State of the World's Human Rights.* London: Amnesty International Publications. 2005. 127.

47 Jaffrelot, Christophe. *Religion, Caste, and Politics in India.* Delhi: Primus Books. 2010. 389.

48 Ibid. 376-377.

49 Human Rights Watch. "India: Gujarat Officials Took Part in Anti-Muslim Violence." April 30, 2002.

50 Goodman. "Explosive."

51 Embassy Mumbai. "Gujarat Chief minister Modi Sets His Sights on National Politics." Wikileaks Cable: 06MUMBAI1986_a. November 2, 2006. Full text available at https://wikileaks.org/plusd/cables/06MUMBAI1986_a.html

52 Mander, Harsh. "Nellie: India's Forgotten Massacre." *Sunday Magazine - The Hindu.* December 14, 2008.

53 Asian Human Rights Commission. "India's Prevention of Torture Bill Requires a Thorough Review." Article 2, Vol. 09, No. 03-04. December 2010.

54 Embassy New Delhi. "ICRC Frustrated With Indian Government." Wikileaks Cable: 05NEWDELHI2606_a. Dated April 6, 2005. Full text available at http://wikileaks.rsf.org/cable/2005/04/05NEWDELHI2606.html

55 Gill, Rahuldeep. "India's Incomplete Democracy." *The Los Angeles Times*. June 18, 2014.

56 United States Commission on International Religious Freedom. *Annual Report: India Chapter*. April 2016. 159.

57 Klostermaier, Klaus. *A Survey of Hinduism*. Albany: State University of New York Press. 2007. 290.

58 European Commission to the International Dalit Solidarity Network. "Caste-based Discrimination in South Asia." June 2009.

59 Izsák, Rita. "Report of the Special Rapporteur on minority issues." United Nations General Assembly. A/HRC/31/56. January 28, 2016.

60 Human Rights Watch. *Cleaning Human Waste: "Manual Scavenging," Caste, and Discrimination in India*. August 25, 2014. 47.

61 United Nations. "Caste systems violate human rights and dignity of millions worldwide – New UN expert report." Office of the High Commissioner of Human Rights. March 21, 2016.

62 Human Rights Watch. *Cleaning*. 12.

63 Ambedkar. *Writings* (vol. 1). 69.

64 Brard, Gurnam Singh Sidhu. *East of Indus: My Memories of Old Punjab*. New Delhi: Hemkunt Publishers (P) Ltd. 2007. 222.

65 Roy. *Seditious*.

66 Rawat. *Dalit*. 132.

67 Arora, Vishal. "UN Official: India's 'Conversion' Laws Threaten Religious Freedom." *The Wall Street Journal* (Blogs). March 10, 2014.

— 7 —
Swaraj Without *Azadi*

Independent India's treatment of non-Hindus as "foreign" to the country is terrifying, but in context of historical realities it is far from surprising. India's indigenous religions — Buddhism and Sikhism — intended to provide the downtrodden masses a path to secure their own future through faiths which teach equality and liberty. However, this goal of emancipating the downtrodden from Brahmanical domination drew the wrath of the elite. Thus, for centuries, the ruling elite have violently harassed adherents of both religions.

In the early 20th century, many intellectuals warned that the *Mulnivasi* risked increased victimization by predatory Brahmanical forces if India became independent. Although they were not against India's independence from foreign rule, they understood independence was not likely to be accompanied by freedom.

Writing in 1909, for instance, Max Arthur Macauliffe compares Hinduism to "the boa constrictor of the Indian forests."

> When a petty enemy appears to worry it, it winds round its opponent, crushes it in its folds, and finally causes it to disappear in its capacious interior. In this way, many centuries ago, Hinduism, on its own ground, disposed of Buddhism.... In this way, it is disposing of the reformed and once hopeful religion of Baba Nanak. Hinduism has embraced Sikhism in its folds.[1]

In 1928, as India's independence movement took root and Britain's Simon Commission discussed granting "home rule," Puran Singh wrote a cautionary letter to Sir John Simon. "He openly expressed his deep concern for the fate of minorities and have-nots after the end of British rule over India," explains American scientist Dr. Baldev Singh. In the letter, Puran Singh describes the Sikhs as a separate people.

The Sikh believes in the inspirations of the Ten Gurus. His past begins from Guru Nanak and his future lies in the progress of his ideals.... They isolated the Sikhs from the disintegrating people called the Hindus who are self-hypnotized slaves of the peculiar theological tyranny of complex intrigue of Brahmanism.[2]

Echoing the concerns voiced by Macauliffe, Puran Singh warns, "The Hindu turned down Buddhism in the past and is thinking of devouring Sikhism because both systems condemn the Hindu tyranny of caste masquerading as a religion of love." He desired independence, stating, "In the verity of things, there is nothing like freedom." Yet he feared that *azadi* would not accompany *swaraj*. Consequently, as the British arranged India's independence, he concludes, "I would request you not to be so small as to be partial in any way to any community and not to be so large as to give over India into the hands of one powerful community and thus reduce the other minor communities to eternal slavery even under democratic institutions."[3]

In 1941, Swami Dharma Theertha also warns that *swaraj* might exclude *azadi*. "Under *swaraj*... caste imperialism may triumph," he writes. "Freedom with caste is a mockery. The Hindu masses who are but pawns in the hands of their caste master will be safer in subjection to a foreign rule than under the free domain of the superior castes." In conclusion, he urges,

> The Hindu masses must be on their guard against Caste-Raj being reestablished in the name of *swaraj*.... Let everyone who dares to demand *swaraj* or independence for India publicly pledge himself to root out caste.... The nation cannot have independence and yet deny freedom and equality.... The revival of Caste-Raj in any form is the greatest menace of the present crisis which all liberty-loving people, Hindus, Sikhs, Muslims, and Christians should unite in combating.[4]

The warnings of Macauliffe, Puran Singh, and Theertha — all of which are summarized in Dr. Bhim Rao Ambedkar's prophetic 1948 warning about the "great danger of things going wrong" — have come to fruition.

"It sometimes happens that a colonial revolt will result in both national independence and increased protections of individual liberty," writes American historian Clarence Carson. "But it hardly follows that one will lead to the other.... However desirable national independence may be, it is something quite different and separable from freedom."[5] In context of India, *swaraj* does not mean *azadi*. Instead, as Arundhati Roy suggests, independent India is a colonial State.

> The Indian State, from the moment it became a sovereign nation, from the moment it shook off the shackles of colonialism, it became a colonial State. If you look at *who* are these people that the Indian State chose to fight — in all the Northeastern states, they were tribal people; in Kashmir, it was the Muslims; in Telangana, it was the tribal people; in Hyderabad, it was the Muslims; in Goa, it's the Christians; in Punjab, it's the Sikhs. So you see this sort of upper-caste Hindu State perpetually at war.[6]

As in any colonial State, the common people suffer the worst. Describing India under the Mughals, Abraham Eraly writes, "Behind the shimmering imperial facade, there was another scene, another life — people in mud hovels, their lives barely distinct from animals, half-naked, half-starved, and from whom every drop of sap had been wrung out by their predatory masters, Muslim as well as Hindu."[7] Little has changed for the masses of modern and independent India. As in the days of the Mughal Emperors, the masses remain in a desperate state of starvation, nakedness, and ignorance.

So little has changed, in fact, that to comprehend the situation in the 21st century we have only to examine the words of two 17th-century European merchants — Francisco Pelsaert and Jean-Baptiste Tavernier — who were in India as contemporaries of Guru Hargobind and Guru Tegh Bahadur, respectively.

Writing in 1626, the Dutch Pelsaert describes a vast contrast between "the manner of life of the rich in their great superfluity and absolute power and the utter subjection and poverty of the common people — poverty so great and miserable that the life of the people can be depicted or accurately described only as the home of stark want and the dwelling-place of bitter woe."[8]

Writing in 1676, the French Tavernier describes how, then just as today, martial law was the first resort of the Central State for sustaining the slavery of the masses.

> The country is ruined by the necessity of defraying the enormous charges required to maintain the splendor of a numerous court,

and to pay a large army maintained for the purpose of keeping the people in subjection. No adequate idea can be conveyed of the sufferings of that people. The cudgel and the whip compel them to incessant labour for the benefit of others; and, driven to despair by every kind of cruel treatment, their revolt or their flight is only prevented by the presence of a military force.[9]

In the 1500s, Guru Nanak laments, "This age is a knife, and the kings are butchers; justice has taken wings and fled. In this completely dark night of falsehood, the moon of truth is never seen to rise."[10] Today, his description of the dark condition of the Indian subcontinent is tragically relevant as the Gandhis, the Dogras, the Chandars, the Chandus, the Birbals, and so many other "Sanskrit thinkers" once again enforce a system of degradation. Like Jahangir, today's ruling elites demand the masses "should be brought into the fold."

This time, however, the religion the State seeks to impose is Hinduism, not Islam. The rulers are no longer collaborating with Brahman advisors. Instead, the Brahman advisors are the rulers. Independent India has developed into a Caste-Raj. A Brahman-Raj. A Hindutva-Raj.

"India is only in the form of a political democracy, where you get to vote," concludes Dr. Manisha Bangar. Speaking in May 2017 as the National Vice President of All India Backward and Minority Communities Employees Federation (BAMCEF), she explains,

> There is no social democracy. There is no representation and so there is no economic democracy in the country. The upper-caste are only three percent. They have been able to bind up the majority in the fallacious and fictitious name of Hinduism — of Hindu identity. The minority Brahmans have super-power and super-control of all the institutions of the country.[11]

As we come face to face with this tragic reality, we are compelled to seek solutions. The history of the Indian subcontinent's struggle for human dignity should be the first place we look. While the common people still suffer under the same dehumanizing sociopolitical structure faced by Guru Arjun and the saints who came before and after him, we must remember that it is only because of their sacrifices that any progress has been made towards achieving the emancipation of the masses.

Therefore, we need to consider what inspired these saints to lay down their lives for the sake of the simple-hearted people. One after another, the Bhagats and Gurus played the "game of love" described by Guru Nanak. Guru Ram Das prepared Arjun to die for the *Panth*. Guru Arjun groomed Hargobind to wage war for the *Panth*. Guru Hargobind prepared Tegh Bahadur to give up his head for the *Panth*. Guru Tegh Bahadur prepared Guru Gobind Singh to sacrifice everything — his mother, his sons, and himself — for the *Panth*. What led the father to nurture the son, the son to nurture the grandson, and the grandson to nurture the great-grandsons to enter the field of battle?

They all heard the battle-drum beating in the sky of their minds. They took aim against false creeds and crooked politics, inflicting wounds as they relentlessly fought in defense of the oppressed. These spiritual warriors never left the field of battle because, as they desired to play the game of love, they accepted the requirement to step onto God's path with their heads in the palms of their hands as they sought the company of the lowest of the low.

These spiritual heroes waged a direct assault on the mighty who wield power to dominate, control, and enslave the weak. In contrast, they stood on the side of the Creator by destroying evil, lifting up the weak and the humble, and dethroning the powerful. In a world full of lies, they spoke truth. To the downtrodden, who were treated as "worms," they taught, "You are the very image of the Luminous Lord; recognize the true origin of yourself."[12]

Before he was murdered by the Indian State for exposing its secret campaign of genocide against the Sikhs, Jaswant Singh Khalra spoke about challenging the darkness.

There is a fable that, when the Sun was setting for the first time, as it was completing its journey, Light was decreasing and the signs of Darkness were appearing. It is said lamentation was rife among the people that the Sun will set, Darkness will spread, no one will be able to see anything. And what will happen to us? Everybody was worried, but the Sun set. In order to show its strength, Darkness set its foot on the earth. But it is said — far away, in some hut — one little Lamp lifted its head. It proclaimed: "I challenge the Darkness. If nothing else, then at least around myself, I will not let it settle. Around myself I will establish Light." And, it is said, watching that one Lamp, in other huts, other Lamps arose. And the world was amazed that these Lamps stopped Darkness from expanding so that people could see.[13]

The Bhagats and the Gurus challenged the Darkness. Caste is a lie, they taught. God made every person forward and free. Politically and socially, all are free by birth. False creeds and crooked politics can be demolished. "Let's go," they said to the sons and daughters of the soil. "Let's separate." Ultimately, they gave a voice to the voiceless, hope to the hopeless, power to the powerless, honor to the despised, and a throne to the throneless.

In place of a dehumanizing sociopolitical structure, they were inspired by a vision of Begampura to introduce a society founded on the politics of liberty. As Puran Singh writes,

> No man or society that has risen from the dead into the life of the spirit can tolerate political subjugation or social slavery to unjust laws or rules. Politics, in the sense of fighting against all social injustice, all tyranny, all wrong taxation of the poor, all subjugation of man to man, were the "politics" of the Guru. Without freedom, no true religion or art can flourish anywhere. Human love, too, degenerates if freedom fails.
>
> Liberty is the very breath of true culture. The Sikhs raised by the Guru fought for freedom. They were defeated, they might be defeated again; all attempts at liberty generally end in defeat. But their very fighting for liberty is the mark of the new soul-consciousness that the Guru had awakened in them.[14]

The lives and legacies of these spiritual heroes should weigh heavily on the *Mulnivasi* conscience. Any activist or institution interested in presenting a true challenge to dehumanizing systems cannot afford to bypass this history of India's freedom struggle. If we fail to learn from past sacrifices, our present struggles are in vain. Thus, as we seek to continue the mission of moving the caravan of freedom forward, we must ask: where are the *Khalsa* today?

Do you hear the battle-drum beating in the sky of your mind? Will you take aim? Will you refuse to leave the field of battle, even though you may be cut apart, piece by piece? Will you challenge the Darkness? Will you establish Light around yourself?

Now is the time to fight. The oppressed must understand their human dignity, learn to have the spines of free people, and recognize the nobility of the common person. The enslaved must hear the liberating message that even a pauper can be king of the whole world if his heart is imbued with the love of God. Those who play the game of love and step onto God's path of friendship with the lowest of the low must do so with head in hand. As Guru Nanak taught, give God your head and do not pay any attention to public opinion.

India's persecuted communities must acknowledge their shared heritage, come together in dialogue, and determine how to continue building Begampura. Now it is our turn to unite with the teachers who offer to liberate the downtrodden, bring relief to the oppressed, and embrace the outcastes. Like Guru Arjun, Guru Tegh Bahadur, and Guru Gobind Singh, we must love others enough to lay down our lives for them. We must be willing to sacrifice. The path is narrow and treacherous, but it is the only way to liberation.

Citations

1 Macauliffe. *Religion* (vol. 1). lvii.
2 Singh, Puran. *Open Letter to Sir John Simon*. October 21, 1928. Full text available at globalsikhstudies.com and archive.org. Introduction by Dr. Baldev Singh.
3 Ibid. Body of letter.
4 Theertha. *History*. 276.
5 Carson, Clarence. *The Beginning of the Republic: 1775-1825* (A Basic History of the United States Vol. 2). Wadley: American Textbook Committee. 1984. 2.
6 Roy, Arundhati. "R. Parekh Annual Lecture." A Conference on Democracy and Dissent in China and India. University of Westminster. June 2, 2011.
7 Eraly. *Mughal*. 520.
8 Pelsaert. *India*. 60.
9 Tavernier. *Travels*. 230.
10 *Granth*. 145.
11 Valmuci, Arvin. "Anglican Church Hosts Indian Human Rights Leader to Discuss Religious Persecution." sikh24.com. May 26, 2017.
12 *Granth*. 441.
13 Khalra. "Speech."
14 Singh, Puran. *Volume One, Part II of Spirit of the Sikh*. Patiala: Punjabi University, Patiala. 1980. 2-3.

Epilogue

"Ideas are very important to the shaping of society. In fact, they are more powerful than bombings or armies or guns. And this is because ideas are capable of spreading without limit. They are behind all the choices we make. They can transform the world in a way that governments and armies cannot. Fighting for liberty with ideas makes more sense to me than fighting with guns or politics or political power. With ideas, we can make real change that lasts."
— **U.S. Congressman Ron Paul** —

After the advent of the Bhagats, the Sikh Gurus successfully institutionalized a consistent and comprehensive ideological solution to the subjugation of the *Mulnivasi*. They united people from all backgrounds — such as "simple-hearted" Hindus and "foolish and stupid" Muslims (in the words of Jahangir) — and developed such an egalitarian ideology that Guru Arjun chose Sufi Muslim saint Mian Mir to lay the foundation stone of Harmandir Sahib. While other movements for independence emerged during India's occupation by the Mughals and the British, the only movement which intentionally pursued the uplift of the "lowest of the low" — and was resisted, harassed, and persecuted specifically for doing so — was the Sikh Revolution.

Guru Arjun fought for the liberation of the downtrodden. He carried the caravan of freedom forward. He was willing to pay any cost in the struggle for human dignity — and he paid the highest cost, sacrificing his life. Likewise, Guru Tegh Bahadur gave his head. Guru Gobind Singh gave his four sons, his mother, and his own life. Throughout their experiences, the Gurus were joined by women and even young children who made the greatest sacrifices as they lived lives of courage and fortitude. These people lived what they taught. They did not just talk, but actually walked the talk. They did not just preach these truths, but they practiced them fearlessly.

Where are the leaders who will follow the example of these men? Where are the *Khalsa*? In this confusing world, how can we truly recognize true leadership?

If nothing else, recognition of the history of the forefathers of the *Mulnivasi* must be a litmus test for anyone who claims to desire sincere, real, *true* change in India. To chart an accurate future, it is crucial to acknowledge the past and how it has led to India's present condition.

The Bhagats introduced teachings of equality and liberty. The Gurus expanded on those teachings and institutionalized the struggle for human dignity. Because of this, the ruling elite attempted but failed to crush the rise of the *Mulnivasi*. The Sikh Empire was a bright point in history, but it crumbled when the Maharaja kept power in the hands of a single individual and failed to create a commonwealth. The saints of the 19th and 20th centuries followed the example of the Gurus, in many ways, and improved the lives of millions. India gained independence from centuries of foreign rule, but failed to gain freedom. *Swaraj* came without *azadi*. Independent India has bled — and continues to bleed — the sons and daughters of the soil. Brahmanism has sunk its roots deep into the Indian soil. The *Mulnivasi* are, today, suffering much like they have for centuries. The country needs hope and change.

Under both major political parties in the Republic of India, religious minorities as well as those people who are historically considered low-caste or outcaste regularly endure both the acute symptom of State-sponsored massacres and the chronic symptom of State-sanctioned discrimination which relegates them to the status of second-class citizenship. Mohandas Gandhi, as the figure-head of the Indian National Congress, endorsed a policy of expansionist Hinduism. The Bharatiya Janata Party has adopted and championed that policy as they pursue the goal of formally declaring India (which they term "Bharat") a "Hindu *Rashtra*" — a Hindu Nation.

In June 2017, over 150 Hindu nationalist organizations gathered for a conclave in Goa to discuss that goal. The conclave was organized by Hindu Janajagruti Samiti (HJS), a group whose stated mission is "To reinstate *dharma*, that is, to establish the Hindu Nation." According to HJS, "To arrest the decline and to bring back the past glory to the Holy land of Bharat, it is imperative to reinstate *dharma* in Bharat." The agenda of the conclave, reports Indian journalist Samar Halarnkar, was,

> How to create an "awakening" of *dharma* (duty), which includes lessons on how to worship, dress, comb one's hair "as per Hindu culture" and the "futility of Bharatiya democracy"; how to count-

er "love jihad," the notion that Muslim men want to marry and convert Hindu women as part of a conspiracy to Islamize India; conversions by Christians and other acts by "anti-Hindu sects"; how to defend yourself — "trainers" are available — with sticks, catapults, nunchakus (to mention anything deadlier may invite unwanted attention, but members of the Samiti's sister organisation, the shadowy Sanatan Sanstha, have dabbled with improvised explosive devices, on which the Maharashtra government, in 2016, sought a ban); how to oppose "symbols of slavery," from trying to stop Valentine's Day to changing the names of some cities, such as Aurangabad and Osmanabad; how to protect temples; and, of course, cows.[1]

The social elevation of "cows" has become a principal wedge issue in 21st-century Indian politics as Hindu nationalists demand the cow be made the national animal, promote the "healing" qualities of cow dung and urine (even at State expense), and institute cow slaughter bans all across the country. Adherents of Hindutva have established countless *Bharatiya Gau Raksha Dals* (Indian Cow Protection Organizations) to field vigilantes who target anyone suspected of not properly "protecting" cows. As a result, multiple people — all Muslims and *Mulnivasi* — have been lynched for transporting cattle, slaughtering cattle, or possessing beef. Mere suspicion of beef possession has motivated many of the lynchings. In a number of cases, the suspicion was later proven wrong.

Meanwhile, the downtrodden remain desperate for real leadership. They are not finding it in any of the Republic of India's multitude of political parties. According to Dr. Manisha Bangar,

The pseudo-nationalism of the Indian National Congress, the Communist Party of India, and Aam Aadmi Party are all almost identical to the *Hindutva* brand of nationalism spread by the RSS [Rashtriya Swayamsevak Sangh] and BJP. If the latter is brutal, the former is akin to slow poison. As such, the so-called secular progressivists in India can never become a force by which radical changes can be brought about to correct the country's worsening sociopolitical scenario. On the surface, they appear to stand in opposition to the rightwing politics of the BJP and RSS, but just one layer down they stand in full support of the caste/*varna* system of graded inequality. They are all against the policy of representation of the Backward Classes and against the emerging independent political leadership of the *Mulnivasi Bahujans*. The reason is that the secular progressivists also come from the same upper-caste, Brahman oppressor class as the right-wingers.[2]

In light of all these issues, many Indians have fled the country to seek refuge in foreign lands. The Western World has become a home to millions of *Mulnivasi* over the past century. In particular, Sikhs have found peace, equality, and liberty in the North American continent.

Punjabi Sikhs paved the way for Indian immigrants to settle in the United States of America when they became the first to emigrate there in 1899. In 1912, they established a *Gurdwara* in Stockton, California, USA — the first in that country. Founded by Baba Jawala Singh and Baba Vasakha Singh, Stockton Gurdwara played a central role in the formation of the Ghadar Party, which conducted the first organized and sustained campaign of resistance against the British Raj. After 1984, when Harmandir Sahib was invaded and thousands of Sikhs were subsequently slaughtered in the streets of Delhi by members of the ruling party, the trickle of Sikh immigration to the USA (as well as Canada and the United Kingdom) transformed into a torrent.

As the Sikhs pioneered Indian immigration to the USA, they were embraced as integral members of a free society — a multicultural society which not only protects, but celebrates, all the basic human rights. They found a home in a country founded on the principle that all people are created equal. As the Sikhs settled into the land, statesmen have identified and called out the compatibility between the foundational principles of the USA and the mission of the Gurus.

In 2012, for instance, as the Sikh-American community celebrated its centennial anniversary, California Congressman Tom McClintock recognized the ideology of liberty undergirding Sikhism.

This is the story of a small group of families who long ago crossed a great ocean in search of religious tolerance and economic liberty; a land where people were free to enjoy the fruit of their own labor, to raise their children according to their own values, to practice their religious beliefs openly, to express their opinions without fear of retribution, to live their lives according to their own best judgment, and not according to the whims and mandates of the powerful.

That is the story of the pilgrims who crossed the Atlantic Ocean on the Mayflower in 1620 seeking a better future in a free land for their descendants. It is the very same story of pilgrims like Baba Vasakha Singh and Baba Jawala Singh who founded the Stockton Gurdwara Sahib a century ago, and all those who have followed since.

One hundred and fifty years ago, Abraham Lincoln said that, although many people who were then in America could trace their families back to the American founding, many more had come since then and could not. But, he said, "when they look through that old Declaration of Independence they find that those old men say that 'We hold these truths to be self-evident, that all men are created equal,' and then they feel that that moral sentiment taught in that day evidences their relation to those men, that it is the father of all moral principle in them, and that they have a right to claim it as though they were blood of the blood, and flesh of the flesh of the men who wrote that Declaration, and so they are."

There is no religion more attuned to the principles of the American Declaration of Independence than the Sikh religion.

Both reject the idea of aristocracy and social class and instead judge every individual on his or her own merit and character.

Both embrace the unique notion that we are born with equal claim to unalienable rights that come directly from the "laws of nature and of nature's God," and not from government — rather, we create governments to protect these God-given rights and whenever any form of government becomes destructive of these rights, it renounces its legitimacy.

And both have inspired and animated the aspirations of those around the world seeking to reclaim, protect, and enjoy these God-given rights.

Individual liberty, personal responsibility, Constitutionally-limited government — these are fundamental both to the Sikh Religion and to the American Founding.

Today, we celebrate not only a century of Sikh immigration and integration into America — together, we celebrate the immortal inscription on the American Liberty Bell to: "Proclaim Liberty

Throughout ALL the Land, and Unto ALL the INHABITANTS Thereof."[3]

Immigration is not, however, an option for everyone. Nor should people be forced to abandon their homeland in order to find freedom abroad. While it is inspiring to see people of Indian origin enjoying the God-given right to life and liberty in welcoming lands like the USA, the masses in India remain trapped within the tragedy of tyranny.

Furthermore, although *Mulnivasi* — with the Sikhs taking the lead — have successfully transplanted into places like the USA, Brahmanism is following close behind. Its advocates have traversed the oceans in order to confront the *Mulnivasi* living abroad by challenging them with their ideology of slavery.

Brahmanical advocates have employed many seemingly innocuous tactics by promoting seemingly mild-mannered ideas such as selective animal rights (as a tool to persecute minorities), the practice of yoga, and Gandhi as an "Apostle of Non-Violence." Through the United Nations, India has achieved declaration of June 21 (the Summer Solstice) as "International Day of Yoga" and October 2 (Gandhi's birthday) as "International Day of Non-Violence." Moreover, on every continent (except Antarctica, to date), the Indian State has initiated and funded installation of Gandhi statues. The Indian Council for Cultural Relations, a State entity, pays for installation of Gandhi statues all around the globe.

In June 2016, Indian President Pranab Mukherjee unveiled a statue of Gandhi in West Africa on the University of Ghana campus. The statue triggered an international incident when, as *The Guardian* reports, "a group of professors started a petition calling for the removal of the statue, saying Gandhi was racist, and that the university should put African heroes and heroines 'first and foremost.'" As the Ghanaian professors opposed the statue, they declared, "It is better to stand up for our dignity than to kowtow to the wishes of a burgeoning Eurasian super power."[4] Yet the Indian State doubled down in defense of the statue and it remained in place.

In October 2016, in Davis, California, Indian Consul General Venkatesan Ashok hosted the unveiling of another statue of Gandhi. Before its unveiling, the statue faced stiff protest by a diverse coalition of *Mulnivasi*-Americans. Sacramento businessman Amar Singh Shergill, for instance, opposed the statue by arguing that "Gandhi — 'who, by his own words, was a bigot and pedophile' — was being used as a propaganda tool by India to obscure, 'in modern times, that there is widespread murder and rape of Muslims, Christians, Sikhs, and Dalits in India.'"[5] Yet, instead of heeding the concerns of local citizens like Shergill, the City of Davis bowed to pressure from the Indian State, which paid for the statue.

Meanwhile, at a national level in the USA, former President Barack Obama, during his inauguration as the chief executive of the largest free country in the world, declares, "We are a nation of Christians and Muslims, Jews and Hindus, and non-believers. We are shaped by every language and culture."[6] Buddhists, Sikhs, and other faiths from the Indian subcontinent, however, drew no mention from him. Instead, all were apparently combined together under a single label of Hindu.

In addition to promoting Brahmanical concepts at an international level, propagandizing the world with installation of a myriad of Gandhi statues, and influencing the President of the United States to declare his country, among other things, "a Hindu nation," a deeper issue is emerging. The caste struggle is crossing oceans. Brahmanism has moved beyond the borders of India in order to demand historical revisionism that erases the truth about caste.

In a 2016 campaign spearheaded by the Hindu American Foundation (HAF), Brahmanical elements have attempted to strip primary school textbooks in California of reference to "caste" as a Hindu practice. HAF, reported *The New York Times*, "seeks to shape the image of Hinduism in the United States." As the *Times* explained, it is "a fight that mirrors similar arguments being made in India, where Hindu nationalist governments have begun overhauls of textbooks in some states." The campaigners "want the caste system to be explained as a phenomenon of the region, not as a Hindu practice."

As readers of this book recognize, such a goal not only rewrites the reality of history and of the *Shastras*, but ironically also directly contradicts the claims of the person whose statues the Indian State installs all around the world. As Gandhi says, "To abolish caste is to demolish Hinduism." Thus, rather than siding with civil rights champions like Dr. Ambedkar in pursuing the annihilation of caste, the forces of *Hindutva* instead seek to justify and perpetuate the system by accusing everyone else of also practicing it. "Every religion has some form of caste and discrimination," insists HAF executive director Suhag Shukla.[7]

The spirit of the *Mulnivasi* was kindled in response to this campaign. Diverse communities united, linking arms across ethnic and religious and national lines, and defeated the HAF. Truth prevailed as the *Mulnivasi* won the textbook battle.

In the words of Guru Nanak: "There is a famine of Truth." Yet, in his wisdom, he also proclaims, "Truth is the medicine for all."[8] Our hope is that, by recognizing the sacrifices of the forefathers of the *Mulnivasi* which are presented within this book, many will be inspired to pick up where they left off, take up the challenge to become spiritual warriors, and enter the field of battle to slay the dragon who is encroaching on the international borders of liberty.

As the Brahmanical caste system attempts to put down roots internationally, it remains entrenched in India and continues to enslave the *Mulnivasi* in the same way it has for ages. Meanwhile, scientists continue to search for evidence of its origins. As Brian K. Smith explained in Chapter 3, many scholars posit the "Aryan Invasion Theory" as the source of Brahmanism. In June 2017, as reported by *The Hindu*, a new discovery appears to confirm the theory of an Aryan invasion.

The thorniest, most fought-over question in Indian history is slowly but surely getting answered: did Indo-European language speakers, who called themselves Aryans, stream into India sometime around 2,000 BC - 1,500 BC when the Indus Valley civilization came to an end, bringing with them Sanskrit and a distinctive set of cultural practices? Genetic research based on an avalanche of new DNA evidence is making scientists around the world converge on an unambiguous answer: yes, they did....

This may come as a surprise to many — and a shock to some — because the dominant narrative in recent years has been that genetics research had thoroughly disproved the Aryan migration theory. This interpretation was always a bit of a stretch as anyone who read the nuanced scientific papers in the original knew. But now it has broken apart altogether under a flood of new data on Y-chromosomes (or chromosomes that are transmitted through the male parental line, from father to son).

Until recently, only data on mtDNA (or matrilineal DNA, transmitted only from mother to daughter) were available and that seemed to suggest there was little external infusion into the Indian gene pool over the last 12,500 years or so. New Y-DNA data has turned that conclusion upside down, with strong evidence of external infusion of genes into the Indian male lineage during the period in question.[9]

In the midst of this, the adherents of Brahmanism within India spew vitriol and sponsor violence against anyone whom they consider to be "foreign" to the land — including Christians, Muslims, and anyone who chooses to self-identify as "non-Hindu." The issue of an Aryan invasion, combined with the long and tragic history of India's foreign occupation by the Delhi Sultanate, the Mughal Empire, and the British Empire, certainly explains why a schism might exist between the indigenous people and foreigners. Yet the evidence suggests that the caste system was invented and imposed by foreign invaders in order to subjugate the indigenous people. If true, then it is Hinduism — or, more accurately, Brahmanism — which is foreign to India.

The "Sanskrit thinkers" have made their path clear. They have declared their policy. They are pursuing a culture of death, slavery, and inequality. The oneness of Brahmanism and the oneness of the Guru's *Panth* are holistically distinct. They are incompatible. They are irreconcilable. They are two divergent paths which cannot ever arrive at the same destination.

However, the core issue is not one of DNA, or of race, ethnicity, language, nationality, or gender. The core issue is one of teachings and principles. The core issue is one of belief.

The Bhagats and the Gurus believed in Begampura — the city without sorrow. They desired "God's Kingdom" in which "there is no second or third status; all are equal there." As Guru Nanak teaches in his writings, "The Brahmans, the Kshatriyas, the Vaishyas, the Shudras, and even the low wretches are all emancipated by contemplating their Lord." Guru Gobind Singh also proclaims, "Let the four Hindu castes, who have different rules for their guidance, abandon them all, adopt the one form of adoration, and become brothers."

The forefathers of the *Mulnivasi* believed in human dignity. "O my mind, you are the embodiment of the Divine Light — recognize your own origin," declares Guru Amar Das. He continues, "Thus says Nanak: O my mind, you are the very image of the Luminous Lord; recognize the true origin of yourself."[10] Thus, the forefathers believed that every individual human being is valuable because all are created in the image of the Creator. This belief, which all the Bhagats and Gurus shared, crafted their characters.

Belief influences behavior. The creeds people embrace mold their character. As India — and the world — cries out for hope and change, one place to look is in the lives and legacies of the originators of the Sikh Revolution.

From their teachings, we must realize that being a *Khalsa* or a *Mulnivasi* is not achieved by birth. The *Mulnivasi* heritage is not hereditary. It is not caste-based. Anyone, as the Gurus believed, can be royalty. A person becomes a king by service, not lineage. Likewise, one is a son or daughter of the soil by principles, not by blood or heritage.

Anyone can be a *Khalsa*. Anyone can be a *Mulnivasi*. It is a matter of what they believe and how they behave. The world must move beyond asking about a person's heritage. As we seek true leadership, the questions we should ask of aspiring leaders are much different. What, we should ask, do the leaders believe? What are their principles? Most importantly, do they put those principles into practice? Do they seek the company of the lowest of the low? Will they die for their principles?

In a world fill with crooked leaders and false teachers, it sometimes seems as though we are wandering in the desert as we search for true leadership. As Guru Nanak declares, "Greed and sin are the king and prime minister; falsehood is the treasurer."[11] Such words are, to one degree or another, as applicable to the governments of the rest of the world as they are to India.

India is a microcosm of the worldwide situation. We are surrounded by sadhus, prophets, preachers, ascetics, fakirs, dervishes, monks, priests, and an assortment of all types of purported holy men. India, like the world, certainly needs holy men. And yet, where are the leaders who are actually holy? Where are the spiritual heroes who fight in defense of righteousness?

We urge you, reader, to enlighten yourself and your companions with this knowledge of the past. Use this history of the *Mulnivasi* as a measuring stick to challenge anyone who steps to the front with ideas and plans for the uplift of the downtrodden. India desperately needs leaders. Are those who want to be leaders willing to speak for justice — even at the cost of their lives?

Standing on the side of the Bhagats and Gurus, there will always be people who are united with the simple-hearted in the battle against the evil, nefarious, and cunning designs of the complex-hearted. How can you identify them? How can you judge them as worthy?

Those who desire to lead must, as Guru Nanak said, step onto the path with their heads in hand. They must hear, as Bhagat Kabir said, the *Gagan Dhamaamaa Baajiou* — the battle-drum beating in the sky of their mind. They must be willing to self-sacrifice. As Kabir asks, "What sort of a hero is one who is afraid to face the battle?" Thus, he urges, "Stop your wavering, O crazy mind! Now that you have taken up the challenge of death, let yourself burn and die, and attain perfection."

The need for heroes in India — and throughout the world — is urgent. The battle-drums must start rolling. We must heed the call of the righteous saints who fought for the indigenous people. "Stop your wavering," they are calling.

The situation is dire, the path appears dark and dangerous, the future sometimes seems dismal and devoid of hope. In the end, however, we can rest assured that the Creator will right all wrongs, that good will be victorious over evil, and that justice will be served. Guru Nanak, who witnessed the brutal invasion and subjugation of the Indian subcontinent, might have had reason to give in to hopelessness. Instead, the Guru spread hope, declaring,

ਰਾਜੇ ਸੀਹ ਮੁਕਦਮ ਕੁਤੇ ॥
ਜਾਇ ਜਗਾਇਨ੍ ਬੈਠੇ ਸੁਤੇ ॥
ਚਾਕਰ ਨਹਦਾ ਪਾਇਨ੍ ਘਾਉ ॥
ਰਤੁ ਪਿਤੁ ਕੁਤਿਹੋ ਚਟਿ ਜਾਹੁ ॥
ਜਿਥੈ ਜੀਆਂ ਹੋਸੀ ਸਾਰ ॥
ਨਕੀ ਵਢੀ ਲਾਇਤਬਾਰ ॥
ਆਪਿ ਉਪਾਏ ਮੇਦਨੀ ਆਪੇ ਕਰਦਾ ਸਾਰ ॥
ਭੈ ਬਿਨੁ ਭਰਮੁ ਨ ਕਟੀਐ ਨਾਮਿ ਨ ਲਗੈ ਪਿਆਰੁ ॥
ਸਤਿਗੁਰ ਤੇ ਭਉ ਉਪਜੈ ਪਾਈਐ ਮੋਖ ਦੁਆਰ ॥

The kings are tigers, and their officials are dogs;
They go out and awaken the sleeping people to harass them.
The public servants inflict wounds with their nails.
The dogs lick up the blood that is spilled.
But there, in the Court of the Lord, all beings will be judged.
Those who have violated the people's trust will be disgraced;
their noses will be cut off.
He Himself creates the world, and He himself takes care of it.
Without the Fear of God, doubt is not dispelled,
and love for the Name is not embraced.
Through the True Guru, the Fear of God wells up,
and the Door of Salvation is found.[12]

Citations

1 Halarnkar, Samar. "Inside the Hindu mind, a battle for a Hindu nation." Scroll.in. June 11, 2017.

2 Valmuci, Arvin. "California Seminar Warns India's 'Brahman Raj.'" sikh24.com. June 1, 2017.

3 Congressional Record. Volume 158, Number 147. 112th Congress. Statement of Congressman Tom McClintock. November 16, 2012.

4 Burke, Jason. "'Racist' Gandhi statue banished from Ghana university campus." *The Guardian*. October 6, 2016.

5 Magagnini, Stephen. "Was Gandhi saint or sinner? Debate rages over new Davis statue." *The Sacramento Bee*. October 2, 2016.

6 Obama, Barack. "President Barack Obama's Inaugural Address." Whitehouse.gov. January 21, 2009.

7 Medina, Jennifer. "Debate Erupts in California Over Curriculum on India's History." *The New York Times*. May 4, 2016.

8 *Granth*. 468.

9 Joseph, Tony. "How genetics is settling the Aryan migration debate." *The Hindu*. June 16, 2017.

10 *Granth*. 441.

11 Ibid., 469.

12 Ibid., 1288.

Glossary

Adi Granth: First Sikh scripture compiled by Guru Arjun in 1604. Contains the hymns of Sikh Gurus and Bhagats.

Adivasi: Indigenous people living in India before the arrival of Indo-Aryans.

Ajit Singh: Eldest son of Guru Gobind Singh.

Akal Takht: Sikh institution founded by Guru Hargobind.

Akbar: Third Mughal Emperor.

Amritsar: City in Punjab, India. Founded by Guru Ram Das.

Anandpur Sahib: City in Punjab, India. Founded by Guru Tegh Bahadur.

Andhra Pradesh: A coastal state in southeastern India.

Arunachal Pradesh: State in northeastern India.

Assam: State in northeastern India.

Ati-Shudras: Also known as Untouchables, Dalits. As the lowest group of Hindu society, they fall outside the caste system.

Aurangzeb: Sixth Mughal Emperor.

Azadi: Freedom.

Badrinath: Town in the state of Uttarakhand in India.

Bahadur Shah: Seventh Mughal Emperor.

Banias: Upper-caste of merchants, bankers, money-lenders, dealers.

Begampura: The city without sorrow. The Bhagats envisioned a place where people are free and everyone has equal rights regardless of their lineage.

Bengal: A geopolitical, cultural and historical region in Asia; today, Bengal is divided between the sovereign Republic of Bangladesh and the Indian States of West Bengal, Tripura, and Assam.

Bhagat Farid: Bhagat whose hymns were incorporated in *Guru Granth Sahib*.

Bhagat Kabir: Bhagat whose hymns were incorporated in *Guru Granth Sahib*.

Bhagat Namdev: Bhagat whose hymns were incorporated in *Guru Granth*

Sahib.

Bhagat Ravidas: Bhagat whose hymns were incorporated in *Guru Granth Sahib.*

Bhagat(s): Holy person. Hymns of fifteen Bhagats were incorporated in *Guru Granth Sahib.*

      Bhagat Jaidev
      Bhagat Namdev
      Bhagat Trilochan
      Bhagat Parmanand
      Bhagat Sadhana
      Bhagat Beni
      Bhagat Ramanand
      Bhagat Dhanna
      Bhagat Pipa
      Bhagat Sain
      Bhagat Kabir
      Bhagat Ravidas
      Bhagat Farid
      Bhagat Bhikhan
      Bhagat Surdas

Bharat: Mythological Hindu nation consisting of modern day India, Pakistan, Bangladesh, Afghanistan and Iraq.

Bihar: State in eastern India, bordering Nepal.

Brahman Raj: Term used to emphasize that power in India is essentially wielded by Brahmans.

Brahmanism: Core ideology of Hinduism which teaches that the Brahmans are "gods on earth."

Brahmans: Highest caste in the Hindu caste-system. They form the priesthood of Hinduism and their religiously-prescribed occupation is performance of religious ceremonies and reception of gifts from kings and merchants.

British East India Company: Privately owned company which was established to create profitable trade with countries in the region of Asia called the "East Indies."

Buddhism: Religion founded by Gautama Buddha.

Buddhist: Follower of the teachings of Gautama Buddha.

Burma: Also known as the Republic of the Union of Myanmar; sovereign state in the region of Southeast Asia.

Caste system: System of birth based social stratification which forms the core of Hinduism.

Caste: Each of the hereditary classes of Hindu society, distinguished by relative degrees of ritual purity or pollution and of social status; in practice, synonymous with *varna*.

Chhattisgarh: State in central India.

Constituent Assembly: Body consisting of indirectly elected representatives established to draft a constitution for India (including the now-separate countries of Pakistan and Bangladesh).

Cow-worship: Refers to the divine treatment of cows in Hinduism.

Dalit: Modern term for those traditionally treated as Untouchables; means "broken."

Delhi Sultanate: Delhi-based Empire that ruled over large parts of the Indian subcontinent for 320 years.

Delhi: Capital of India.

Dharma: Doctrine of Hinduism according to which one's duties in life are dictated by the caste into which they are born; caste duties.

Dharmashastras: *Shastras* dealing with *dharma*.

Dogra: Indo-Aryan ethno-linguistic group in India and Pakistan.

Dowry system in India: Refers to the durable goods, cash, and real or movable property that the bride's family gives to the bridegroom, his parents, or his relatives as a condition of the marriage.

Dravidian: Native speaker of a Dravidian language.

Farrukhsiyar: Ninth Mughal Emperor.

Fateh Singh: Youngest son of Guru Gobind Singh.

Feringhee: Foreigner, especially one with white skin.

Gautama Buddha: Founder of Buddhism.

Gaya: Town close to Bodh Gaya, the place where Buddha attained enlightenment.

General Hari Singh Nalwa: Commander-in-chief of the Sikh Khalsa Army.

Goa: A coastal state in central India.

Gujarat: India's westernmost state.

Gurdaspur: City in Punjab, India.

Guru Arjun: Fifth Sikh Guru.

Guru Gobind Singh: Tenth Sikh Guru.

Guru Granth Sahib: *Adi Granth* combined with the hymns of Guru Tegh Bahadur; viewed by Sikhs as their living Guru.

Guru Har Krishan: Eighth Sikh Guru.

Guru Har Rai: Seventh Sikh Guru.

Guru Hargobind: Sixth Sikh Guru.

Guru Nanak: Founder and first Guru of Sikhism.

Guru Tegh Bahadur: Ninth Sikh Guru.

Gurdwara: Sikh place of worship.

Harmandir Sahib: Also known as Darbar Sahib or Golden Temple; *Gurdwara* founded by Guru Ram Das in Amritsar.

Haryana: State in northern India.

Hill Rajas: Refers to the historical upper-caste Hindu rulers of princely states in northern India.

Himachal Pradesh: State in northern India in the Himalayas.

Hindu: Derogatory term used by the Persians to refer to all non-Muslims living in the Indian subcontinent. In the modern sense, refers to person following the religion of Hinduism.

Hinduism: Term used by the British to refer to the collection of various doctrines and religious ideologies of British India which were not a part of other religions (i.e. Islam, Sikhism, Buddhism, or Jainism). In the words of Gandhi, "Brahmanism is synonymous with Hinduism."

Hindustan: Geographical term, with unspecified boundaries; historically used by Muslim invaders to refer to the region of the northern Indian subcontinent east of the Indus River. In the modern sense, technically refers to the area between Punjab and Bengal.

Hindutva: Ideology seeking to establish the hegemony of Hindus and the Hindu way of life.

Huns: Nomadic people who lived in Eastern Europe, the Caucasus, and Central Asia between the 1st century AD and the 7th century AD.

Indus: South-flowing river in the Indian subcontinent, originating in Tibet and terminating in Sindh, it is the namesake of India; historically, areas east of the Indus are identified as belonging to the Indian subcontinent.

Hyderabad: A city in Telangana and an historical region.

Jahandar Shah: Eighth Mughal Emperor.

Jahangir: Fourth Mughal Emperor.

Jammu: City in the state of Jammu and Kashmir in India.

Jammu and Kashmir: Northernmost state of India; territorial control of J&K is contested by China, Pakistan, and local movements for sovereignty.

Jat: An agricultural community in northern India and Pakistan.

Jharkhand: State in eastern India.

Jujhar Singh: Second son of Guru Gobind Singh.

Junagadh: A city in Gujarat.

Kapilvastu: Buddha's hometown.

Karma: Doctrine of Hinduism according to which one's fulfillment (or failure to fulfill) *dharma* in one's "past" life dictates one's caste in the "current" life.

Karnataka: State in southwestern India.

Kashmir: Northernmost geographical region of the Indian subcontinent.

Kerala: A coastal state in southwestern India.

Khalsa: Sikh institution founded by Guru Gobind Singh.

Khatri: Upper-caste of merchants and soldiers from the northern Indian subcontinent.

Kshatriyas: Second caste of the Hindu caste system. They form the ruling class, and their duty is to protect Brahmans.

Kushans: Indo-European nomadic people.

Lahore: Historical capital of the Punjab region; presently located in modern day Pakistan.

Madhya Pradesh: State in central India.

Maharashtra: State in western India.

Manipur: State in northeastern India.

Manusmriti: Hindu law scripture.

Mecca: City in western Saudi Arabia which is the birthplace of Prophet Muhammad.

Miri Piri: Term used to connote the nexus between the temporal and the spiritual.

Misl: Sovereign state of the 18th-century Sikh Confederacy.

Mizoram: State in northeastern India.

Mughal Empire: Empire founded by Babur.

Muhammad Shah: Twelfth Mughal Emperor.

Mulnivasi Bahujan: Victims of caste violence and untouchability who are the aboriginals of the land and comprise approximately 85% of the Indian subcontinent's population.

Mulnivasi: Aboriginals of South Asia before it was colonized by Indo-Aryan invaders.

Nagaland: State in northeastern India.

Nagarjunakonda: Historical Buddhist town in Andhra Pradesh, India.

Nanded: City in Maharashtra, India.

Nishan Sahib: Sikh flag.

Orissa: Now Odisha; state in eastern India.

Pandit: Hindu scholar; the term generally refers to Brahmans specializing in Hindu law.

Panth: The collective Sikh body; also, the Sikh ideology.

Pataliputra: Historical city in Bihar, India.

Punjab: State in northwestern India and an historical region. Historical Punjab was partitioned in 1947 and is now split by the India/Pakistan border.

Punjabi: Residents of or the language of Punjab.

Qazi: Islamic legal scholar and judge.

Rajasthan: State in northwestern India.

Rigveda: Most sacred and probably oldest *Shastra*.

Sacha Padshah: Title accorded to Guru Hargobind and Guru Tegh Bahadur by *Mulnivasi*; means "True King."

Sanatanism: Hinduism.

Sangat: Sikh congregation.

Sanskrit: Ancient Indo-Aryan language in which *Shastras* were written and which only Brahmans were allowed to read, write, or speak. It is also known as the "language of gods."

Sarvodaya: Universal uplift; term used by Gandhi to describe his political philosophy, which emphasized anti-individualism, collectivism, and eradication of private property.

Sati: Hindu practice according to which a widow immolates herself in the cremation fire of her dead husband.

Shabad: Hymn in *Guru Granth Sahib*.

Shastras: The Hindu scriptures.

Shiva-linga: Idol representing the penis of the Hindu god, Shiva.

Shudras: Fourth and lowest caste in the Hindu caste system. Occupation is to be slaves to other three castes.

Sikh: Follower of the Sikh religion; means "disciple" or "student."

Sikh Gurus: Ten Sikh Gurus (spiritual teachers) who established the Sikh religion.

    1) Guru Nanak
    2) Guru Angad
    3) Guru Amar Das
    4) Guru Ram Das
    5) Guru Arjun

6) Guru Hargobind
7) Guru Har Rai
8) Guru Har Krishan
9) Guru Tegh Bahadur
10) Guru Gobind Singh

Sindh: State in southeastern Pakistan and an historical region.
Sirhind: City in Punjab, India.
Sons of Guru Gobind Singh:
>Baba Ajit Singh
>Baba Jujhar Singh
>Baba Zorawar Singh
>Baba Fateh Singh

Sri Lanka: Island country in South Asia.
Sutlej: River in Punjab.
Swaraj: Independence.
Tamil Nadu: A coastal state in southeastern India.
Telangana: State in southern India.
Tibet: Autonomous region of China on the northern side of the Himalayas.
Touchables: People belonging to the four castes of the Hindu caste system.
Travancore: A historical region of southwestern India which currently includes most of the State of Kerala.
Turban: Headdress worn by Sikhs; historically, attire reserved for royalty.
Untouchable: Person outside the caste system; an "Ati-Shudra" or "Dalit."
Uttar Pradesh: State in northern India.
Uttarakhand: State in northern India.
West Bengal: State in eastern India.
Vaishyas: Third caste of the Hindu caste system. Occupation is to be traders, money lenders, and farmers.
Varna: Caste.
Varnashrama Dharma: Caste ordinances or laws; duties of each caste in each "stage" of life. Refers to classification of society in four *varnas* (castes).
Zorawar Singh: Third son of Guru Gobind Singh.

Bibliography

Authors' Note: The integrity and original verbiage of all sources cited within the text have been retained exactly with the exception of occasional grammatical edits (such as the inclusion or exclusion of commas) and the standardization of spelling for the sake of clarity. Thus, for instance, "Brahman" has replaced "Brahmin" and "Brahmen"; "Shudra" has replaced "Sudra" and "Soodra"; "Nanak" has replaced "Nanuk"; "Arjun" has replaced "Arjan"; "Gobind" has replaced "Govind"; "Sikh" has replaced "Seik"; "Guru" has replaced "Gooroo"; "Punjabi" has replaced "Punjabee"; and so on and so forth. We believe doing so provides a consistency, clarity, and ease of comprehension which in no way impacts the academic value of the book.

Agnihotri, V. K. (ed.). *Indian History with Objective Questions and Historical Maps*. 1981. New Delhi: Allied Publishers Private Limited. 2010.

Ambedkar, Bhim Rao. *Thoughts of Dr. Baba Saheb Ambedkar*. Y. D. Sontakke (ed.). New Delhi: Samyak Prakashan. 2004.
— *Dr. Babasaheb Ambedkar: Writings and Speeches* (vol. 1). Vasant Moon (ed.). Bombay: Education Department, Government of Maharashtra. 1979.
— *Dr. Babasaheb Ambedkar: Writings and Speeches* (vol. 3). Vasant Moon (ed.). Bombay: Education Department, Government of Maharashtra. 1987.
— "Mohandas Karamchand Gandhi: Memories of the Mahatma, by Bhimrao Ramji Ambedkar." Francis Watson (int.). British Broadcasting Corporation Sound Archive. February 26, 1955.
— *What Congress and Gandhi Have Done to the Untouchables?* 1945. Delhi: Gautam Book Centre. 2009.

Amnesty International. *Report 2005: The State of the World's Human Rights*. London: Amnesty International Publications. 2005.

Arora, Vishal. "UN Official: India's 'Conversion' Laws Threaten Religious Freedom." *The Wall Street Journal* (Blogs). March 10, 2014.

Asian Human Rights Commission. "India's Prevention of Torture Bill Requires a Thorough Review." Article 2, Vol. 09, No. 03-04. December 2010.

Bamzai, P. N. K. *Culture and Political History of Kashmir: Medieval Kashmir* (vol. 2). New Delhi: M. D. Publications Pvt Ltd. 1994.
— *Culture and Political History of Kashmir: Modern Kashmir* (vol. 3). New Delhi: M. D. Publications Pvt Ltd. 1994.

Basu, Amrita. *Violent Conjectures in Democratic India*. New York: Cambridge University Press. 2015.

Basu, Manisha. *The Rhetoric of Hindu India: Language and Urban Nationalism*. Delhi: Cambridge University Press. 2017.

Bernier, François. *Travels in the Mogul Empire: A.D. 1656-1668*. Archibald Constable (Tr.). London: Oxford University Press. 1916.

Bhangoo, Rattan Singh. *Sri Gur Panth Prakash* (vol. 1). Kulwant Singh (tr.). Chandigarh: Institute of Sikh Studies. 2006.

Bloom, Irene and J. Paul Martin and Wayne L. Proudfoot (eds.). *Religious Diversity and Human Rights*. New York: Columbia University Press, 1996.

Brard, Gurnam Singh Sidhu. *East of Indus: My Memories of Old Punjab*. New Delhi: Hemkunt Publishers (P) Ltd. 2007.

British Indian Empire. *The Imperial Gazetteer of India* (vol. 20). Oxford: Clarendon Press. 1908.
— *Report on the Administration of Punjab and Its Dependencies for 1901-1902*. Lahore: Punjab Government Press. 1902.

Browne, James. *India Tracts: Containing a Description of the Jungle Terry Districts, Their Revenues, Trade, and Government: With a Plan for the Improvement of Them; Also An History of the Origin and Progress of the Sicks*. London: Logographic Press. 1788.

Burke, Jason. "'Racist' Gandhi statue banished from Ghana university campus." *The Guardian*. October 6, 2016.

California State Assembly. Concurrent Resolution No. 34, Chapter 36. "Relative to the November 1984 anti-Sikh pogroms." May 5, 2015.

Carson, Clarence. *The Beginning of the Republic: 1775-1825* (A Basic History of the United States Vol. 2). Wadley: American Textbook Committee. 1984.

Chandra, Satish. *Medieval India: From Sultanat to the Mughals* (vol. 2). 1999. Har-Anand Publications Pvt. Ltd. 2006.

Cole, W. Owen and Piara Singh Sambhi. *A Popular Dictionary of Sikhism*. 1990. London: Routledge. 1997.

Congressional Record. Volume 158, Number 147. 112th Congress.

Constituent Assembly of India Debates (Proceedings). Vol. 11. 1946-1950. Full text available at http://parliamentofindia.nic.in/ls/debates/debates.htm.

Crossette, Barbara. "New Delhi Journal; The Sikh's Hour of Horror, Relived After 5 Years." *The New York Times*. September 7, 1989.
— "India Uproots Thousands Living Near Sikh Temple." *The New York Times*. June 3, 1990.

Cunningham, Joseph Davey. *A History of the Sikhs From the Origin of the Nation to the Battles of the Sutlej*. London: John Murray. 1849.

Dhami, Sukhman. "Confront India on Poor Human Rights Record." TheHill.com. January 26, 2015.

Dubois, Jean A. *Hindu Manners, Customs and Ceremonies*. Henry K. Beauchamp (tr.). 1897. Oxford: Clarendon Press. 1906.

Elphinstone, Mountstuart. *The History of India* (vol. 1). London: John Murray. 1843.
— *The History of India*, (vol. 2). London: John Murray. 1843.

194   Captivating the Simple-Hearted

Embassy Mumbai. "Gujarat Chief Minister Modi Sets His Sights on National Politics." Wikileaks Cable: 06MUMBAI1986_a. November 2, 2006. Full text available at https://wikileaks.org/plusd/cables/06MUMBAI1986_a.html

Embassy New Delhi. "ICRC Frustrated With Indian Government." Wikileaks Cable: 05NEWDELHI2606_a. Dated April 6, 2005. Full text available at http://wikileaks.rsf.org/cable/2005/04/05NEWDELHI2606.html
— "Manmohan Singh a True Statesman in Reacting to Sikh Riot Report." Wikileaks Cable: 05NEWDELHI6310_a. August 12, 2005. Full text available at https://wikileaks.org/plusd/cables/05NEWDELHI6310_a.html

Eraly, Abraham. *The Mughal Throne: The Saga of India's Great Emperors*. 1997. London: Phoenix. 2004.
— "Just A Legal Indian." *Outlook*. August 20, 2001.

European Commission to the International Dalit Solidarity Network. "Caste-based Discrimination in South Asia." June 2009.

Farquhar, J. N. *The Religious Quest of India: An Outline of the Religious Literature of India*. London: Oxford University Press. 1920.

Faruki, Zahiruddin. *Aurangzeb & His Times*. Bombay: D.B. Taraporevala Sons & Co. 1935.

Gandhi, Mohandas. *The Collected Works of Mahatma Gandhi*. 100 Volumes. Delhi: Publications Division, Ministry of Information and Broadcasting, Government of India. 1958-1994.

Gandhi, Surjit Singh. *History of the Sikh Gurus (A Comprehensive Study)*. Delhi: Gur Das Kapur & Sons (P) Ltd. 1978.
— *History of Sikh Gurus Retold: 1606-1708 CE*, Vol. 2. New Delhi: Atlantic Publishers & Distributors. 2007.

Ghosh, S. K. *Torture and Rape in Police Custody: An Analysis*. New Delhi: Ashish Publishing House. 1993

Gill, Rahuldeep. "India's Incomplete Democracy." *The Los Angeles Times*.

June 18, 2014.

Goodman, Amy. "Explosive Report by Indian Magazine Exposes Those Responsible for 2002 Gujarat Massacre." Democracy Now! December 5, 2007.

Gossman, Patricia. *Human Rights in India: Punjab in Crisis*. Human Rights Watch. 1991.

Gregg, Heather Selma. *The Path to Salvation: Religious Violence from the Crusades to Jihad*. 2014. Lincoln: University of Nebraska Press.

Grewal, J.S. (ed). *Sikh History from Persian Sources*. Irfan Habib (tr.). 2001. New Delhi: Tulika Books, 2011.

Griffith, Ralph T.H. (tr.). *Rigveda*. 1896. Santa Cruz: Evinity Publishing, Inc. 2009.

Gupta, Hari Ram. *History of the Sikhs* (vol. 1). New Delhi: Munshiram Manoharlal. 1978.

Guru Nanak Khalsa College of Arts, Science & Commerce. gnkhalsa.edu.in. Vision.

Halarnkar, Samar. "Inside the Hindu mind, a battle for a Hindu nation." Scroll.in. June 11, 2017.

Human Rights Watch. *Cleaning Human Waste:"Manual Scavenging," Caste, and Discrimination in India*. August 25, 2014.
— *India: Investigate Unmarked Graves in Jammu and Kashmir*. August 24, 2011.
— "India: Gujarat Officials Took Part in Anti-Muslim Violence." April 30, 2002.

Irvine, William. *Later Mughals: 1707-1720*, Vol. 1. London: Luzac & Co. 1922.

Izsák, Rita. "Report of the Special Rapporteur on minority issues." United

Nations General Assembly. A/HRC/31/56. January 28, 2016.

Jackson, A. V. Williams (ed). *A History of India* (vol. 9). London: The Grolier Society. 1906.

Jackson, Richard and Eamon Murphy and Scott Poynting (eds.). *Contemporary State Terrorism: Theory and Practice*. London: Routledge. 2010.

Jaffrelot, Christophe. *Religion, Caste, and Politics in India*. Delhi: Primus Books. 2010.

Joseph, Tony. "How genetics is settling the Aryan migration debate." *The Hindu*. June 16, 2017.

Juergensmeyer, Mark. *The New Cold War? Religious Nationalism Confronts the Secular State*. Berkeley: University of California Press. 1993.

Kaur, Jaskaran. *Protecting the Killers: A Policy of Impunity in Punjab, India*. Human Rights Watch and Ensaaf. October 2007.
— *Twenty Years of Impunity*. Ensaaf. October 2006.

Khalra, Jaswant Singh. "Last International Speech — The Struggle for Truth." Ensaaf. April 1995.

Kinra, Rajeev. *Writing Self, Writing Empire: Chandar Bhan Brahman and the Cultural World of the Indo-Persian State Secretary*. Oakland: University of California Press. 2015.

Klostermaier, Klaus. *A Survey of Hinduism*. Albany: State University of New York Press. 2007.

Kohli, Mohindar Pal. *Guru Tegh Bahadur: Testimony of Conscience*. New Delhi: Sahitya Akademi. 1992.

Kollar, Nathan R. and Muhammad Shafiq (eds.). *Poverty & Wealth in Judaism, Christianity, & Islam*. Rochester: Palgrave Macmillan. 2016.

Kuiper, Kathleen (ed.) *Understanding India: The Culture of India*. New

York: Britannica Educational Publishing. 2011.

Kumar, Ram Narayan and Amrik Singh. *Reduced to Ashes: The Insurgency and Human Rights in Punjab*. Kathmandu: South Asia Forum for Human Rights. 2003.

Lawrence, Walter R. *The Valley of Kashmir*. London: Oxford University Press. 1895.

Macauliffe, Max Arthur. *The Sikh Religion: Its Gurus, Sacred Writings, and Authors*. Six Volumes. Oxford: Clarendon Press. 1909.

Madra, Amandeep Singh and Parmjit Singh (eds.). *"Sicques, Tigers, or Thieves": Eyewitness Accounts of the Sikhs*. New York: Palgrave MacMillan. 2004.

Magagnini, Stephen. "Was Gandhi saint or sinner? Debate rages over new Davis statue." *The Sacramento Bee*. October 2, 2016.

Mahmood, Cynthia Keppley. *Fighting for Faith and Nation: Dialogues With Sikh Militants*. Philadelphia: University of Pennsylvania Press. 1996.

Malcolm, John. *Sketch of the Sikhs*. Prithipal Singh Kapur (ed.). Amritsar: Satvic Media Pvt. Limited. 2007.

Mander, Harsh. "Nellie: India's Forgotten Massacre." *Sunday Magazine - The Hindu*. December 14, 2008.

Manucci, Niccolao. *Storia do Mogul or Mogul India: 1653-1708*. William Irvine (tr.). London: John Murray. 1907.

Mathur, Shubh. *The Human Toll of the Kashmir Conflict: Grief and Courage in a South Asian Borderland*. New York: Palgrave MacMillan. 2016.

Mayo, Katherine. *Slaves of the Gods*. New York: Harcourt, Brace and Company, Inc. 1929.

Medina, Jennifer. "Debate Erupts in California Over Curriculum on India's

History." *The New York Times*. May 4, 2016.

Metcalf, Barbara D. and Thomas R. Metcalf. *A Concise History of Modern India*. 2001. Cambridge: Cambridge University Press. 2012.

Mohamad, Malik. *The Foundations of Composite Culture in India*. Delhi: Aakar Books. 2007.

Mohammed, Shah. *The First Punjab War: Shah Mohammed's Jangnama*. P. K. Nijhawan (ed. and tr.). Amritsar: Singh Brothers, 2001.

Mugali, Shiladhar Yallappa and Priyadarshini Sharanappa Amadihal. "Mahatma Jyotirao Phule's Views on Upliftment of Women as Reflected in Sarvajanik Stayadharma." *Proceedings of the Indian History Congress* (vol. 69). 2008.

Muller, F. Max and George Bühler (eds.). *The Sacred Books of the East: The Laws of Manu*, Vol. 25. Oxford: Clarendon Press. 1886.

Nahal, Tarlochan Singh. *Miri and Piri: Religion and Politics in Sikhism with Special Reference to the Sikh Struggle (1947-1999)*. Paper presented at International Sikh Conference. 2000. Vancouver, British Columbia.

Nicoll, Fergus. *Shah Jahan: The Rise and Fall of the Mughal Emperor*. London: Haus Publishing Ltd. 2009.

Obama, Barack. "President Barack Obama's Inaugural Address." Whitehouse.gov. January 21, 2009.

Ontario Legislative Assembly. Private Members' Public Business, Ballot Item Number 47, Private Members' Notice of Motion Number 46. Ms. Malhi.

Pelsaert, Francisco. *Jahangir's India*. Cambridge: W. Heffer & Sons Ltd. 1925.

Pföstl, Eva (ed.). *Between Ethics and Politics: Gandhi Today*. New Delhi: Routledge. 2014.

Phule, Jyotirao. 1891. *Collected Works: The Book of the True Faith* (vol. 2). 1991.
— *Slavery: In This Civilised British Government Under the Cloak of Brahmanism*. 1873. Full text available at velivada.com.

Rawat, S. Ramnarayan and K. Satyanarayana (eds.). *Dalit Studies*. Durham: Duke University Press. 2016.

Richards, John F. *The Mughal Empire*. Cambridge: Cambridge University Press. 1995.

Rigoglioso, Marguerite. "Stanford scholar casts new light on Hindu-Muslim relations." stanford.edu. September 9, 2015.

Robinson, Francis. *The Mughal Emperors And The Islamic Dynasties of India, Iran and Central Asia, 1206-1925*. New York: Thames & Hudson, Inc. 2007.

Roe, Thomas. *The Embassy of Sir Thomas Roe to the Court of the Great Mogul, 1615-1619 as Narrated in His Journal and Correspondence* (vol. 1). William Foster (ed.). London: Redford Press. 1899.

Rothbard, Murray. *The Libertarian Forum*. Volume VII, NO.7. July 1975.

Royal Asiatic Society of Bengal. *Journal of the Royal Asiatic Society of Bengal: Letters*. Vol. XV, 1949, No. 1. July 1949.

Roy, Arundhati. *Field Notes on Democracy: Listening to Grasshoppers*. Chicago: Haymarket Books. 2009.
— "My Seditious Heart." *The Caravan*. May 1, 2016.
— "R. Parekh Annual Lecture." A Conference on Democracy and Dissent in China and India. University of Westminster. June 2, 2011.

Sappenfield, Mark. "Obama's new India problem: What to do with Narendra Modi?" *The Christian Science Monitor*. May 18, 2014.

Saraswati, Maharishi Swami Dayanand. *The Satyartha Prakasha*. 1975. New Delhi: Sarvadeshik Arya Pratinidhi Sabha. 1984.

Scott-Clark, Cathy. "The mass graves of Kashmir." *The Guardian*. July 9, 2012.

Singh, Gopal. *The Religion of the Sikhs*. 1971. New Delhi: Allied Publishers Private Limited. 1981.

Singh, Gurmit. *History of Sikh Struggles* (vol. 1). New Delhi: Atlantic Publishers & Distributors 1989.

Singh, Guru Gobind. *Zafarnama*. Jasbir Singh (tr.). 1705. Full text available at zafarnama.com.

Singh, Harbans. *The Heritage of the Sikhs*. New York: Asia Publishing House. 1964.

Singh, Harinder. "Nash Doctrine: Five Freedoms of Vaisakhi 1699." Sikh Research Institute. April 16, 2017. Full text available at http://www.sikhri.org/nash_doctrine_five_freedoms_of_vaisakhi_1699.
— "The Emergency & The Sikhs." Sikh Research Institute. Full text available at http://www.sikhri.org/the_emergency_the_sikhs.

Singh, Kanwarjit. *Political Philosophy of the Sikh Gurus*. New Delhi: Atlantic Publishers & Distributors. 1989.

Singh, Kapur. *Sikhism: An Oecumenical Religion*. Gurtej Singh (ed.). Chandigarh: Institute of Sikh Studies. 1993.
— "The Golden Temple: Its Theo-Political Status." 1960. Sikh Research Institute. April 25, 2016. Full text available at http://www.sikhri.org/the_golden_temple_its_theo_political_status

Singh, Prithi Pal. *The History of Sikh Gurus*. New Delhi: Lotus Press. 2006.

Singh, Puran. *Volume One, Part II of Spirit of the Sikh*. Patiala: Punjabi University, Patiala. 1980.
— *Volume Two, Part II of Spirit of the Sikh*. Patiala: Punjabi University, Patiala. 1981.
— *Open Letter to Sir John Simon*. October 21, 1928. Full text available at globalsikhstudies.com and archive.org.

Singh, Sangat. *The Sikhs in History*. 1995. Amritsar: Singh Brothers. 2005.

Singh, Sardar Harjeet. *Faith and Philosophy of Sikhism*. Delhi: Kalpaz Publications. 2009.

Smith, Brian K. *Classifying the Universe: The Ancient Indian* Varna *System and the Origins of Caste*. New York: Oxford University Press. 1994.

Smith, Vincent A. *Akbar the Great Mogul*, 1542-1605. Oxford: Clarendon Press. 1917.

Srivastava, Ashirbadi Lal. *The Sultanate of Delhi*. 1950. Agra: Shiva Lal Agarwala & Company. 1966.

Steinbach, Henry. *The Punjab: Being a Brief Account of the Country of the Sikhs*. London: Smith, Elder, & Co. 1845.

Sullivan, Richard Joseph. *An analysis of the political history of India. In which is considered, the present situation of the East, and the connection of its several powers with the Empire of Great Britain*. 1779. London: T. Beckett. 1784.

Swift, E.P. *The Foreign Missionary Chronicle: Containing a Particular Account of the Proceedings of the Western Foreign Missionary Society and a General View of the Transactions of Other Similar Institutions* (vols. 1 and 2). Pittsburgh: Christian Herald. 1834.

The Imperial Gazetteer of India (vol. 20). Oxford: Clarendon Press. 1908.

Tavernier, Jean Baptiste. *Travels in India* (vol. 2). V. Ball (tr.). London: Macmillan and Co. 1889.

Theertha, Dharma Swami. *History of Hindu Imperialism*. 1941. Kottayam: Babasaheb Ambedkar Foundation. 1992.

Thorn, William. *Memoir of the War in India*. London: Military Library. 1818.

Captivating the Simple-Hearted

Thornton, Edward. *A Gazetteer of the Territories Under the Government of the East-India Company and of the Native States on the Continent of India.* London: Wm. H. Allen & Co. 1858.

Truschke, Audrey. *Culture of Encounters: Sanskrit at the Mughal Court.* Ebook. New York: Columbia University Press, 2016.
— *Aurangzeb: The Life and Legacy of India's Most Controversial King.* Ebook. Stanford: Stanford University Press, 2017.

United Nations. "Convention on the Prevention and Punishment of the Crime of Genocide." United Nations General Assembly. December 9, 1948. Article 2.
— "Final Report of the Commission of Experts Established Pursuant to Security Council Resolution 780 (1992)." United Nations Commission of Experts. 27 May 1994, section III.
— "Caste systems violate human rights and dignity of millions worldwide — New UN expert report." Office of the High Commissioner of Human Rights. March 21, 2016.

United States Commission on International Religious Freedom. *Annual Report: India Chapter.* May 2010.
— *Annual Report: India Chapter.* April 2016.

Valmuci, Arvin. "Anglican Church Hosts Indian Human Rights Leader to Discuss Religious Persecution." sikh24.com. May 26, 2017.
— "California Seminar Warns India's 'Brahman Raj.'" sikh24.com. June 1, 2017.

Weber, Max. *The Religion of India: The Sociology Of Hinduism And Buddhism.* Hans Gerth and Don Martindale (trs.). Glencoe: The Free Press. 1958.

Wheeler, James Talboys. *India Under British Rule From the Foundation of the East India Company.* London: Macmillan and Co. 1886.

X, Malcolm. "The Race Problem." African Students Association and NAACP Campus Chapter. Michigan State University, East Lansing, Michigan. 23 January 1963.

Yong, Tan Tai. *The Garrison State: The Military, Government, and Society in Colonial Punjab, 1849-1947*. New Delhi: Sage Publications. 2005.

Zubrin, Robert. "The Population Control Holocaust." *The New Atlantis*. Number 35. Spring 2012.

Acknowledgements

We extend our deepest regards to those many people who have supported us throughout the development of this book. Several friends read portions of the manuscript at various stages and gave invaluable feedback and encouragement. You know who you are.

In particular, we acknowledge the efforts of Anmol Singh for helping create the infrastructure of this book. His efforts are tireless. We also acknowledge the creativity of Rakind Kaur for helping to develop the cover. Her abilities are superb. Our gratitude to Elizabeth Barnard for her insightful eye for editing.

From Pieter Friedrich: "I want to thank the *Mulnivasi* community for encouraging me in the creation of this book. I also extend my gratitude to the many European adventurers who traveled to the Indian subcontinent in centuries past and recorded their experiences. My indebtedness to C. for her unwavering encouragement and support. Finally, I thank the Sikh Gurus for the inspiration of their unshakeable courage and commitment."

From Bhajan Singh: "I want to thank my family, especially my dear wife, who has stood by me, supported me, and allowed me to accomplish this book. In service to the humanity of this planet, I hope this humble effort will be a beacon of learning for all the world's oppressed."

About the Authors

Pieter Friedrich is a journalist and activist living in California, USA. He is author of *Gandhi: Racist or Revolutionary* (2017), co-author of *Faces of Terror in India* (2011) and *Demons Within: The Systematic Practice of Torture by Indian Police* (2011), as well as editor of several books. He serves as an Advisory Director to Organization for Minorities of India. He is a student of world religions, human liberties, eco- nomic action, imperialism, and South Asian history and culture.

Bhajan Singh is a humanitarian and community activist living in California, USA. He is co-author of *Faces of Terror in India* (2011) and *Demons Within: The Systematic Practice of Torture by Indian Police* (2011). He is Founding Director of Organization for Minorities of India.